ALSO BY JENNIFER TOTH

The Mole People: Life in the Tunnels Beneath New York City

ORPHANS
OF THE
LIVING

Stories of America's

Children in Foster Care

JENNIFER
TOTH

A TOUCHSTONE BOOK
Published by Simon & Schuster

TOUCHSTONE
Rockefeller Center
1230 Avenue of the Americas
New York, NY 10020

First Touchsone Edition 1998

TOUCHSTONE and colophon are registered trademarks
of Simon & Schuster Inc.

Designed by Karolina Harris

Manufactured in the United States of America

10 9 8 7 6 5 4 3 2 1

The Library of Congress has cataloged the Simon & Schuster edition as follows:
Toth, Jennifer.
    Orphans of the living: stories of America's children in
foster care / Jennifer Toth.
        p.   cm.
      1. Foster children — United States — Case studies.   I. Title.
HV881.T67   1997
362.73'3'0973 — dc21   96-40316   CIP
ISBN 0-684-80097-7
ISBN 0-684-84480-X (Pbk)

For Mom, Dad, Jess, and John,
who taught me love,
and
for Craig,
who deepens and enriches that meaning every day
and
for Angel, Bryan, Jamie, Crystal, Damien, and Sebastian,
whose strength, resilience, and honesty have taught me so
much and given me the greatest hope for the future

CONTENTS

PART II: JAMIE
Lumberton, North Carolina

PART III: ANGEL
Los Angeles, California

PART IV: BRYAN
Chicago, Illinois

The primary job that any writer faces is to tell you a story out of human experiences — I mean by that, universal mutual experience, the anguishes and troubles and griefs of the human heart, which is universal, without regard to race or time or human condition. He wants to tell you something that has seemed to him so true, so moving, either comic or tragic, that it's worth preserving.

WILLIAM FAULKNER, 1962

AUTHOR'S NOTE

※

IN the course of researching this book I came across evidence of appalling violations of children's basic rights. Much of this I could not use, because my access to files was limited or, more commonly, adults were afraid to go on the record with the facts. At stake were their jobs, their reputations, their community and church affiliations. One supervisor explained that if she came forward, she would not only lose her job but also forgo the possibility of any other job in the state, because she would be breaking the code of silence that appears to be so pervasive. Another administrator confirmed those fears: "She'd be fired and then blacklisted in the state and probably beyond" for going public with her criticisms.

Among the stories for which I found evidence were those of teenage girls in foster care literally tied down for forced abortions, and of children's homes that routinely drugged all their children with Ritalin to subdue and control them, because of inadequate staff. I have seen children crying and spitting out drugs that I was later told had not been prescribed for them. While such violations of human rights are sometimes exceptions to general practice, others are tolerated as basic, systematic policy.

One director of a children's home acknowledged that immediately after a girl in his home begins menstruating, she is taken to the local Planned Parenthood clinic once a month for Depo-Provera shots to prevent pregnancy. Female residential supervisors nearly mutinied over this practice because they saw the damaging side effects of the drug on the girls, many of whom were not yet sexually active. Nonetheless, the home's board of directors reaffirmed the practice, in part because the drug also lessened the girls' sex drives. Only after a doctor at the clinic refused to administer the drugs because she considered their use inhumane were the injections halted and birth control pills provided instead. All pubescent girls are required to take the pills now, though several of the female houseparents break the rules by turning away before they have seen the girls swallow them. In this birth control program, the director and his board are succumbing to the pressures of state and federal funding and the ratings of caseworkers when they consider the home as a place for their children. A high number of pregnancies per year in a children's home is a negative factor in choosing foster care homes.

I am very grateful to those who did come forward with their experiences. They did so because they believe the system needs radical reform. Recounting their criticism, they sometimes acknowledged mistakes for which they are responsible. But by admitting to these mistakes and flaws, they expose details of a desperate and destructive system, and in the process they make the larger case that the abuses are often the fault of the substitute child care system itself, not just of the individuals within it.

But most brave and admirable are the children who came forth in honesty with their pain and hope—at the risk of scrutiny and harsh judgment—because they believe in making a better future for the next generation of social orphans. All of their stories are true. "Damien" and "Sebastian" are not the real names of those two boys, nor are the true names of their siblings used. They have been changed at the request of the homes involved to avoid identifying the children. A few other names and details were also changed in their story for the same reason. Angel, Jamie, and Bryan chose to have their true names used, though Bryan asked that the spelling of his name be changed in the book back to his mother's original spelling. Social services mistakenly converted his name to "Brian" when registering him, and though he complained throughout his years as a ward of that department, his teachers and caretakers did not permit him to spell his name as he believes his mother intended. His reasons for using his true name now as well as for cooperating in this project are as simple and direct as Angel's and Jamie's.

"It's taken me this long to face the truth head-on and become who I am," Bryan said. "I don't want to change now."

Angel's reason is perhaps the most immediate.

"My kids are in foster care now," she said. "I don't want them to live the way I lived. No way."

Jamie was more hesitant; she worried about hurting her family. But over the course of two years' work, she decided without reading the text that her real name should be used.

"I want to help so that no other kid or family has to go through what I went through," she said. "I can do that by telling the truth and putting my name to it, by making me real."

This is the crisis of our times. See those children there? Look into their faces. Their eyes will tell you, these are the orphans of the living. I almost got fired calling them that. But that's what they are, and it's important that they recognize that fact. Most of these children would rather say their parents are dead than say their parents don't want them. This is a way of making them acknowledge that they've got parents too, no matter how sorry their parents are. They got parents, the rascals, oh yeah, they got them. They're drug addicts, or abusive, or homeless, or they just don't want their kids. These children are the victims of that mess. Their numbers are growing faster than anyone could have imagined. Society doesn't seem to care. Go ahead, look into their eyes, talk to them. You won't believe what you'll find. You won't believe their stories, but you go out there and see. It's time someone starts telling the truth about this. Check it out. See how we're failing these orphans of the living.

MIKE ALSTON,
Director of Central Children's Home,
Oxford, North Carolina

INTRODUCTION

❈

A HALF million children are now consigned to the substitute child care system, a chaotic, prisonlike system intended to raise children whose parents and relatives cannot or will not care for them. I wish I could meet Mike Alston's challenge to tell each child's story. The details of their lives are more gripping and more revealing than any psychological studies or welfare statistics available.

Their stories cry out for an overhaul of today's tired and destructive foster care system—a system that feeds 40 percent of its children onto welfare rolls or into prison, according to a study commissioned by the U.S. Department of Health and Human Services. Only 17 percent of foster care "graduates" become completely self-supporting two and one half to four years after discharge. While more than half (54 percent) finish high school, a little less than half (49 percent) are gainfully employed as adults. Almost 60 percent of the girls give birth within a few years of leaving the system. Most enter another program of the welfare system, Aid to Families with Dependent Children (AFDC).

Without the backbone of a stable childhood environment and the opportunity to bond with responsible adults, these children are at great risk of falling through society's safety nets. Former foster kids are three times more likely to become homeless. Major metropolitan areas report that as much as 30 to 40 percent of their shelter population has passed through the foster care system. And the new welfare reform laws could vastly increase the number of foster children, since AFDC funds have been severely cut back. Already in crisis, the foster care system may well collapse under the strain.

The substitute child care system is trying to provide parenting for children of unproductive and dependent adults—society's "lower rung." Looking into the bright eyes of many kids in the system today, with their heart-tugging smiles, their impressionable intelligence, and their often amazing resilience, it is difficult to believe they will in turn become their parents, as studies and statistics dolefully predict. Something is very wrong.

Most child care workers in the system agree that the federal and state governments' substitute child care system, costing between $6 billion and $10 billion a year, is a failure. For the youngest children, it defies the underlying precept of modern pediatric thought, that infants and small children require nurturing and love, consistency and permanency, and a reliable opportunity to identify with a responsible adult. It fails to bring older children who are traumatized, abused, and neglected back into society's mainstream. It even marginalizes those who are simply parentless but swept up into the system's bureaucratic currents.

Several caseworkers and social workers told me flatly that the substitute child care system does more harm than good. One Baltimore study found that maltreatment reports are three times more frequent from *foster care homes* than biological homes. The primary complaint in biological families is neglect, which is closely associated with poverty, while the main complaint in foster homes is abuse, sexual and physical. In fact, the same Baltimore study found the rate of physical abuse was seven times greater in foster care than in biological homes. In most cases, the abuser was a foster parent.

Children's homes—a more modern and politically correct term for orphanages—fare little better. Many children tell of being abused in the homes not only by staff but also by other kids, who have been abused, too, and in turn act out their trauma and rage on other children. "These children, removed from their biological families, often because of allegations of abuse and neglect, are further harmed, physically and emotionally, while in state custody," one 1986 study concluded.

But handing them back to their parents is not necessarily the answer. Child care workers complain that they are continually pressured to return children to dangerous biological homes because substitute child care costs more; it can be afforded only for children in the most life-threatening situations. About two thirds of children in foster care are eventually returned to their biological homes. But half of them are later returned to the system more physically or sexually abused, further neglected, or again rejected by mothers and fathers who can't or won't cope with the responsibility of parenthood.

National statistics on the number of children in foster care are suspect. Figures may appear inconsistent because key definitions (that is, what constitutes "foster care" and "abuse"), as well as the policies that led to them, vary not only from state to state but even, at times, from county to county. Moreover, until a decade ago, the number of children in substitute child care nationally was extrapolated from small random surveys. Results were at times unbelievable. For example, reports for 1977 and 1980 claimed the number of children in foster care had actually dropped by over one hundred thousand, even though the foster care population had clearly increased in the intervening years as the primary causes for children being placed in foster care— drugs and crumbling families—grew enormously in frequency and severity.

Today most data on substitute child care comes from Toshio Tatara, who is in charge of the only national database of children in state care, the

Voluntary Cooperative Information System. Federal funding for VCIS was cut in 1996, so the most recent VCIS data is for 1990. Tatara now struggles on his own time to keep a rough estimate of the growing number of kids in substitute child care. He warns that even his 1990 figures are not without flaws. Among the difficulties is that overworked and understaffed child care offices in many jurisdictions cannot or will not take the time to complete his questionnaire. Nonetheless, Tatara is confident that the number of children filling the system has increased steadily since 1982, with a nearly 60 percent leap from 1986 to 1990, to 400,000. Since then, Tatara estimates the number has increased about 5 percent each year, or twice the growth rate of welfare rolls. There were 494,000 children in care according to his most recent estimates for 1995. If his estimates are correct, there are well over half a million children in foster care today.

The types of care in which children find themselves vary. About fifteen years ago, Congress enacted the concept of family preservation into law. The idea was to spend government money to fix the child's biological family by offering counseling, parenting classes, housing, and whatever else was needed to keep the family together. The program costs far less per year than taking a child into state custody, the cost of which in most states is about equal to the annual tuition and board at Harvard, Yale, Dartmouth, or Duke.

But the number of children entering substitute care is still growing. Each year about two hundred thousand new children enter the system, according to Tatara's figures, while half that number leave.* Of the entering children, fully three quarters (75 percent) go to foster homes, usually consisting of a family of two parents (sometimes one parent) in a home environment. Foster families are paid as much as $40,000 and as little as $7,000 per year per child, depending on the disabilities and needs of the child as well as the whims of local social services budgets. Some states argue that more money attracts higher-quality foster parents; others argue that keeping the amount low assures a more selfless parent. *Kinship care,* recently popular but controversial, consists of paying a child's relative for foster care.

About one sixth (16 percent) of the children are placed in group homes, emergency shelters, children's homes, or residential treatment centers. *Group homes* are often homelike environments for more than one child, with more than one or two parentlike figures and counselors on hand. Therapeutic group homes usually have psychiatric workers on staff. *Emergency shelters* are the most expensive form of care. Children are expected to stay no more than thirty days because of demand. Because of the expense, most caseworkers hastily send them to longer-term placements. Nonetheless, many children remain in emergency shelters for more than a month. Because of shortages

---

* Most are placed back with their biological families or relatives and return to foster care later. Some "age out" of foster care and are considered independent adults. Others find their way into the juvenile penal system.

in foster families or because of disruptive behavior, a child may be placed in a *children's home*. Most often, the children in children's homes are divided by age and sex into cottages of ten to twelve each. One or two houseparents care for the children. Some homes have begun to mix children of different ages and gender, in hopes of establishing a more familylike atmosphere.

Almost 3 percent of the kids who are available for adoption live in foster homes that may adopt them. Less than 1 percent are living independently, with social workers checking on them in their apartments and offering aid when needed, or they are living in transitional programs. A final 5 percent are living in maternity homes, hospitals, college dormitories, mental retardation facilities, or correctional institutions.

Tatara's statistics confirm what Central's director, Mike Alston, knows from experience: the children in substitute child care today are not orphans in the traditional, narrow meaning of the word. They usually have one, sometimes two, parents, who can't or won't care for them. Most are the victims of drug-abusing adults, poverty, and dysfunctional families. Tatara's 1990 data from nineteen states (covering about 46 percent of the estimated number of children in care that year) show that over half the children were in foster care for protective reasons—because child protective service workers had found them living in unsafe environments or with dangerous people. Just over 20 percent of the children were placed in substitute care because of parental conditions, such as financial hardship, incarceration, illness, handicap, or death. About 13 percent of the children were placed in state hands because of a troubled relationship with their parent or parents, or they were put up for adoption, or they became pregnant. Almost 2 percent of parents turned their children over to the state because the child had a disability or handicap, including physical, mental, or emotional problems. Almost 1 percent of the kids entered because their parents simply relinquished their parental rights—and this number is increasing. Far more children have entered state custody after their parents simply disappeared from their lives without legally freeing them for adoption.

Once in the system, these children have less chance of being adopted than they do of becoming homeless, getting pregnant as a teen, dropping out of school, or winding up in prison. Fewer than 8 percent of these children filling emergency shelters, foster care homes, children's homes, group homes, and mental hospitals are ever adopted. Most of the children are younger than twelve, and 16 percent are infants under the age of one. The U.S. Department of Health and Human Services found that even children with parents waiting to adopt them are held up in foster care for three and one half to five and one half years.

A common belief is that Americans want to adopt babies instead of older children, and it is supposedly for this reason that children remain in the system so long. More likely it is because the children are bound to the system by endless reams of paperwork and miles of red tape. Many foster parents have fought to adopt older children. But in most states, passing adoptive standards is more difficult than passing foster parent standards. There are several cases in which couples who have foster-parented children for years are refused permission to adopt them because, ironically, they fail the standards.

Another reason why children remain suspended in the limbo of substitute care is that most parents do not relinquish their rights to the children. Sometimes they drop off the child and disappear without signing the necessary legal papers. And often, overworked social workers do not have the time to track the parent down and free the child for adoption.

Yet another reason is that bureaucratic rules require caseworkers, before recommending adoption, to make often unrealistic attempts to put the biological family back together. Only when that fails in a rare and definitive way are they then permitted to solicit adoption permission from the biological parents, who are often uncooperative or difficult to find.

A final reason is that caseworkers charged with placing children are often undertrained and overburdened. A federal report found that fewer than half of caseworkers have had any training or experience with children before becoming responsible for children in the system. The Association of American Social Workers recommends a caseload of up to seven children. But in fact, caseworkers carry far more cases, as many as 150 at a time. With such a load, attention is focused on the most difficult child or the crisis of the moment, and the "good kids" get ignored. The average child in substitute care drifts through three or four placements in foster families, group homes, or children's homes. The situation is worse for infants, who are likely to experience even more dislocations.

White children have made up the largest proportion of children in the system until very recently. Now African-American children comprise the greatest number, and they remain in the system twice as long as white children.

EACH of the half million children in substitute child care today is a story. Most of their experiences would help us to understand the system. I chose to focus on five children and their siblings to explain the crisis at hand. Through them I hope the reader sees how the system parents and whom it parents, as well as how it works—or more often, how it does not.

My conclusion is that the accepted generalizations are badly and dangerously flawed. For example, it is said that only those children who "fail out" of three or four foster care home placements end up in children's homes. But two of the children I profile were placed in children's homes *before* they were put in foster homes. Jamie was a difficult child only by her mother's standards. A foster home could not be found to accept Damien together with his five siblings, so at the children's insistence the caseworker chose to keep them together. Only a children's home could accommodate them.

Another conventional belief is that, statistically, only a small percentage of children in care have been sexually abused. But Central Children's Home director Mike Alston estimates that *all* of the girls and *more than half* the boys in his children's home were sexually violated before they entered foster care. Sexual abuse, his social workers say, is highly underreported by child protective service workers because they are looking for the most expedient way to remove a child from a harmful environment. Neglect is far quicker and easier to prove than sexual abuse.

Sometimes tragic oversight of abuse occurs when caseworkers fail to be thorough and persevering in examining all the fragmented case records available to them. Reflecting conditions repeatedly found across the country, Kathryn Croft, executive deputy commissioner of New York City's Child Welfare Administration, complained that cuts in resources and staff have made it impossible to train caseworkers to spot abusive parents and even to measure the competence of the child protective service workers themselves. Sometimes fundamental safeguards, such as checking to see whether the prospective foster parents have criminal records, are not carried out. In some states, such checks are not even required.

Pervasive and just as disturbing is the readiness of caseworkers, under pressure to clear their caseloads, to put children in the first available placement rather than one that the child deserves or that would best serve his or her needs. The system, in its desperate shortage of resources, is geared to the fastest rather than the best disposition of cases. The placement system is not built even on compromises, but on urgency and minimal standards of care. Children often have little voice in where they go, and when they speak up, they are usually ignored.

These problems span the country. In Washington, D.C., the child welfare system was found to be in such chaos that, in 1995, a federal judge ordered it taken out of the District's hands and put into private receivership. Four months after the appointed receiver, Jerome G. Miller, took control, he reported that his staff was still trying to account for all the children in the agency's custody, as well as for how its budget was being spent. He estimated that there was a total of twenty-four hundred children in D.C. custody. But his most recent effort to track the children—every social worker filed a form on every child in his or her care—resulted in a flood of nine thousand forms. Miller speculated that thousands of cases had become inactive but were never formally closed; but he added that he really doesn't know. He faces, he told a federal judge, "a bureaucratic malaise [that] routinely sabotages and undermines the agency's capacity to deliver effective services to families and children at risk."*

Removing the foster care system from the District's hands was unprecedented but may not remain unique for long. Children's Rights Inc., the non-profit group whose lawsuit against the District of Columbia prompted the takeover, has filed similar suits challenging child welfare procedures in New York, Connecticut, New Mexico, and the cities of Philadelphia, Kansas City, and Milwaukee.

The failings of foster care may well be compounded by congressional action to slash funding for welfare in an effort to break the cycle of generational poverty. If fewer funds are available for foster care, the theory goes, poor adults will give birth to fewer children who are odds-on favorites to replace them on welfare. But while the approach is intended to change adult behavior, it will penalize the children already with us as well as the ones who will be born to adults who refuse to be parents. In most cases, the foster care system proves to be as poor a parent to these orphans of the living as the biological parents. That is not to say that children in jeopardy should be kept with their biological family at all costs. It is only to point out the extent of foster care's failure. If we are going to entrust children to the state, in order to reform the welfare cycle we must be willing to make the system capable of providing responsible care. Right now, it can barely feed and clothe the children.

I intended this book to be about the kids and their lives in foster care. *Orphans of the Living* would describe the system as I had learned it from them—undernourished, overburdened, and understaffed. It was falling apart as I watched, and damaging children not just by simple errors but by systemic failures as well. It is so dangerously flawed in structure and operation that some caseworkers choose to keep children with neglectful or even abusive parents rather than trust them to foster care. The bureaucracy seems almost designed to entrap and then prohibit a healthy outcome for its wards.

But Susan Zuravin, a dynamic professor of social work at the University of Maryland with thirty years' experience in the field, took me a step further. Beyond fixing the system for tomorrow's children, the equally daunting challenge is to save the children already in the system, to give them the necessary psychological as well as physical nourishment to survive the profound trauma of separation from family. The quality that separates those who overcome their trauma from those who do not is, to her, resilience.

A framework within which to consider this challenge is a fairly young field sometimes called "risk research." Described by Marian Radke-Yarrow of the National Institute of Mental Health in *Hard Growing: Children Who Survive,* risk research focuses on an individual's vulnerability and resistance to risk

---

* Miller later found evidence that some children who were victims of abuse and neglect were mistakenly taken into the District's foster care system in handcuffs.

and stress. The earliest work dealt with disturbances such as anaclitic depression, found in infants who were institutionalized and lacked mothering during and immediately after World War II. In some babies the depression was so severe that they died. Harry Harlow gave further impetus to the field in 1958 with studies showing that severe nurturing deprivation has profound effects on infants' social, emotional, cognitive, and physical development and well-being. The fundamental conclusion is that human infants require love and psychological nurture as well as physical shelter for their survival.

More recently researchers have approached the issue from another direction. Why, they ask, do some children in the same environment cope better than others? It is a question I heard often in my own work. Social workers, caseworkers, teachers, directors, and administrators all spent the final few minutes of interviews musing about why, given the same substandard conditions, some kids make it and others do not.

Developmental psychopathologists have found that the intelligence, sex, age, and family socioeconomic status of the child help to predict which children will weather stress better. But how and why is not always clear. Resilience and survival appear to be rooted in the relationship the child develops with his or her nurturer; specifically, the child satisfies some need in the nurturer and thereby finds a place for and value in himself or herself. Radke-Yarrow wrote, for example, that a boy is more likely to succeed than a girl in a situation where he is the only boy in a family that has always wanted a boy. His age may not be significant. The study concludes that the successful child develops a belief that there is something good and special about him- or herself.

In my stories, Jamie was nurtured in this regard by her grandfather and perhaps her aunts. Angel had no one except Mr. Brown, her foster father, who violated (or complicated) that relationship by becoming her husband. Bryan had his sister Crystal. Damien and Sebastian had no one at all.

None of the studies on resilience offers a cheap or quick cure for the hundreds of thousands of children drifting through foster care. But they point directly to where the system is going wrong. The children in substitute child care today have all suffered trauma. They are all at greater risk than the general child population. Yet they are given less care, when they need more care. Many thousands of children are lost and millions of dollars are wasted each year because no one—not the caseworker, not the foster home—takes full responsibility for them. Instead, each is passed from one caseload and placement to another, with too many kids and too little attention to go around. When these children look to adults for help, no one is there. Only when their situation becomes desperate, when they also fail, are they awarded the attention they crave.

The bottom line is that the children are fed into an antiquated system designed merely to provide physical shelter for literal orphans. Most need much more. They need a bridge to relate the horrors of abuse and neglect they have experienced to the society we wish them to join. They need love and counseling to understand that their experiences have made them different. They need to be shown that the tricks of survival learned in foster care are not necessary or desirable for success outside the system. They need to be enveloped in the "normal," everyday standards by which they will be judged outside. They also need to know that while those standards are unfair now, the goals are achievable.

The stories in *Orphans of the Living* prove that children are resilient. They can survive and succeed. But those who succeed do so despite the foster care system today, not thanks to it.

So we turn to the children for their stories. Each of them is different, from their age to their color to their family background, but their experiences have made them kin. They were all parented by the system. They may react differently, but they all understand one another better than those of us outside the system can know them. Some have learned how to adapt to society; others have not and perhaps, now, cannot. Their parent, the system, has failed.

I

DAMIEN
AND
SEBASTIAN

Oxford,
North Carolina

1

Oxford

❉

Two green highway signs along Interstate 85 in North Carolina alert travelers, as they approach Oxford, to two unique establishments in the town of eight thousand people. The first sign is for Oxford Orphanage, the state's first and the nation's second home for orphaned children, founded in 1873. The next is for Central Children's Home, founded a decade later by prominent members of the state's African-American community to care for orphaned black children, who were excluded from Oxford and, until then, leased out for work rather than cared for as the white children were. In town and among social workers, the two children's homes are still distinguished as the "white" orphanage and the "black" one. The institutions meet, briefly, on one exit sign. Then, just past the thick covering of pines and maples that hide Oxford from the highway, separate signs point in opposite directions to their separate worlds.

To the north, beyond genteel neighborhoods of whitewashed houses rimmed with fresh black shutters, expansive porches, breezy porch swings, and bright American flags, stands Oxford Orphanage. Centuries-old oak trees shelter its well-tended lawns and handsome brick buildings to suggest a small boarding school rather than a children's home.

Oxford opened too late to accomplish its initial purpose of soaking up the thousands of children left orphaned after the Civil War. But it is still as independent as it was a century ago. It is still privately funded and thus free and exempt from government oversight. It was founded and is still supported exclusively by the Masonic order, and Oxford's children are referred to the home by members of the Masons, rather than by the state.

The state has virtually no part to play at the orphanage. Neither Oxford's facilities nor its programs are approved or examined by state licensers. It opened its doors a few years before legislation requiring child care facilities to be inspected to insure the safety of the children, and thus the orphanage escapes its provisions.

If it chose to, the orphanage could join the state foster care system. But Oxford, as it is commonly known, still refuses to sign on to the 1964 Civil

Rights Act. Signing would enable Oxford to receive state and federal money, but would also require it to open admission to children of all races and accept state inspection.

Oxford claims it thrives on its autonomy. It argues that without state interference, it can provide a genuine family atmosphere and better programs for its children. With annual revenues of $2.8 million, it is one of the richest children's homes in North Carolina and arguably in the country. There is no financial pressure to comply with the Civil Rights Act. Oxford is so well off, in fact, it pays the tuition of its children who go on to the local community college, and even helps them finance their first cars.

Recently there have been signs of discomfort that Oxford is not inspected by the state. After years of persistent rumors of physical abuse, particularly that Oxford still takes the paddle to wayward children, Oxford director Rev. David Grissolm invited state license supervisor Elsie Roane to tour part of the facilities with him. There she saw nothing out of line. To the contrary, she was impressed.

"There was a real family atmosphere," Roane says. "Many homes strive for it, but Oxford seems to have achieved it. It really is a better home . . . ," she says, falling just short of comparing it to the black home down the road.

Oxford finally yielded further to social pressures in 1995 by admitting its first African-American children, a family of five siblings (thereby reducing to seven the number of white-only orphanages in the United States). That year, too, it changed its name to the Oxford Masonic Home for Children.

The town of Oxford remains largely unofficially segregated, but children from Oxford and Central are sent to the same public high school. Color seems to be no barrier in friendships. In fact, children from the homes seem drawn to one another because of their similar backgrounds. But in town there is considerable opposition to interracial dating, particularly of white girls with black boys.

ON the other side of town, about three miles down the same road but a world apart, is Central Children's Home, a state-, county-, and federally funded institution that accepts children of all races but has remained since its founding an almost all-black institution. Per child, it survives on less than one third the budget of Oxford, according to Roane.

Before a 1994 federal General Accounting Office report on unfit child care facilities shamed North Carolina into increasing Central's funding, its director was making monthly trips to the bank for loans to feed the children. Central's support from the state and county is prorated on the number of children it houses. It is critical for Central to keep its forty-six beds full. The economics of operating the home thus counters its goal for the children—to reunite them with their families.

Central was not identified by name in the GAO report, but Central director

Mike Alston and Elsie Roane's state licensing office found it easily enough in the section dealing with sanitary and safety violations in children's homes —burst sewer pipe, unlocked medicine cabinets, unrefrigerated medicine, unlabeled medicine, crumbling and leaking roof, torn curtains, dead trees falling on campus.

"The only thing those devils missed is that we don't have enough money to feed the children," Alston says of the report.

Following its publication, the North Carolina General Assembly appropriated a half million dollars to improve conditions at Central.

Alston's first move was to raise the starting salaries of his residential counselors (who live in cottages of twelve children each) from $5,200 a year plus board, but not always including medical insurance, to $13,000 and medical insurance. He still has trouble attracting qualified staff. While Oxford's staff is college educated, Central is lucky to have staff with high school diplomas. "And staff is everything," Alston says. "If you have a good staff, you know good services are going to be rendered."

Despite the disparity in the budgets of Oxford and Central, the black orphanage usually sends a greater percentage of its graduates to college and military service than Oxford. Of Central's three graduates in 1994, two went to college and one into the military. Of Oxford's ten graduates that year, one went on to college and two to the military. While that may be an immediate measure of success, Central social worker William Marrow says that final judgment in this regard must wait several years. The results are usually disheartening. Adrift, without the structure and support they have learned to depend on in the homes, most of the kids drop out of college or are discharged early from the military. Oxford's director says he considers his graduates successful if they pay their taxes, maintain a home and a job. Most of Oxford's graduates are successful by that measure, he says.

The facilities, staff-to-child ratio, programs, environment, and attention are far better at Oxford. Looking beyond race, Alston wants the best care for every child. He doesn't want less for Oxford; he wants more for Central. If a white child staying at Central has the opportunity to be placed at Oxford, he won't stand in the way.

"Every child, black or white, deserves the best placement they can get," Alston explains.

Alston knows Grissolm personally and considers him a friend. Long before Oxford opened its doors to black children, Alston knew that Grissolm sought to desegregate the home. But Alston still cringes at the segregation practiced at the institutions for over a century and the patronage system he has had to take advantage of for the children in his care. For as long as he can remember, Oxford has sent excess clothes to Central. And recently its maintenance crew was offered to repair Central's pipes, after Grissolm got wind of the GAO report.

As different as the two homes are, their directors see things much the same. Oxford's Grissolm, for example, speaks of the 171 children in his care as "social orphans," a phrase remarkably similar to Alston's "orphans of the living." But Alston is extremely unsympathetic to the whites who determined Oxford's white-only policy for more than a century.

"Until the older generation of white devils dies out, there won't be any real changes," he says, leaning over his wide oak desk with anger flashing in his dark eyes.

CENTRAL Children's Home is remarkable not only for surviving the difficult environment. Much like Oxford, it also boasts a place in history. It is the second-oldest orphanage in the state (after Oxford) and one of the first in the country created specially to serve black children.

Two prominent black community leaders from Henderson, a town just east of Oxford, founded the home. One was Rev. Augustus Shepard, pastor of a Baptist church, and the other, Henry Cheatham, then a teacher in the local public schools. Cheatham, the son of a slave and a slave owner, went on to become the first black man elected to the U.S. House of Representatives and served two terms during Reconstruction. Initially the home was called the Grant Colored Asylum (for U.S. president Ulysses S. Grant), then the Colored Orphan Asylum, and then the Central Orphanage.

Through the last two decades of the nineteenth century, the orphanage was entirely dependent on donations of churches and benevolent individuals for support to augment money the children earned cultivating the twenty-three acres of land that belonged to the home. Bessie Hockins, a white woman from Canada, provided furniture and a house, for example, and Henry Hester, a black businessman, promised to pay for the children's food. In 1892, the grand lodge of black Masons of North Carolina allotted 10 percent of its gross receipts annually to the home.

The children at Central worked hard in the early years of the home's existence. Besides farming, the boys labored over bricklaying for the growing home, while the girls took in sewing and washing. Some of the boys were also hired out to local farmers to supplement the home's income. The practice stopped after 1918, when the superintendent complained that the local farmers hired away some of his best workers. But as with many institutional-ized children's homes, complaints that the children were used as labor inside the home continued into the 1960s.

Licensing of residential child care began nationwide in 1910 to regulate this activity and afford protection to children living apart from their parents. But state officials in 1917 exempted Central from inspection and standardized child care practices by declaring it part of the state government. Central was not licensed until 1974, so was not subjected to the same standards as white children's homes. Central has been playing catch-up ever since.

The Depression hit the home brutally. A drop in funding reduced the number of children in Central's care from 250 to 160, even though the needs of impoverished families rose. Records show the home was forced to turn away orphaned children in need. During this time, the home attempted to feed, clothe, and house all the children for thirty-eight cents a day. Some argue that Central never recovered from the Depression. For lack of funds and unequal state licensing standards, it failed to keep up with advances in child care found at other homes, such as employing trained staff and professional social workers.

In 1965, Central opened its doors officially to white children, but it was nearly twenty years before the first white child was placed there. In recent years Central's population has decreased, and so has the amount of funding from the N.C. General Assembly.

Today, "Central is a shoestring operation, which is a pretty strong thing to say about a children's institution," says Roane. "It does amazingly well with what it's got, but it has to survive on thirty cents to the dollar of what a white institution gets."

2

Damien's Arrival

A MONTH shy of his thirteenth birthday, Damien Mangum sits in a white van that is covered by a layer of fine brown dust, and scans the dry August grounds of Central Children's Home. His four younger brothers and a sister wriggle about beside him. "Home" seems to him a strange word for the place. The acres of short-cropped grass are punctuated by a tumbling shed, a tobacco field, a chapel, some big trees, and about five squat brick buildings. It isn't exactly what came to mind when his caseworker said he and his siblings were going to their "new home." No, he thinks, the caseworker was wrong. This is only where they'll stay for now.

The Mangums were taken from their mother's home and her custody because of "neglect," a broad term that encompasses just about any unacceptable living environment for a child. The protective services worker who investigated the Mangums' case told one social worker, on the side, that it was the single worst living environment he had ever seen. But that was all he said. There is no record as to whether the children were beaten or sexually abused. All that would come out later. The protective services worker did his job: he removed the children from an unhealthy and perhaps dangerous environment as quickly and efficiently as possible, and went on to his next case.

Central Children's Home is the Mangums' second placement away from their mother. The first was with their maternal grandparents. The caseworker assigned to the Mangums knew the extended-family placement was a long shot; nevertheless he hoped it would keep the children out of official foster care homes long enough for their mother to pull herself together. But he was not optimistic that the Mangums' mother would obey court-ordered measures required to reclaim her children.

His gut was right. After a year, the caseworker found the grandparents "too infirm to care for the children." Damien had begun skipping school. The grandparents could not get him to attend. Teachers complained that he had the ability to do well but refused to apply himself to anything but lunch. When Damien got "involved with a negative peer group," his file said, the caseworker looked for another foster placement. He sought a temporary home with "security, structure, and discipline" until Damien and his siblings could be reunited with their mother.

"However," the caseworker noted in the case plan, his mother "is not taking the necessary steps that should precede reunification."

DAMIEN steps out of the van first, onto Central Children's Home's pocked dirt-and-gravel driveway. His soft frame, large only in its defiant stance but average by every other twelve-year-old measure, blocks the van's door. He surveys their new home long enough to glare at the nosy young faces staring back at him from the grounds, and then watch a heat mirage quiver on the still road—a road he wishes they had continued down, passing by this place without stopping.

Standing there, stopping the process on his time, he grabs at some control. No one moves for the moment; he rules. If he wants to, he could climb back into the van and tell the driver they aren't going to stay. It is an illusion, but image is everything in Damien's book. He knows he has no choice but to go where he and his siblings are sent. But he doesn't have to surrender, either. He doesn't have to like Central Children's Home. He doesn't have to trust the adults he is told to obey. They lie most of the time anyway, saying it will be OK when they don't even know what OK is. They don't have to be him, in charge of a family. That lesson he has learned the hard way.

Finally, on his terms, he moves casually from the door, ignoring his siblings' impatience. As they empty the van, he feels his control slipping. He fights back for it, lagging behind as his brothers and sister are herded into a 1970s ranch-style brick building.

Once inside, Damien looks at the staff skeptically, then falls into his routine. When they are kind, he is hard; when they are tough, he is gentle. They know the game as well as he does. It is so familiar that they pass it off almost unnoticed.

What strikes the staff first about Damien is not his boundary-testing games or attitude but the way his eyebrows rise at the ends. He looks devious and sometimes mean beyond his years. His dark brown eyes hide his thoughts well. At times they are unfathomable black pools, indecipherable and impenetrable. To a sympathetic young staffer, they tell of a soul old in ugly experiences, caught in a child's body. To an older, more experienced and tired staffer, they warn of trouble.

"He was not a very likable child," one social worker will remember a year later. "There are some children who are somewhat receptive to kindness. Damien wasn't one of them. He was always looking for an angle. And he could be mean. You could see that the moment you looked at him."

The Mangums are processed in the first building they enter at Central. In a conference room they are given a brief explanation of their case. They will be staying at Central "for some time," a Central social worker tells them.

"How long?" Damien asks.

"It's a temporary placement," the social worker answers. He pauses, and then explains further. "That means that the plan is to reunite you with your mother."

"How long will that be?"

"We don't know. Your mother has to be able to take you back."

"But we will go back."

"If she does what she's supposed to," the worker says, nodding.

"What is she supposed to do?" one of the younger children asks.

"Hush up," his older brother says. "She'll do it, you know it. She said she'd get us back if she has to steal us."

Damien's words ease the younger children. The social worker asks if there are any questions. The children look around. They don't know what questions to ask.

A Polaroid camera is brought out. Snapshots of the children will be attached to the files to identify each child for social workers and staff during meetings.

The social worker asks for a volunteer for the first picture.

Damien moves forward. He smiles a little for the camera. But his smile doesn't light up his face. Instead it draws out the lines and circles, making him look unreasonably old and angry. It could be a beautiful face if it weren't so warped by abuse and anger, a counselor whispers. The children are divided between three cottages.

Damien's file says he was taken into Wake County Department of Social Services' custody "due to lack of proper care, supervision, and discipline from his alcoholic mother." His siblings were taken for similar reasons, though their records have a hit-and-miss quality. Some mention physical abuse of the child while others do not. Their mother's alcoholism is cited in some records, but not others. What drew and cemented DSS attention to the Mangums was the common denominator of neglect. It wasn't that the children did or did not want to be with their mother or even that their mother's alcoholism often exploded into violence. Those were details buttressing the fundamental claim. She was simply found by a child protective service worker "not responsive to the needs of Damien and his siblings."

Child neglect affects more families than any other form of child mistreatment, yet it receives far less attention than child abuse. North Carolina's central registry recorded ten thousand substantiated reports of child neglect for 1994, and less than a quarter that number of child abuse. Part of the reason for this huge disparity is not the absence of abuse but the fact that neglect is far more broadly defined in law and much easier to prove than abuse.*

North Carolina general statutes legally define a neglected juvenile as one "who does not receive proper care, supervision or discipline from his parent, custodian, or caretaker; or who has been abandoned; or who is not provided necessary medical care or other remedial care recognized under State law, or who lives in an environment injurious to his welfare."

Neglect is the easiest and most efficient reason to remove a child in jeopardy. And when the child is in danger, the reasons for removal are clearly secondary to keeping the child safe. But focusing on immediate placement often causes vital details of the child's history to be lost and his or her needs overlooked.

Nowhere in Damien's record, for example, is mention of the sexual abuse he experienced throughout his childhood. But the staff at Central was not surprised when disturbing symptoms of sexual trauma surfaced in Damien a couple of months later. Sexual abuse is virtually the norm in Central's children. Director Alston estimates that virtually all the girls and slightly more than half the boys have been sexually abused, though most of their case files don't record it.

"Girls who are being sexually abused are usually easier to keep around," he says. "A family won't give them up unless they're in extreme danger and might talk about it, or are promiscuous and the family doesn't want to deal with the rumors. But being promiscuous is also a symptom of previous sexual abuse. Those kids think that to get attention and love—well, to them, that's sex because that's what they've known."

---

* The most common reason given for the half million children placed in foster care throughout the country is neglect, though in many of these cases there may also have been signs of abuse. Neglect is the most difficult problem facing family reunification because it is so tied to poverty and impoverished families' generational practices in child rearing. According to the American Humane Association's report "Trends in Child Abuse and Neglect," 45 percent of neglected children live in single-parent households and are on public assistance. In North Carolina, Elsie Roane found that families in which maltreatment occurs are four times more likely to receive public assistance and almost twice as likely to be black.

Sexual abuse of boys is even more underreported than it is with girls. Boys are often more reticent to report or confirm being abused because they sense a greater stigma in being weak enough to be sexually victimized.

"And there's seldom proof," one social worker explains. "When a twelve-year-old girl is pregnant, you know where that's coming from. A boy doesn't have that. And boys are different. They aren't going to lie to you if you ask them if someone has molested or abused them, but it's more of a disgrace for them to admit it than girls. Boys think they're supposed to be cool; they're even supposed to like it and be big men about it. They're supposed to know about sex."

All forms of abuse—physical, sexual, and emotional—are more difficult to document than neglect. A social worker can use his or her judgment in reporting neglect. But unless the social worker actually witnesses abuse, either the abuser must admit mistreating the victim or hospital records must certify abuse.

Sometimes the social worker will even make a deal with the parents. To get the children away as soon as possible, he or she will agree to ignore signs of sexual abuse if the children are released to foster care immediately and the abuser ejected from their family. In such cases, the parents are much more likely to regain custody of the child than if the sexual abuse was charged. Unfortunately, the children in these cases suffer the effects of the abuse and of the trauma of separation from their parents without treatment. Only when they later begin to act out, as almost all victims eventually do, does the staff at the foster home suspect the truth and call for professional help. Evidence of abuse often remains submerged for years, as in Damien's case. When it surfaces, it may be too late for the child.

THOMAS is photographed next. Though younger than Damien, he looms larger in the picture because before the snap of the shutter he lurches forward with a tough and angry expression. With his bold-striped T-shirt, he appears to be the toughest as well as the biggest of the Mangum clan, although his looks are deceiving. He is something of a gentle giant. His file chronicles the problems arising from his tough facade, although the reports may reflect the prejudices of weary caseworkers toward mean-looking kids. His mother is homeless, alcoholic, and violent, his records say.* He makes no effort in school, and for a while, C's and D's are his usual grades. Central will find that Thomas's IQ falters along the borderline between normal and retarded.

---

* Differences such as these point to the sympathies and prejudices of many child care workers in the system. Favoritism runs through the system as it does through classrooms. Some caseworkers are more open about it than others. They are influenced by race, by cleanliness, by age. But most, as in the Mangums' case, form their first telling impression by the child's attitude during their initial brief meeting.

His sister Julia is sweet and docile. Unlike her brothers', her smile opens her face; though, like them, she barely parts her lips. She wears her brothers' hand-me-downs and her coltish frame swims in them. Her hair had been tied back carefully that morning, but by afternoon it is in need of a brush—"raggedy," the girls in her cottage later call it.

Michael Mangum comes to Central Children's Home in his favorite green Godzilla T-shirt. He has a bright, fresh face. To the camera he shows the same skepticism as his brothers and sister, but like Julia's, it's a mask that slips often into playfulness. He does very well in school, despite a bad temper.

Michael and Jefferson tumble like bear cubs most of the day. Though they are a few years apart, they are about the same size. Jefferson stands a full four feet five and weighs fifty-two pounds. His orange shirt and jeans are unwashed and grungy. His hobbies are basketball and reading, and like Michael, he will do well in school while at Central: A's in English and reading, C's in math and science. His teachers will complain that he's hyperactive. Like Thomas, he fights anyone who slights his family, no matter their size.

Fred, the youngest child, stays quiet next to Julia all day. His wide eyes soak up everything, yet he hardly speaks and never in full sentences. An accidental head injury when he was a baby has left him virtually deaf.

Central will find out about that later. For now, all they know is the faces and sizes of the children standing before them and what's written on the children's applications for admittance. Unfortunately those applications are only as honest as any applications. The facts that might cause the Mangums to be rejected are phrased in the least inflammatory way, if not blatantly ignored. With each new child, staffers must learn as they go.

WITHIN the first week at Central, Damien makes it clear that he is democratic in his distrust. It is not reserved for adults or authority figures; he distrusts everyone. He fights with the other kids until he establishes himself as one to be reckoned with. Although not large or particularly strong, he knows how to fight mean.

"You don't want to mess with Damien," says a boy two years older and twice his size. "It's his eyes, maybe. Angry. He got control. You mess with him and he'll get mad, wild mad, and he'll get you. If he has to sneak into your room at night with a knife, he'll get you."

"What alerted us to trouble first is that it took Damien a long time to process his anger," says Emeron Cash, a Central social worker.

Damien can be cunningly patient as the anger eats at his insides, until it bursts. Hours after an argument with one boy, he ransacks the boy's room. Aware of his volatility, a residential parent stays with Damien and another boy after their argument in a kitchen, until it appears Damien has calmed down. But as soon as he leaves, Damien grabs a butcher knife. A serious incident is only narrowly avoided.

Only his siblings are safe from his fury. They are the only ones he cares about. He fights to protect them from other children's taunts and even staff members' discipline. He fights with his brother or his sister, but only in quick spats. Damien and his siblings hold together as a family. They look out for one another, they draw pictures for one another, and they fight for one another. When Thomas, who is larger than most children his age, is ridiculed, his smaller brothers are quick to jump to his aid and fight for him. Thomas's gentle nature is accepted by the Mangums even as they come to his defense.

"I don't think he's ever fought anyone, and if I have it my way, he never will," Damien says.

Julia adjusts well with the girls in the cottages, on the far side of the campus from the boys. Her only complaint is that she is not living with her brothers. She draws pictures and writes notes to them.

All five Mangum children have private and family counseling (without a parent but with siblings). In several sessions, Julia becomes upset at her brothers when their behavior is criticized.

"Why you do that?" she scolds Michael in one session. "They'll make you leave and put you in a different place and we'll never see you again."

Then she bursts into tears.

Julia is the only Mangum who heeds their caseworker's warning that if one child is expelled from Central, the children will be split up because it is too difficult to accommodate all six of them together. In fact, that's why they are at Central. Their caseworker could not find a foster family that would take all six siblings.*

The stress of her brothers' behavior and the fear of separation causes Julia to nibble at her fingers until they bleed. On her own, she is a gentle and giving child. Residential staff find her "easy to deal with and happy." Most of the time, she is laughing—if not at something, then at nothing, it seems.

Though Julia is only eight years old, Damien, at thirteen, wants to insure that no boys in the home have their eyes on his little sister. Sex is dirty, violent, and ugly, he feels.

"It's for boys," he says, "not for girls."

Later, the staff learns that Damien was sexually abused by several adult men, including a relative and several of his mother's boyfriends.

"We think that the other children were OK," Alston says after the discovery. "Oftentimes in that situation, there's a target child. He absorbs all the negative behavior. The abusers focus on him and ignore the other children."

But with Damien's family there is no way to be certain. A child may not be physically molested, but seeing or hearing others being sexually abused

---

* The difficulty is greater for the Mangums because they are African-American. North Carolina policy is that African-American children should be placed with African-American foster families, and the state has relatively few African-American foster families.

can be extremely traumatic. If Damien's younger siblings have also been sexually victimized, they don't talk about it, or perhaps even remember it—yet.

3

Adjusting

▓

DAMIEN does not accept Central as readily as his younger and more pliant brothers and sister. Like many older children in the system, Damien has had more than a few bad experiences with adults. So trust and adapting to staff rules are just not on his agenda. His first job is to take care of himself and his siblings, and maybe then see how the staff figures into the picture and how he can use them. The staff sees Damien's attitude as the cause of their broken relationship with him. But Damien doesn't see any correlation between his self-preservationist attitude and the problems he later experiences with the staff.

He doesn't plan to be bad, he says. Trouble just has a way of attaching itself to him. And trouble grabs on to Damien almost immediately. The day after he arrives at Central, he steals $1.50 and a pack of cigarettes from a counselor. A counselor reprimands him. One week later another counselor disciplines Damien for being sassy to his residential advisor.

Damien works at establishing himself, both with the staff and other children in the home. He tests the limits and demonstrates his own. His frequent cursing, his angry outbursts, his sass are all part of the image he wants to project to the other boys, most of whom are bigger, to preclude them from preying on him or his siblings. Or so he says, perhaps rationalizing his anger and the purging effect violent behavior has on it.

Bravado and dare taking are the beginning of Damien's serious estrangement from Central. All of the new children are subjected to hazing in one form or another, particularly the older ones. For girls, it often takes the form of threatening to cut off the new girl's hair when she's asleep.

"If she gets scared and you see it, you know you can't trust her," one girl explains. "She either gonna rat, or someone gonna get her because they know she scared."

New boys, much as in Dickens's *Oliver Twist,* are often told they are permitted to do something, like walk off campus, that in fact is expressly forbidden by the rules. Michael is the first victim of this form of hazing. On a $10 dare, the seven-year-old runs away from school for one day. He gets off with a stern warning after he says he wanted the $10 to buy a doll for his sister.

More serious breaches of conduct include visits by girls to the boys' cottages and vice versa, or abetting such behavior by acting as lookout or leaving basement doors open. In his first month at Central, Damien is caught and punished for all infractions. Rather than showing fear, he brazenly acts as if he doesn't care.

Initially Damien's residential counselor, Mr. Brown, allows Damien's minor violations to slip by unreported.* Like other good residential cottage counselors, he tries to shield Damien from complaints of other staff members. Brown's motive is not limited to saving Damien from punishment. Reported violations, no matter how minor, can damage the child's chances of a good foster placement in the future. And Brown also hopes to win Damien's trust and respect by protecting him. But after one month, the staff gets fed up with Damien's behavior and his only defender, Mr. Brown, shifts toward their side in frustration. Damien, he complains after several difficult and even unnerving incidents, prides himself on being "stubborn and bullheaded."

Damien does not fare any better at school. In fact, he spirals downward. By trial, Damien finds that the town's public school, which Central's children attend, is less patient and understanding than the staff at Central.

In early September, a teacher takes a bracelet away from Damien because he fidgets with it constantly and refuses to pay attention in class.

"I'm going to beat your ass if you don't give me my bracelet back," Damien threatens.

He later admits that while he doesn't remember the threat, he did get out of hand. He keeps his eyes lowered and shuffles his feet with his hands behind his back, but offers no excuses. Still later, his brother explains that their mother had made the bracelet for Damien. Personal possessions are vitally important to children in a new home setting, particularly if they were given by a person significant to them.†

A few days later, Damien leaves his cottage at 7:50 P.M. without permission

---

* Many, if not most, children get into some trouble defining their limits and adjusting to their new environment. Generally it is accepted that recorded misbehavior is understated and underreported. A new or overzealous staffer, one simply doing his or her job but unfamiliar with the unspoken understanding that only serious problems are actually reported, can do great damage to a child's future. There are other reasons for not formally reporting the child. It saves overworked houseparents time from clerical work—time they can spend with the children or on their own.

† Bryan, a foster kid now twenty years old, is keenly aware when the door to his room is slightly ajar when he returns from school or work. He paces around nervously, looking for items missing or out of place. "These are my things," he says. "I know I go overboard, but I don't have many things that I've been able to keep, and I don't like things taken from me. It's real personal to me. A real violation." He walks around agitated the rest of the day if anything has been disturbed.

and wanders off campus. When staff catch up with him, they describe him as "in a daze." At first he does not recognize them. But he is easily guided into their car and back onto campus.

"I don't know what I'm thinking at times," he says. "I just go off. My head is full of clouds and I can't think."

He wanders off on other occasions, particularly during stressful times. One night he leaves after midnight. But he never goes far away.

"It's hard to call it running away," one supervisor explains. "He wanders around like in circles."

Damien's psychologist ties this daze to the trauma of having witnessed violence. The therapist later discovers just how violent Damien's family life has been. His early records suggest that brutality was a companion from infancy. So frequent were the violent episodes that he stopped flinching when those he cared about were beaten. To some degree, he is immune to pain when beaten. It may even be comforting to be struck. It means he is not being ignored, that perhaps he is cared about, and is worthy of some kind of emotion. Subtly, abuse became indistinguishable from care and love in Damien's mind, the psychologist concludes. But now, at Central, what were common and everyday events in his home—violence, cursing, shouting—are unacceptable. Each time he is disciplined, he slips further from understanding his place and deeper into cynicism about the world.

In October a staffer reports him for "use of profanity and being noisy." A dollar is deducted from his allowance, which Central gives the children weekly.

By the time November's chill blows through campus, Damien feels totally alienated. When the other children draw up lists for Christmas presents, Damien writes down nothing. "I was bad," Damien explains with no trace of self-pity. "I wasn't gonna get no Christmas present because I was bad." So he leaves his list blank.

Julia writes down a request for her brother: a new bike. And he receives it on Christmas from a group of local charities that donate presents each year.

Damien's behavior now undergoes an unexpected change. He loves his bike, and he begins to pay more attention and even deference and respect to the staff workers. His teachers report that he is doing better in school. Instead of failing three classes, he is passing all of them. For the first time, he actually wants to learn. When told the roads might ice with a coming snowstorm and that school might be canceled, Damien says he'll get a blowtorch to clear the way.

Damien is proud of his positive attitude and behavior at school and home, he says. He even apologizes to a teacher after harsh words spring out. To his psychologist, he volunteers "that he is glad he had decided to do right" and that he feels good about school and personal relationships.

And he continues to press staff about visiting his mother. He asks the therapist who has been counseling him for any word from his guardian *ad litem* (the court-appointed advocate who is expected to keep in close touch with him and speak in court on his behalf). The therapist hasn't heard from the guardian but assures Damien that he will pass on word of Damien's desire to visit his mother with his siblings.

Uncovering the early violence in Damien's life is easing him away from violent impulses, the therapist believes. Damien is learning to come forward with his needs and desires by simply asking, without anger.

"Damien was very appropriate in presenting his thoughts about wanting to have a home visit with his siblings," the therapist records. "In addition he was very appropriate in stating that he wanted to see his mother and that not seeing her affects how he feels."

Damien misses his mother a great deal more than the therapist's report suggests. He recognizes that she beat and neglected him and the other children. He knows that while in her home he was sexually abused by other adults. But he loves her still and seems willing to give her limitless chances. His love for her appears untarnished. And he reserves his trust only for her, refusing to share it with other adults, even those who have never harmed him.

"No matter how abused these children are, they still want to go home," Alston explains. "I don't care what happened to them, most of them only talk about going home."

But Damien does not get the visit—his mother is barred legally from seeing them—and his behavior backslides. In February, he ransacks another boy's room. Soon after, he seizes a butcher knife after an argument with another boy. Staff tries to control his outbursts by telling him that he will have a better chance of being reunited with his mother if he behaves well.

Damien tries even harder to convince staff that returning home would be best for him and his siblings. He tells the therapist he doesn't believe his mother would beat them again, and convinced of that, he doesn't understand why she can't see them. He mentions that on a recent visit to his grandparents, his mother stopped by to see the children despite the court order. The psychologist reports her visit to a Central social worker. Damien is angered by what he sees as the therapist's betrayal and decides not to speak freely to him again.

He begins to think that all the talk of reuniting the family is just talk and he has to do something to make it happen.

Damien asks to see his guardian *ad litem* almost desperately now. The guardian *ad litem* had been presented to Damien as his unconditional advocate. It was promised that he would keep in close touch with Damien. But the guardian has not visited Damien since the Mangums arrived at Central, and Damien has no way to contact him. When the guardian was first introduced to the Mangum children, Damien did not trust him. He understood that the guardian was a volunteer, and that raised his suspicion. No one does something for nothing, Damien believes. However, after a few meetings at his grandparents' home, in which the guardian seemed sympathetic, Damien came to believe this advocate could be his way out of Central. But now, frustrated in his efforts to reach the man, Damien never again asks to see the guardian.

Instead, Damien now decides to play the game. He will not speak openly about his feelings and will simply do as he is told. That way, maybe, the home will reunite him with his mother. He promises his siblings that because of their good behavior, they will almost certainly be reunited with their mother by Easter.

In his excitement at the prospect, Jefferson sends a letter home full of his dreams and hopes:

Dear Family
   How are you doing? I hop you are dig fine and I really do hope momma is doing fine probably we will be coming home friday and if we do i will be happy to see all of you and if i see momma i will faint and she will have to carry me in the house

"I wouldn't really faint," Jefferson says later, with a wink. "I'd pretend to so that Mama would carry me again like I was her baby, like she used to."

It is a distant memory, one that he holds closer and firmer than the ones of flying dishes, sharp slaps, cigarette burns, and perhaps rape.

A week later, at the end of March, the children are brought together with the therapist to discuss the plans for Easter break. A Central social worker tells them that because their mother has still not complied with the court order for abuse counseling, they cannot go home to her, but that there is a chance that they can go to their aunt's for that week. Damien, Julia, and Jefferson complain about the decision and are told to leave the session because they become disruptive. A file also notes their increasing "anxiety regarding the home situation."

Anxiety soon turns to resentment. The Mangum children had come to Central believing, as many children in foster care do, that in some way it was their fault that they were taken from their mother. Now they believe that they have done something wrong to be kept away from her. They cannot believe that she would fail to do everything she could to get them back. But they don't know what wrongs they have committed. The guilt thaws into anger. Maybe it isn't their fault, but why are they being punished so much? For months they have been waiting to be released into their mother's arms. Those months now seem like forever. Their frustration and confusion feeds resentment and then fury. In this tornado of emotions, all that Central has built for the Mangums crashes to the ground.

Central has filled its role well as surrogate parent for most of the Mangums. The children have adjusted to Central and accepted their new authority figures. But now they feel fooled. Damien especially feels duped. And furious.

"Man," he says, throwing his math book across the floor, "they told us this was just going to be for a while and then we'd get to go back home. They told us to be good. They told us if we was good they'd let us go back to Mama. We been good. We been bustin' good, and they ain't lettin' us go back. We just fools."

Damien cannot point toward any one person who told him that his behavior determined whether he would be reunited with his mother. Most child care workers are careful not to make such statements. Experts say it is vital to convince children that their behavior in foster care and in their past is unrelated to their future. And yet their behavior in foster placements does affect their future. But rather than offer a carrot of reunification in exchange for good behavior, good caretakers recognize that the children need unconditional love and care and an outlet for their anger. They also recognize that it is almost impossible to find such caring in the system.

Damien's disillusion turns sour and angry—emotions that an institution constantly struggling to meet the minimum required number of staff for a growing number of hurt and troubled children in their care has no room for. Anger in such an institution threatens control.

"What's the point of being good anyway?" Damien spits. "It don't do no good anyway. If anything they don't treat you no better when you're good. They treat you worse."

His eyes light up as if he has discovered a truth.

4

Slipping

DAMIEN'S behavior worsens significantly over the next week and then plunges despairingly in the weeks that follow. No longer satisfied to push Central's boundaries, he rails against the stricter confines of the public school at Oxford, whose PTA regularly grumbles about the disruption "home kids" pose to their small school. He doesn't care about anything anymore, he says. Just the thought of being good or trying to please anyone angers him. He regularly disrupts classes. Profanity spills out of him like a busted water pipe. He is angry and doesn't care to hide it anymore.

Central allows him his tantrums, to a point. "If cursing relieves him of some of the anger, then that's fine in my book," a Central social worker says. "It's a whole lot better than getting violent."

The public school is less understanding. Damien is suspended for two days for saying "shit." "We don't want *our* children to start using that language," one teacher explains. "And besides, suspension is a good way to get a disruptive child out of the way for a while."

Her comment hints at the tension between the school and its Parent-Teacher Association, on the one hand, and, on the other hand, Oxford's two children's homes, particularly Central with its overwhelmingly black population. Many of the teachers and parents in Oxford see Central's children as trouble, rather than just as troubled, and treat them as inferior. Mary Ann Lumpkins, who serves as the liaison between the homes and the schools, acknowledges the bias of some teachers.

"The kids pick it up right away," she says. "They know which teachers look down on them and treat them badly. Sometimes they try to use that when they get in trouble with the teacher, that she's prejudiced."

It is an atmosphere ready made to come down hard on Damien with his new hostility. In mid-April, he is suspended for four days "for severe disrespectful behavior toward Mr. X and failure to follow requirements of Miss Y."

His grades suffer with the suspension, and the lower grades reduce his earlier determination to succeed in school. Teachers no longer go out of their way to help him. They see him as a lost kid.

"Once they've slipped beyond detention into suspension, we've lost them," says one teacher who is sympathetic toward Central's kids. "It's time then to redirect your attention to other kids who are slipping toward detention."

In seventh grade now, Damien is averaging 60s in reading, language arts, and social studies, with some effort. In science and physical education, his grades reach into the 70s, and they pinnacle even higher in math. But after Easter, Damien fails even math. His teacher complains of his malaise. Damien is making "no effort" in the subject.

"Shit," he replies to her comment, and is suspended again before he completes the sentence.

"This," he says later with angry bravado, "is only the beginning."

Whether a promise or a threat, his prediction turns out to be accurate.

5

Sebastian's Home

SEBASTIAN was born to a fragile home in the spring of 1978. Even before he was conceived, social services considered his mother to be mentally and physically unstable. At times a white mist would roll through her mind. It was something she could sense but never stop. One doctor prescribed Valium, but she used heroin most of the time. She wandered around some then. Before and between the times one of her children took her in, she was on the streets, homeless.

Sebastian doesn't know his father. If his mother knows, she did not use his name on Sebastian's birth certificate. It is only the first of many blanks in his files. The man he calls his father died when Sebastian was eight.

Something must have been right, a caseworker once told him, for him to turn out as well as he did. And Sebastian agrees. On paper it all looks worse than it was, he says. When they were together, it was *almost* like *The Cosby Show. Almost.* His much older brothers and sisters and his uncles have been around, on and off, for him. His mother was loving toward him, caring for him when she could. Only she can't even care for herself anymore. Her daughter Alice cares for her now.

Even at its best, Sebastian's family was anything but tight. His two older brothers are more than fifteen years older than Sebastian. They showed up occasionally and taught him how to take care of himself at school and in sports. His three sisters, Fran, Ann, and Alice, more than ten years older, helped out some, too. But the attention from his siblings was even more sporadic and random than from his mother. Moreover, Sebastian felt lost in his older family. He knew he had been a surprise and often he felt—and was told so by his siblings when he was bad—that he had been a mistake.

Teachers saw the obvious neglect in his appearance. He came to kindergarten without shoes some days. In first grade he wore two shoes, but often mismatching ones. In second grade his clothes were unwashed and often torn, and his hair was dirty and unbrushed. The teachers considered reporting his case to family services. But they didn't. In this poor, rural county in the North Carolina Piedmont, school authorities are understanding toward the needy and disheveled children who parade through their doors. They know that both parents are often so busy working, in order to feed their family, that they have neither the time nor the energy to monitor their children as closely as the teachers would like. But they do not equate loose oversight with lack of love for the children. They also know that even in some cases of neglect, the children are better off at home, with family and a familiar and relatively stable environment, than in the foster care system.

Once, in junior high school, a teacher sat Sebastian down to talk about his home life. He was intelligent and capable, with a certain presence, a dignity, that suggested a potential to rise above his environment. Perhaps he would benefit from the advantages of foster care or even a children's home. He would be exposed to more possibilities. He might even get a shot at college and be able to focus on his future if he weren't so distracted and exhausted by the struggle to feed and clothe himself. Would he want to go into foster care? the teacher asked.

Sebastian squirmed in his seat and sucked his thumb nervously, clearly distraught at the idea of leaving what he had.

"No," he replied. "My mama's a good mama. She takes care of me. She mends my clothes, minds my studies, and teaches me good manners."

The teacher concluded that Sebastian knew how to lie to cover for his mother. "Mends" was a word he had probably read in an old book. But if he wished to cover for his mother, he clearly wanted to stay where he was. The teacher dropped the subject.

Sebastian has sucked his thumb for comfort throughout adolescence. He knows how to take care of himself in every way, he believes, but he can't give up the solace his thumb provides. Whenever the subject of his family comes up, he sucks voraciously. He doesn't know why. He only knows that he can't help it. He slips back to when he was nine years old and he knew inside that every mention of his mother or family by an outsider was the last warning of what was to come.

6

Alice Takes Over

❖

WHEN he was nine, Sebastian's mom really started messing up. She'd walk off in a daze and disappear for days. Sebastian was frightened to be alone, mostly because he was unsure that she would return. He was even more afraid for her, and when he was so worried, he could not concentrate on anything for long. He never called the police for help. Police were as much an enemy as anything his mother might come across on the streets. If they found his mother he feared they would take her away, probably forever.

"When I do that craziness," she told her son, "you don't tell no one, hear? They'll put me in a loony bin and then you be alone. I don't want my baby to be alone."

She had returned one Saturday morning to find him curled in a fetal position in the corner of his room with a blanket pulled over his head, sucking his thumb. His eyes were squeezed tightly shut when she uncovered him. When she said his name, they opened wide and terrified. She held him then, rocking and stroking him while he sucked his thumb. Tears filled his eyes and washed over his face, but no sound came from him.

Occasionally there was a man in the house. The boyfriend controlled his mother by beating her and verbally degrading her until she fell miserably to the floor, shoulders hunched, hands hiding her face. That dominance earned Sebastian's respect—and his hatred.

"Why does he beat you, Mama?" Sebastian asked.

"Because he stronger than me," she replied.

He beat Sebastian too, but not often. Sebastian didn't understand the boyfriend, but he understood how he felt when he was beaten and when he watched his mother being beaten. Humiliation first. Then awe. The man standing with his hand raised ready to knock anyone down, to subjugate them, was full of power. Everyone listened when he spoke. Everyone gave him full attention.

One day, when Sebastian was eleven and a half, he watched the man beat his mother through her screaming to submission. It had happened before, many times. Usually he felt scared when it happened. This time he felt a wild mixture of rage and envy. He desperately wanted to beat that man. Instead he went outside, found a dog, tied him to a tree, and beat the yelping dog to death with a bat. Every bone in the young dog's body was broken. But Sebastian's rage had not yet broken. He tried to set the dog on fire. Afterward, he felt no remorse. He felt powerful. He felt good.

His mother cried when she saw the dog. "Monster," she screamed at him.

Sebastian knew he had done wrong, and even that he should feel guilty, penitent. But he didn't. Instead, he felt a rush of power. The guiltless freedom after brutal actions would resurface hauntingly throughout his adolescence. He would dream of committing a murder or murders, and when he awoke, he'd feel good. They weren't nightmares, they were dreams. Only sometimes he'd remember his mother's look when she saw that dog, and then he believed he was a monster.

Sebastian, a psychologist later noted, seemed "to know the difference between good and evil, and right and wrong. But he worries that he does not have feeling of remorse and worries about controlling his impulses."

He would beat no more animals. His mother asked him not to. Instead, he found release in watching the violence of street fights, TV wrestling, and sometimes, when his brother treated him, a boxing match. He'd imagine he was the winning fighter, the one administering the beating, and he'd feel much bigger, stronger, powerful, and capable.

SEBASTIAN'S home life deteriorated rapidly after he turned twelve. He cared for himself and his mother more as she cared less. When she did not wander off, she sat in her rocking chair for hours, staring off into space. She forgot to eat unless Sebastian brought food to her. Sometimes she cried. And some days she laughed aloud as she spoke to mermaids floating through the air.

Twice the police picked her up off a street corner where she had been haranguing passersby, including Sebastian's friends, in nonsensical gibberish. She was sent to a drug rehabilitation program. But drugs weren't the problem. After the third time, the authorities suggested permanent hospitalization for the mentally ill.

Her children cut a deal to keep their mother out of the hospital. They promised social service workers that they would care for their mother. Alice, twenty-two at the time, returned home to look after her mother and Sebastian, who was now twelve.

THAT'S when things started falling apart, Sebastian says. He was accustomed to caring for himself and for his mother. He resented Alice and refused to obey her. He often threw a tantrum. She slapped him, he slapped her back. On a psychiatric evaluation years later, Sebastian related the word "fight" with Alice.

Sebastian's mother, slowly losing her grip on reality, began embarrassing him in public. Just the unruly sight of her talking to air, shouting at trees, threw his friends into bouts of howling laughter. "Yo' mama is a case," they'd say. And Sebastian shrunk further from her love in embarrassment.

At the same time, she would side with Alice in her efforts to discipline Sebastian. He was infuriated by what he saw as his mother's betrayal. Alice was stealing his mother's love from him. He was the man of the house. He was strong. He should make the decisions. Women are weak and need direction. They should not have authority over him. He would overpower his mother and sister as he had seen the other men do it. Angry words, profanity. A slap, sometimes a punch.

He was wild. Each time Alice tried to control him, he went crazy. Twice she called police to subdue him.

7

Probation

❊

SEBASTIAN turned particularly violent one night, ripping the television out of the wall, grabbing a knife, and hurtling furniture. Before the police arrived, he fled. The family's mobile home looked like a tornado had torn through it, according to one officer.

This time Alice pressed charges against her brother.

Juvenile court found Sebastian, now fourteen years old, guilty of injury to personal property, and placed him on probation. His sister and mother dropped the assault charges, but he was no longer welcome to live at home, and his aunts and uncles refused to take him in.

Sebastian's caseworker placed him in an emergency shelter in Sanford, North Carolina. According to his case plan, Sebastian would eventually be reunited with his mother. But before that could happen, the shelter expelled him because of "behavioral problems." Sebastian's caseworker placed him in another emergency shelter, where Sebastian was "defiant, particularly toward white female authority," his files say. White women, Sebastian tried to explain, were snobbish and weak. They really have no power or strength. They never really tried to get to know him. They just put him down. He was thrown out for "behavioral problems." In both cases, no specific incident was described.

At his caseworker's urging, Sebastian's uncle relented enough to take him in until another placement could be found. Sebastian did well in his new home. Grateful to be out of the children's homes and determined to stay out, he impressed his teachers as good-natured and amiable. His grades rose to B's and C's—the highest they had ever been. He found anger less necessary and inviting as he thrived on the structure and stability of his new home. He believed that if he did well in school and stayed clear of trouble, his uncle and aunt would let him stay.

During this time, Sebastian's mother became more enfeebled, mentally and physically. Alice also began to show signs of mental instability and was hospitalized for several months. Embarrassed by their illnesses, Sebastian no longer wanted to return to his mother or his old school. His caseworker recognized that reuniting Sebastian and his mother or sister had become improbable at the least.

She began looking for alternatives. Her first choice was to keep Sebastian with his uncle and aunt. They refused. She argued, but they told her bluntly that they did not want to keep Sebastian any longer than necessary.

The rejection hurt Sebastian.

"I was good," he says. "I was very good. I tried hard. I did everything my uncle said. But that didn't matter none. None of what I did mattered to anything."

Like many children in the homes, Sebastian feels responsible for events that were in fact out of his control, such as his mother's illness. But he doesn't believe that his actions have any effect on the decisions made by the Department of Social Services. He began to believe he had no control of his future. When told that he would be leaving his uncle's home, he cut school, ignored homework, and turned away from his "good" friends.

8

Sebastian's Arrival

SEBASTIAN'S case worker mentioned only his difficulty accepting white authority when she presented him to Central. She did not warn them of anything else in his past.* He was presented in an application to Central social worker William Marrow as a healthy, athletic fourteen-year-old boy. While earlier tests qualified Sebastian as learning disabled, he was attending

---

* Caseworkers are under a great deal of pressure to place children. They are not always totally frank about a child's problems and needs in their desire to find a home for their children. But withholding information often proves damaging not only to the child but also to other children, who may be victimized if counselors are not aware of the child's propensity toward certain behavioral disorders. "It's placement pressure," one home's admission officer says forgivingly. "Let me put it this way. If you don't ask the right questions, the caseworkers won't volunteer the information." He pulls a file from the top of a stack on his desk. "Take this one," he says, scanning it. "A caseworker sent in an application for a child. The form said he had little or no information about the child. I called and said we needed more. He said the child had a problem with aggressive behavior. He didn't have any more information. We came to find out, finally, that the kid beat up his grandfather when his grandfather told him to get off the phone. That kid would be like a bomb in here. But he'd be out of the caseworker's hands and in ours."

regular ninth-grade classes in Sanford, earning average or slightly below-average grades before his performance deteriorated. At the first children's home he was placed in after he assaulted his mother and sister and before his uncle took him in, Sebastian had tested as behaviorally-emotionally handicapped (BEH). But his behavior and grades dramatically improved in the months he spent living with his uncle and aunt. His verbal IQ was relatively high at 108. But Burk's Behavior Rating Scales found he had poor attention span, poor impulse control, poor reality contact, excessive sense of persecution, excessive aggressiveness, excessive resistance, and poor ego strength.

On an identification test he responded to word cues as follows:

sad—"unfamiliar surroundings"
mad—"Alice, authority figures"
fight—"Alice"
glad—"sports and girls"

Sebastian's weaknesses are "racist and sexist attitudes" toward people with skin lighter than his dark color, particularly whites, and that he "feels he doesn't have to follow rules," an evaluator wrote.

His strengths: "intelligent, catches on quickly, athletic, and somewhat ambitious."

In an interview, Sebastian tells Central social worker Willie Marrow he wants to be a sports commentator or policeman when he grows up. Despite his dysfunctional home life, his case plan is still to reunite him with his mother eventually.

Central's administrators debate whether or not to accept Sebastian. A bed is open in the older boys' cottage, which they need to fill. But his assault on his mother and sister, which they find out about through their own investigation, disturbs them. Sebastian could very well be a difficult child, they all agree. Nonetheless Alston and his staff decide to risk it. Some of the most difficult children turn out the most determined and successful. Sebastian has displayed some of the qualities that indicate this potential—intelligence, ambition—and they hope his anger will translate into tenacity and drive.

IN early 1994, at fourteen years old, Sebastian completes Central's entrance physical. He is five feet two and 112.5 pounds with 20/40-20/20 vision and no trace of drugs in his system.*

Sebastian tries to project an image of sophistication from the first moment

---

* If he were a girl, he would have been given a pregnancy test as well, no matter what the age. "Some of these rascals have sneaked in here pregnant, even eleven- and twelve-year-old girls who we didn't test because we thought they were too young," Central director Alston says. "These kids aren't young in anything but age."

he enters Central. His Polaroid portrait looks like a full-length mug shot. He stands in the long hallway in Central's administration building with his hands behind his back. Like most of the kids who have some experience with the juvenile justice system, but unlike most of the children in the home, he doesn't smile. Still, his face is intelligent and open, his eyes wary. In his dapper gangsta sweat suit he looks smart and tightly athletic, but with a babyish quality, like a pretty boy trying to discard any sense of innocence in his soft cheeks. I'm ready and I'm tough, his expression and cool stance seem to say. But it doesn't quite overcome the doubt that flickers in his deep brown eyes or roughen the softness in his cheeks. Not quite yet.

9

The "Incident"

A YOUNG spring breeze filters through an open window, flirting with the light curtains beside Sebastian's assigned bed. It is his third day at Central and he is tired of learning the ropes. He flops onto the thin mustard-colored bed covering, still wearing the untied Pumas his uncle gave him as a going away present three days earlier. He's worn out from the long day and the intrusive staff. Sebastian is used to being left alone. But now no one leaves him alone.

At 6 A.M. he's forced to get out of bed, wash up with the twelve other boys in Shepard Cottage, and do his chores. By six-thirty, Mr. Phillips, the cottage supervisor, inspects him for school, sometimes even looking in his mouth to make sure his teeth are clean. Then to the cafeteria for a nasty breakfast of grits or oatmeal. Then at seven-thirty the bus, then school, then the bus home, then more chores. And as the new kid, lots of ragging by the other boys.

For three days Sebastian has been on guard, even through the night, alert for trouble and the quickest escape. If he weren't so pretty, he might have avoided the harsh initiation by his cottage mates. But his features are soft and, he thinks, unnervingly slow to develop into handsome.

Five to six is study time, when all the boys gather in one room under Mr. Phillips's supervision. But Sebastian asks to be excused for a nap. Mr. Phillips sees the exhaustion ringing Sebastian's eyes and weighing down his shoulders, and says OK.

Sebastian's tense body bounces when it first hits the hard mattress. He can relax, he tells himself. Everyone is downstairs. He is finally alone. He takes a deep breath and melts into the mattress. He watches, briefly, the shadowy designs cast by the fluttering curtains on the bare walls. The breeze kisses his face gently, as his mother once did, softening his scowl. He feels warm and smiles. The last yellow rays of the setting sun lie like a blanket across his skinny legs.

He dreams of drifting on dark water. His body starts to tingle. Something feels wet, warm, and tugging, like the ocean he swam in when he was seven with his uncle. Like a dolphin he dives deep as the current pulls and tugs at him. Soon, he floats to the top again. He doesn't want to wake up. The rhythmic rise and fall of the waves excites him.

In a panic, he realizes that his penis is hard. He's afraid he will explode all over the sheets. He can't come over the sheets, he tells himself. They might send him to jail or something. Some of the other boys warned him about punishment like that.

Sebastian opens his eyes to a flash of sunlight. The silhouette of a boy leaning over him slowly comes into focus. He wants to scream, but he doesn't or he can't; he's too freaked by the boy's head as it lifts its mouth from his open fly.

The wind whips the curtain back and sunlight falls on thirteen-year-old Damien's face.

The boys stare at each other for a moment without a word.

Damien smiles dolefully.

"You like that?" he asks in a whisper as Sebastian fights with the zipper of his black shorts.

"Shit, man, you better not tell anyone I was part of this mess," Sebastian says, fight edging in through his disbelief. He feels more awake than he has been in several years. And he is terrified, but somehow powerful.

"You better not, Damien man, or I'll kill you, you . . ."

Sebastian's voice shakes as it rises to a shout.

Damien doesn't flinch at Sebastian's anger. He just smiles, a smile that confuses and terrifies Sebastian.

"I know you liked it. I know you like me," Damien says in another whisper.

Sebastian swings his bony fist at Damien, catching him in the ear.

Tinker Fielding, a building superintendent, is checking a broken faucet when she hears the thud of Damien's falling body. She rocks her large round figure as fast as she can walk to the boys' room.

"What's going on?" she bellows, eyeing Sebastian's half-open fly and the white semen around it.

"He!" Sebastian says shaking, almost tongue-tied. "He blew me. I was asleep. I swear I don't get it off with no perverts!"

Fielding gasps loudly as Mr. Phillips, an athletic twenty-nine-year-old, bounds up the stairs. A handful of boys follow. Phillips fills the doorway but boys peek around his side and between his legs.

"Come in here, Mr. Phillips, please," Miss Fielding says, regaining stern composure. She is angry, in a chilling way.

The door closes.

Ten minutes later, Damien and Sebastian join the other boys for dinner.

"What happened, man?" one boy after another asks as they buddy up to Sebastian.

Sebastian shies away, unsure. Then he decides to take advantage of the attention they offer.

"Damien tried to rape me until I beat his sorry ass off," he says, at first quiet and then louder, enjoying the spotlight. He feels a little guilty. While he is disgusted with Damien, he also senses a kind of closeness with the younger boy. They shared something but he didn't know what.

AT Fielding's urging, Phillips reports the "incident" the same afternoon. "While sleeping, he was awakened abruptly by Damien performing oral sex on him," the counselor writes, "which he immediately stopped upon recognition."

There is a heated discussion at the weekly staff meeting.*

"What's this," Alston asks from the head of the table, looking at the report, "about Damien and the new boy?"

The counselors pass around looks. None want to begin.

"Deviant sexual behavior," one says in a low tone.

"What's that?" Alston asks sharply.

The counselor repeats his answer.

"I know what you said. I want to know what you're talking about," Alston says with a laugh ringing of intimidation. "You talking sheep, what?"

The counselors don't laugh.

Vanessa Hall's voice comes forward bravely, in a cool tone, with her explanation. "Sebastian, the new boy, was sleeping and Damien took advantage of him," she says.

A murmur among the male counselors, on the far left corner from where Alston sits, rumbles through the room.

"What you all saying?" Alston asks. No one speaks up, so he returns to the report. "What we do about it?"

"He needs stricter discipline," Hall suggests.

The murmurs grow louder from shaking heads.

---

* Alston and the entire residential staff at Central meet regularly on Wednesday mornings while the children are at school, to update one another on the children's behavior. Typically each residential counselor gives a brief report on the week's low points—which children behaved poorly and their punishment.

"What?" Alston asks, now looking directly at the young male residential counselors at his left.

"We just saying that he couldn't be asleep through all that," one says. "He just couldn't."

"Sure he could," Hall interjects.

"No," another man says. "He couldn't."

The counselors are divided. One group believes that Sebastian was a consenting partner but tried to escape trouble by pointing the finger at Damien. The other camp believes that Sebastian was purely a victim and that Damien needs more stringent discipline.

"But Sebastian is almost fifteen years old," one man points out.

"So," Hall shoots back.

"Damien is thirteen. No way he could take on almost a fifteen-year-old. Sebastian is big for his age and Damien is a small guy. No way Damien could take advantage of him," the male counselor explains.

Alston searches the scant two-sentence report for some clues and finds none.

"Is Damien seeing someone?" Alston asks, referring to a psychotherapist.

"Yes," Phillips says. "Damien is."

"And the new boy?"

The counselors look at one another. No one knows for sure.

"Let Damien's therapist know about this and check for sexual abuse in Damien's past," Alston says. "Was he sexually abused?"

No one seems to know.

"It's not in the files," one counselor says.

"I bet it happened, though," Alston says. "Also see about Sebastian."

The discipline would have to wait another week. But as with a hung jury, the matter is in effect dropped. The therapist is left to deal with the incident.

Damien is told what constitutes "appropriate cottage behavior and sexual discretion." He had been restricted to the building for talking back to a counselor. That restriction is extended.

Eventually the incident is dismissed by Central as boyish experimentation. It is not normal, but it does not have to be rape. It could be that Damien had suppressed these problems and that he is beginning to act out, but that would be the worst case. Central decides to provide special services and counseling to Damien, and they hope that will clarify the problem to him and prevent such problems in the future. It is not fair to kick Damien out, they reason, not knowing exactly what happened and not giving him a chance to understand either. If Damien is forced to leave, he will not have a chance to get treatment, because in an effort to find him a home, the incident would be downplayed so that it would seem Damien had merely had some sort of behavioral problem. If Central keeps Damien, they have a shot at intervention. At least they can be sure the incident is addressed. A general hush prevails over the incident.

But weeks later, Sebastian tells his county caseworker about it while being driven back to campus. She demands that Central report the matter to the county that is responsible for Damien and his siblings.

"It's not for the kids' sake," another professional complains critically. "She did it as a matter of punishment, so Sebastian won't think Damien got away unpunished. But it won't do either kid any good. Pressing charges won't solve the problem of placement. It doesn't mean that either kid is going to get better treatment or services. And the courts don't feel that their job is to discipline children. They resent it. It's like taking your kid to court because he took some money out of your purse. The judge will look at you and say, How come you can't care for your kid? So reporting it is just a formality. It's just paperwork. It doesn't do anyone any good."

The incident is reported. Nothing more is heard of it.

Damien's therapist never discussed the incident with him, he says. "I don't think he even knew about it," Damien says, lifting his shoulders in a shrug. "They put me on building restriction, which I was already on."

A week later, Sebastian is playing basketball. Damien stands at the side of the court, kicking dirt as he explains how he sees it.

"Sebastian was sad all the time and I wanted to make him happy, but I got in trouble," he says. "They do it all the time at the other homes, even the counselors do it. That's what this boy told me. But Sebastian is mad. He don't talk to me none. He be telling the other boys I tried to rape him.

"Ms. Fielding says I'm a deviant. I snuck out of study hall so she says I'm a deviant," he says sadly.

Damien has no greater understanding of his actions than that.

10

Thirteen Days

THE confusion and frustration swirling inside of Damien swiftly turn to anger. He doesn't remember much of the next thirteen days following the incident, except that he is stiff with anger. He can't say why.

"It's like another part of me took over," he tries to explain.

He doesn't remember if he saw his therapist. He just remembers that he was angry, really angry.

What happened on the thirteenth day he doesn't seem to have a problem talking about. That more than anything raised a red flag.

"He showed no remorse," says Central social worker Emeron Cash, shaking his head somberly. "We knew we had a problem then. He needed help."

11

Martin Gets Hurt

▓

AT three o'clock on a Sunday afternoon, Daryl walks by the basement television room of Shepard Cottage. He has been playing basketball, and though it is only the first of May, North Carolina's summer heat has kicked in for the day. Daryl is looking for a cool drink from the kitchen. As he passes by the basement room, his eyes dimmed by the white sunlight flooding the grounds outside, he catches a glimpse of Damien doing pushups. Daryl pauses. Something isn't right. He goes back and looks again.

Panic strikes his eyes first, then his heart, and before he knows it, he is running across the campus for a counselor.

"He's humping Martin!" Daryl breathlessly cries out to a residential counselor.

"Who?"

"Damien!"

By the time the counselor arrives, thirteen-year-old Damien is riding his bike away from the cottage, and eight-year-old Martin is on the basketball court.

The counselor sends Daryl to get Martin.

Martin stands before the counselor dazed. He is slower than most children his age, but this is different. He looks down at the floor when he answers questions. He is afraid he is in trouble, so he tells Mr. Powers the story.

He was watching *Power Rangers* on TV when Damien came in the room. They watched together for a while. Then Damien told Martin to pull his pants down. Martin did what Damien told him to do. He didn't cry out because he was afraid he'd get in trouble.

"When Damien finished," Martin says with unintentional doe-eyed innocence, "I went out to the basketball court."

Damien tells essentially the same story when he stands before the counselor. He is told to write out a confession, including what happened and what he thinks about it. Damien sits down with a black ballpoint pen and writes on a sheet of clean white paper:

> I told Martin to lay down on his stomach he laid down then my Dick get hard and then it stuck im Dick in his butt.
>
> The head of my Dick went in his butt. He was kind of squirming around but he said nothing.
>
> I hunched about 10 times.
>
> After it was over I felt that I had done something wrong.
>
> Martin went out side to play basketball, I went to get my bike and I went up stairs with my bike to ride it and Martin came out to tell me that Mr. [Powers] wanted me and then I knew what it was about.
>
> Damien Mangum

Martin is taken to the hospital, where doctors find no tissue damage. About half of all sexually abused boys show no physical damage upon examination. "I could do more damage with my finger probing around," the doctor tells Central staff. Central is relieved to find an understanding doctor, one who does not overplay the incident.

"Some of the young doctors don't understand," Alston explains. "They take staff aside and talk about neglect and ask us about possible abuse. They don't understand that with fifty rascals running around like that, there are going to be a lot of trips to the hospital."

Martin is sent to therapy the next week. Because of his submissive and dazed reaction, it is assumed that this is not the first time Martin has been raped.

A week later, Damien still cannot explain his actions. He just shrugs when asked why he did it. He couldn't help it, Damien says, and then he starts to cry.

After this second incident, Central has no choice but to have Damien removed from the home. They have tried to intervene and failed. They do not believe they ignored warnings so much as gave Damien a second chance, and a chance to understand what was wrong in his behavior. They could not have known in advance that Damien was suppressing his problems. Most of the children suffer from post-traumatic stress when they arrive at Central, and almost always it is only after their acting out exposes their condition that they are provided therapy to help them understand and cope with their submerged horrors. The staff is again struck that it all happened so fast. Before the special therapeutic services could intervene, another incident occured.

"Damien's behavior went from A to F so fast," one social worker says, shaking his head. "Then he went from F to Z like that," he adds with a sharp snap of his fingers.

Because Martin was taken to the hospital, the incident must be reported to the local police.

Damien admits guilt to the police detective assigned to the case. Damien was raped when he was eight, he tells the detective, by an older relative. Though they did not know this, the staff at Central is not surprised.

Under police questioning, Damien is aware but detached, slumped in his chair, as if insulated from events. Nothing more could be done to him, he thinks.

He is wrong. He has to leave Central, he is told.

"What?" He sits erect now.

Even when the police arrived to question him, he had not recognized the seriousness of his action. Now it is slammed home to him in the words of his counselor.

"I don't want to leave my family," Damien pleads.

"You don't want to leave Central but you have to because of what happened."

"I don't care about leaving here," he says. "I don't want to leave my family."

"You need help and we can't give it to you here," a counselor explains.

"I need to take care of my family," Damien repeats.

"You aren't doing that," the counselor says. "You're getting into trouble. You want them to go with you?"

"Is it better than here?"

"No."

"I guess not, then. You gonna take care of them good?" he asks.

"Yes."

Damien shrugs cool again, sinking back into apathy, resigned to a hopeless future.

12

Damien Has to Go

▓

DAMIEN has made the priority list finally. His troubles graduate him to emergency of the week. Staff scurry about seeking a new place for him to go to. Even before a new home is found, his files are prepared for transfer. Damien's departure is to be fast, before the story seeps out into the community to damage Central. If people ask, Central wants to be able to say the matter was taken care of some time ago. The child has been placed out, away from Central.

"It has to do with reputation, and it has to do with business," one staffer says. "Get them out quick so we can say, He's not ours."

All too often, as it is with Damien, the child is the last to know where he is going. Social workers and staff focus on completing applications for the new home, collecting school transcripts, packing the child's belongings. In the rush, the child is almost forgotten, then rushed off to a new home without understanding why. Rarely is he or she prepared for the change.

Damien knows he has to leave because of Martin. He does not know where he is going. Nor does he know how far he will be from his siblings. He dreams that he will be sent home to his mother, that the system will throw him out and he can finally go home. He knows it is not likely, but he is afraid to ask what will happen to him. He does not want to know. He doesn't want to think about what his brothers and sister will do without him. So he lets it just happen.

Emeron Cash, a Central social worker, worries about the rest of the Mangum family. They have a closeness that few sibling groups maintain in the homes. He does not want their trust of one another and the home to diminish. He is uncertain about how to break the news of their brother's departure. Aside from Damien, the Mangum children are adapting well to Central.

He calls on the children's therapist. Four days after the incident, the therapist talks first to Damien, and then to all the Mangums as a group.

In the individual session, Damien tells the therapist that he doesn't want his siblings to know why he must leave Central. He doesn't want to tell them he is leaving at all. But he is told that it is best for his younger brothers and sister to know what is happening. The therapist suggests that Damien tell his siblings he is leaving either because of his sexual behavior or for some reason he will explain in the future.

Damien is still hesitant. The therapist argues that informing his siblings of his departure will provide the support he needs for the move.

But Damien is far more concerned about the welfare of his siblings. Finally he agrees to tell them the reason for his departure. Maybe, he thinks, it will teach them a lesson. He doesn't know what lesson, he says later. He just knew something went wrong with him.

IMMEDIATELY after Damien meets with the therapist, his siblings are brought into the room. They sit around the table, arguing about who gets to sit nearest to Damien.

Once they settle, Dr. Isaac, the psychologist, announces that Damien will be leaving Central.

The children become disruptive. Thomas, Jefferson, and Julia threaten to stop eating and going to school if Damien leaves.

After the eruption subsides, Isaac asks if they know why Damien has to go.

Thomas says he knows why. Jefferson says that he does not know why but he wonders if it is related to what people are saying about his brother. Julia says that she does not know why, although there is a hint that she has some idea of the reason. Michael refuses to speak. He sits, arms folded across his chest, lower lip jutting forward and at times trembling. Fred remains quiet.

Damien has been silent. Now he breaks into the conversation firmly. He has changed his mind, he announces. He will not tell them why he is leaving. He senses from their reactions to Isaac's question that although they have heard something about the incident, they really do not want to know the truth. It is easier sometimes when inside you do not know the truth, he thinks.

Isaac ignores Damien, arguing that the information will help the remaining Mangums to support one another. He also reasons that understanding the situation, no matter how painful, will help them continue to trust their environment rather than falling back, as Damien has, to believing that decisions concerning them are random and chaotic.

But the children refuse to listen to him when he tries to describe Damien's "inappropriate sexual behavior," even when he tries to discuss ways for the family to remain in contact with one another.

Afterward the Mangum kids swear not to believe what the therapist has said, and not to trust adults, whatever they say.

"It's just another lie," Michael says, a ready tear dissolving into anger.

13

Therapy

D<small>R</small>. Isaac concludes that Damien needs to live in a therapeutic group home. Damien's caseworker applies to several on his behalf.

"Central seeks a structured environment for Damien," he writes on one application. "He needs supervision of his behavior and a place that provides treatment that addresses his sexual behavior and issues related to his history of chronic and severe neglect, exposure to domestic violence and family involvement with alcoholism and psychiatric problems."

No mention is made of the sexual abuse Damien experienced repeatedly throughout his childhood, nor does the caseworker reflect the urgent warning in Dr. Isaac's final report: "Damien presents as being at high risk of continuing inappropriate sexual behavior should he not receive appropriate intervention."

ONE week later and barely two weeks since he sodomized Martin, Damien is placed at Wake House, an emergency shelter for children in need of an immediate transition. Wake House is not restricted to high-risk children.

Within a month, Damien finds a twelve-year-old boy alone in a room and orders him to lie on his stomach. Like Martin, the boy submits without questioning. A staff member walks in on the boys. Damien seems not to care. The other boy is embarrassed and scared. He would not have told the staff, he later says. He is embarrassed, afraid of Damien, and terrified that the staff might blame him as well as Damien.

Two weeks later, Damien turns fourteen and declares he is gay. He begins curling his hair. Looking back, the Central staff can see how Damien's early outburst of anger may have come out of his past sexual abuse and his private struggles to understand it. When Damien drew the butcher knife in his cottage, his first serious offense recorded by Central, it was against a boy who had declared himself gay. There had probably been some sexual encounter between them.

Damien is sent to a psychiatric hospital. There he receives a letter, forwarded by a Central social worker, from his sister, Julia:

Dear Damien
   I love you very much. I miss you and where ever you are I still love you. I no you didn't mean it but i still love you.

Damien cries when he reads the letter. He worries about his siblings. They can't afford the long distance call from Oxford, and he is permitted only local calls.

The Mangums are not faring well back at Central.

Julia, who had been cheerful and eager, has turned sullen and defiant. She eventually accepts what the therapist and social workers tell her, that Damien was not a bad person; he just needed some extra special attention and they could not give it to him at Central. She had been allowed to call her brother at Wake House. But when she wants to phone him at the hospital, she is told he is not allowed to receive calls.

"Why you all say he crazy?" she shouts suddenly. "He not crazy."

She turns then and refuses to listen to whatever anyone has to say. They lie and betray her.

She sucks her thumb, almost viciously, angry that Damien has been taken from her. Never before has she used profanity; now it spills out of her almost as readily as it had from Damien. She goes to school tired and angry. There she is teased about Damien. She tells the therapist that sadness fills her all the time. Rarely does anyone hear Julia's infectious laugh anymore.

Her brothers constantly fight with the other children, again because of Damien. Julia wants to help them but she is on the girls' side of campus and learns of the fights only later. She feels more cut off than ever from her brothers.

Then another incident occurs at Central. An eight-year-old claims that ten-year-old Michael Mangum "tried to penetrate him." Counselors might not believe the eight-year-old at first, except that he describes Michael's actions exactly as Martin described Damien's. Both times each of the Mangum brothers told their victims to lean over exactly the same way. Damien and Michael even used the same words.

Central staff now believes that the Mangums' family trauma has gone well beyond the recorded neglect, to impact more than Damien. At least Michael also has been sexually abused or has repeatedly witnessed sexual abuse. Central is not equipped to handle these problems, though they are constantly faced with ones just like the Mangums' tragedy. Meanwhile, the Mangums and other unknown victims of abuse like them put other children in the home at risk.

In January, Julia refuses to go to school. Her house supervisor is "unable to determine why."

"I think," Julia whispers one afternoon, "that if we're bad and we get kicked out of here, maybe we can go be with Damien where he is. He was bad. So now if we act bad, maybe we can be with him."

She thinks for a moment, and then snatches it up as her plan.

14

Julia's Rescue

❖

HER plan works. Julia's poor behavior draws attention and breeds frustration. After two weeks of Julia's refusing to attend school, Central begins asking the Mangums' caseworker to find Julia another placement.

The Mangums' caseworker accuses Central of failing Julia. When first placed at Central, she was a good child and a bright one. She never belonged at Central, her caseworker fumes. She was placed there only because it would keep all the Mangums together. She should have been placed in a nurturing foster family that might have adopted her. Only if she had failed out of that placement and several more might she come so far down the ladder as Central. Now expelled from Central, Julia's chances of a good placement are significantly lower. The caseworker cringes at the thought of the poor quality of homes that will accept her now that Central is discharging her.

The caseworker finds a Mangum aunt willing to take Julia, at least temporarily—then the aunt goes further, with the urging from the caseworker, and agrees to take all four of the Mangums still at Central.

Julia wriggles with excitement. She feels that she has saved her family. Though she understands Damien will not be with them, she knows that her aunt will make an effort to reunite the family on long weekends or even just for a single visitation day.

INSIDE his office, Central social worker Cash shakes his head. In foster care, kids learn that they are more likely to get attention if they are bad. The system is so overburdened and in such a state of crisis that the good kids like Julia get overlooked. Now she has learned that acting out, breaking rules, gets her what she wants, while all the good behavior in the world got her nowhere.*

"If a kid is good and not causing trouble, the social worker will forget about reuniting him with his parents no matter how much the kid wants that," Cash says. "They've just got too much other stuff to deal with."

But when the child is creating problems in a home, the caseworker makes a much greater effort to reunite the family.

Still, Cash is anxious about the hurried placement of the Mangums. He hangs the phone up gently and shakes his head, which seems heavy with concern.

"The aunt just called me," he says. "She's worried about caring for six young kids."

He tried to reassure her and held his concern to himself. The stress of a young family could divide the most stable households. The Mangums and their aunt are starting out with less than that. Suddenly their young aunt will become a single parent, working full-time at a low-wage job. There will be no extra child support for the children. The house is not in the best of

---

* Some children sabotage their placement because they feel betrayed by the system. For example, Sam was taken from his mother because of her addiction to crack cocaine. When his mother overcame her addiction, he was not allowed to return to her because of her low income. Sam and his mother were furious. Sam unleashed his anger on the counselors and social workers at his home. He made no effort to curb his anger because he had seen other children, like Julia, get reunited with their family after being kicked out of the home. The experience teaches such children not to trust and even, some argue, not to be good.

neighborhoods. Bad influences take control in the absence of care and attention there, he says.

Cash shakes his head again. "The last thing these kids need is another unstable placement," he says.

He's seen it before. Like Alston, he can predict the outcome of this case with disturbing accuracy. But he hedges, for the sake of optimism.

"Maybe it won't happen that way," he says with an unconvincing shrug. "Maybe they'll surprise us."

The wheels are turning and the train is pulling out. They've seen it many times. They can't stop it.

THE phone rings in Alston's office. Alston sighs and leans across his wide oak desk. He knows what this is about. The school principal asks if the Mangum children could finish the rest of the school year. Their teachers have developed plans for each of the children and the children are responding well. Why disrupt them three quarters of the way through the year?

Alston is sorry. There is nothing he can do. The Mangum's caseworker has made the decision to place them at the aunt's home as soon as possible, which means within the week. She says it is for the children's sake, but everyone suspects she is punishing the home for allegedly not handling Julia properly. The Mangums' departure will mean five empty beds. No monthly income from those empty beds means that Alston will have to go to the bank for another loan this month.

"The children are the victims here," the principal says angrily.

"I'm sure the caseworker is doing what she believes is in the children's best interest," Alston responds diplomatically.

But in the privacy of his office, he nods his head. He knows the victims and he knows the game.

15

The Killing Feeling

▓

THE Damien-Sebastian incident is recorded in Damien's file but appears nowhere in Sebastian's record. He was judged not to be at fault. Fading in the high counselor-turnover rate, the incident becomes a distant memory to the counselors. The new supervisor at Sebastian's cottage is only vaguely aware that Sebastian was involved in something sexual his first week at Central, but he doesn't know what.

Sebastian does get therapeutic counseling, but not because of the incident. Rather, Central complies with a suggestion from Sebastian's first children's home that he receive counseling for an unrelated attitude: his hostility and anxiety.*

SEBASTIAN, shoulders forward and head down, walks into the psychotherapist's room. He slumps casually in his chair, but knees and elbows jut out sharply, betraying his discomfort. As they talk, he draws his thumb to his mouth and sucks it for most of the session. He is barely aware of the act. When he does notice it, he hides his hand under his sport shirt, which is open at the waist, then lifts it to the neck opening so he can continue to suck it by lowering his face into his chest.

Suddenly he pulls his head up and away from that comfort.

"I feel like killing someone," he announces.

"Who?" the therapist asks.

"I don't know, just someone. It doesn't matter. I just feel like killing someone."

"Do you have anyone in mind?"

"No."

"Why do you want to kill someone?"

"Don't know," he says, puzzled. Then he shrugs. "I just do."

"Do you know what they look like?"

"No."

The therapist passes on to other subjects, dismissing the concern as a ploy for attention or simple bravado.

In his report, the therapist describes Sebastian as "an angry, sullen, black adolescent. Sloppily dressed, poorly groomed. He seemed ready for a fight at the slightest provocation."

His memory is not impaired, his judgment is adequate, but his information

* It is difficult to get children good counseling because resources are so limited, one social worker complains. Medicaid pays for children's mental health services but it must be provided by the county. There is often a three-month waiting list for the children to get such services. So Central, like many such homes, contracts on its own for therapists and a psychologist. The expense—$1,352 a month, or $45 per hour of therapy—is from its own funds and is not reimbursed. For severe cases, requiring a psychiatrist and psychotherapeutic drugs, Central takes its children to the Granville County Mental Health Department, where the county pays for the children's care. Most of the children resist being sent there, feeling stigmatized by the children in the home who watch them get herded off. "A lot of kids equate therapy with being crazy," explains one social worker. "As long as they see it that way, they can't be helped."

processing is "slightly off." Sebastian appears resistant but answers questions readily. He appears uncertain about whether to trust the therapist.

At the next session, Sebastian repeats his concern about his violent urges. The therapist encourages him to stick with his junior varsity football, believing that playing football will alleviate some of the violent urges. Soon Sebastian is the star of the team.

16

Impulses

▓

SEBASTIAN's violent urges, as noted by the therapist, are a surprise to his counselors at Central. They have not seen any evidence of them. The staff think of him as a good kid. If anything, one counselor says, "that boy wants to be liked too much. To an extreme. That kind of susceptibility to peer pressure can destroy a good kid in less than a year."

The therapist has a different view.

"Sebastian was very upset by this Damien incident," he notes. "He is increasingly troubled by his own sexual identity."

Soon after the incident, Sebastian's behavior changes. He misses homework, his grades drop, he procrastinates with his chores, he misses school, and more than once he sleeps through church. One exasperated teacher notes that "there hasn't been a single hour in the last three days when Sebastian hasn't been in trouble."

The other children at Central tease him about his sexual preference. In response, it seems, he starts spreading tales about his sexual prowess with females. In May, a few weeks after the Damien incident, Sebastian is caught in a girl's bedroom after bedtime with a condom over his erect penis.

But around campus, countering that macho gossip, the first girl Sebastian has intercourse with calls him a pickaninny and laughs with her friends about how small his penis is. The laughter echoes through the cottages at Central.

The therapist now notes that Sebastian suffers from low self-esteem and rage. His thumb sucking and talk about killing continue. He tells the therapist he worries especially about not being remorseful about his feelings of wanting to hurt someone.

Football does not reduce his expressions of rage, and he begins to act "bizarre" and "weird," one social worker says, and to ask questions such as what is the "right time to have sex." Sebastian is caught repeatedly sneaking around the girls' cottages.

"He was obsessed with sex," Central social worker Cash later remembers. "I thought it was just an image thing for the other boys. I'm not sure. But suddenly everything was sex."

In August, Sebastian refuses to go to his weekly therapy session. The therapist misses the next two weeks because of an illness. By the end of the month, Sebastian is anxious to talk. He is troubled by nightmares of being jumped and beat on, even raped, he says. He dreams again about killing people.

He wants to feel remorseful about his dreams, hoping that might restrain him from extreme violence. But he fears he has no remorse.

"Sebastian has strong notions about death and killing," the therapist reports. "But he knows the difference between good and evil. There is no strong evidence that he is likely to act on these impulses."

17

Sex

▨

When school starts in September, Sebastian is "increasingly concerned about his lack of impulse control," the therapist writes. In their conversations, Sebastian wants to talk about sex. The therapist wants to talk about violence. Each time Sebastian speaks of his concerns and asks about sex, the therapist guides him back to discuss violence.

A week later Sebastian sits next to a girl on the backseat of the Central van filled with children going to a Saturday night movie. Sebastian slips his hand down the girl's pants. She screams and pushes it out. He then holds his hand to the nose of a friend.

"See that," he boasts to his friend. "Smell that. That's pussy."

Sebastian is penalized with a week of extra chores and a day of room restriction.

18

Walking Time Bomb

❋

SEBASTIAN'S friends are in awe after the van incident.

"He knew how to do girls," one says later. "He could get away with a lot."

Another nods and sucks air through his teeth. "He was mean to girls but they liked him for it," he adds coolly.

A third boy twists the bill of his Durham Bulls baseball cap from the side to the back.

"Maybe cuz he so good looking," he says. "Or they think that."

The other boys look at him as if he is crazy. "He wasn't all that," another boy argues.

"Yes, he was. He was all that," the defender retorts. "He was a brother."

"No," the first boy argues. "He just know how to do girls. That's all. He'd tell us stories. At first we thought he made them up."

"It didn't matter none if he did," the second boy concludes. And they all laugh. "Sebastian told good stories for a while."

WITHOUT staff knowledge, Sebastian leads other boys in snooping expeditions through the girls' cottages.

But he knows he is going too far.

"They thought I knew it all," he says. "They thought I could help them have sex. I didn't know what to do or how to, but I couldn't stop. I thought they wouldn't like me then, and they'd call me a homo again."

Sebastian even calculates that Xavion, a boy known for his mouth, will be useful. Xavion will broadcast and even embellish Sebastian's exploits. It works pretty well until thirteen-year-old Katrina sneaks into Xavion's room one afternoon and Sebastian is there.

Katrina likes Xavion. She wanted to impress him in the brazen way many kids in the home admire, by nonchalantly breaking cottage rules. And she wants to see him. She doesn't know Sebastian is visiting. If she did, she probably would have stayed away. Instead, she climbs through the window. The boys are impressed. They whisper together until footsteps approach. Xavion pushes Katrina into the closet.

Craig, Xavion's roommate, comes in. Sebastian and Xavion play it cool, but Craig goes to the closet for a sweatshirt and finds Katrina.

"Whatcha doing here, girl?!" he demands.

"Nothing!" she says defensively, her head high.

"You get out of here." He grabs her wrist and pulls her to the door. "You get in trouble here with these boys, c'mon."

Katrina is indignant, knowing Craig thinks she can't take care of herself. She doesn't want Xavion or Sebastian to think that she is scared of anything, least of all them. Snapping her wrist free, she tells Craig to get out.

Craig listens to his favorite song, "Don't Wanna Lose Your Love," on his Walkman for fifteen minutes as he worries about what might be happening to Katrina in that room. "She's a little girl," Craig says in a gentle way. "She don't know what she getting into. She just looking to be liked."

"You gonna give him some pussy?" Sebastian asks Katrina after Craig leaves. The air feels tight and severe.

"No." She backs away.

What happened in the room next differs by each account. The only thing certain is that Katrina was raped.

Sebastian tells the staff later that he crawled under a bed after Craig left because he thought he heard someone coming. From there he saw "Xavion sucking Katrina's breasts and humping her."

But Xavion's account is more like Katrina's. Katrina says Xavion tried to pull her pants down. She tried to hold them up. Xavion succeeded in pulling them down and entering her "halfway."

"I pushed him out of me," she says. "And then Sebastian held my arms down. When Xavion was through I ran away. Sebastian said it was his turn but I was hitting out at them like wild. I just ran. At first I didn't care if anyone saw me cuz I just had to get out. But then I didn't tell no one because I didn't want to get in trouble."

Three months pass before Central staff learn of the rape. Katrina has been silent for fear of getting into trouble. She has not told her friends because she is embarrassed that she was overpowered. She believes it is better to maintain the sex was consensual than to say she fought and lost. That would only make her a target of more abuse.

Only when a counselor overhears Sebastian and Xavion bragging and ribbing each other do they learn about the rape.

"No, she didn't scream out," Sebastian says. "She liked it too much. She would have liked it more if I had been in there, but I coached Xavion. She wanted it. Sometimes you just got to push a little harder."

Sebastian and Xavion admit the incident when questioned by staff. Sebastian now admits he touched Katrina's arms. He does not "see it as assault," he says.

• • •

CENTRAL files no complaint against Sebastian or Xavion. They have heard the gossip, spread by a girl with whom Sebastian had consensual sex, that Sebastian has a very small penis. That kind of belittling could bring out the very worst in a guy, one counselor says. The boy talk swirling around campus about Katrina being easy does not help either. It has dehumanized her further. And in the end, Central concludes that Sebastian did not realize that it was "offender-type behavior" to hold a girl down while having sex with her.

But the staff begins working immediately to get Sebastian, Xavion, and then Katrina out of the home.

Katrina's caseworker is angry that Central is asking to have Katrina removed. The caseworker says Katrina was not at fault and should stay. Central says Katrina would do better with a fresh start somewhere else. While Katrina is eager to leave, her caseworker moves slowly. Katrina is not a priority or an emergency, as several of her other cases are at the time.

As for Sebastian, Central's position is more complicated.

"First of all, as I understand it, the girl was party to it but then changed her mind," one administrator explains about not reporting the crime.

"Second, we have to be both the accuser and defender of the child in our home.

"And third, you know what would happen to a kid like Sebastian if he were charged and found guilty in this state? Let me put it this way. We have a black boy of thirteen serving a life sentence for raping a white woman in Durham. And then in Chapel Hill, we have a white man who stalked a student while she was jogging, viciously raped her, tortured her really, and killed her. He's getting ready to go free on probation after two years' incarceration. Tell me what about Sebastian?"

19

Expelled

THREE months after the rape of Katrina, but only three days after the incident is confirmed by staff, Central discharges Sebastian. Initially his caseworker is given one week to find him a new placement. But during that week, Sebastian lashes out at staff. His caseworker is told to remove him the next day. She begs Central to keep him until another home can be found.

But again, Central feels the need to get the ugly incident behind it and to protect the rest of its children.

The caseworker is angry at Central for discharging Sebastian. "We do not know the whole story, her side or his. [Katrina] should not have been in that cottage. And as I understand it, the week Sebastian left she was caught sneaking out of her cottage again," she says, as if to indicate Katrina was in part responsible for being raped.

The caseworker tries urgently to get Sebastian into several homes, including one in central North Carolina that is infamous among the state licensers.

"The last of the worst," is how one licenser describes it.

Eight days after Sebastian is officially discharged, the social worker picks him up from Central and takes him to live with an aunt while his application is being considered.

"We know what that means," one Central staffer says, nodding at another. The other nods back sourly.

"He ain't even going to get [in there] with his record. The caseworker just has to find a place for him to live," he says. "No one's taking him."

But as with Julia Mangum, it appears to kids at Central that Sebastian has been rewarded for bad behavior. The system sends him to relatives, where he wanted to go from the first.

Alston knows, however, that this new chapter in Sebastian's life will not be one he expects.

"When we kick them out of here, we're basically handing them over to the juvenile penal system," he says. "No, it's not right. But there's nowhere for them to go. So everyone waits for the crime."

Eventually the home admits Sebastian. But not long after, Sebastian fulfills Alston's prediction. In less than a year, Sebastian is in trouble at school there. Then after a series of aggressive acts by him toward girls, the home debates whether it should allow him to stay. Before it can decide, a violent outburst, which no one wants to talk about and only his closed juvenile records can reveal, lands him in a juvenile detention facility.

"I don't care," he says with a shrug and a finality that betray no fear or remorse, if in fact he feels any at all.

Alston's prediction has come true. And Central social worker Marrow knows for sure then that Sebastian will not be coming back to him in two years to say hi and refresh the bond that gives Marrow incentive for his work.

"The most important thing is forming a bond with a child," Marrow explains. "Good kids and ones with behavioral problems—it doesn't matter. They've got to be able to come to you and tell you when they need help or to talk or anything. Otherwise there's no way to figure them out or predict how they're going to be. The most important thing is good communication among the child, caretaker, therapist, and counselors. If that breaks down, the kid is lost."

• • •

LIKE the others, I had chosen Sebastian to profile almost at random. I had no idea how his story would end but I would have bet, with his above-average IQ (at 108 it was well above that of the other kids at Central, where the range is generally in the 80s and 90s), his good looks, athletic ability, and generally pleasing personality, he had a good chance at success. I chose him because he was a soft, warm young boy, struggling to control the rage inside, and motivated to emerge from the foster care system as one of its success stories.

In the end, his eyes were distant and removed. His seventeen-year-old face was lined with fatigue and worry, and finally he looked old, the way he had wanted to look three years earlier. He also looked to be in pain, but he said he wasn't. He said he didn't feel anything anymore.

II

JAMIE
Lumberton, North Carolina

1

Lumberton

❖

LUMBERTON, North Carolina, is famous for the wrong reasons. On July 23, 1993, two local teenagers shot to death James Jordan, the father of basketball superstar Michael Jordan, while he slept alongside a rural highway. When Larry Demery and Daniel Green realized whom they had killed, they dumped Jordan's corpse in a South Carolina creek, then spent three days joyriding in his $45,000 Lexus and flaunting the NBA championship ring his son had given him.

While the crime sent shudders across country, the city of Lumberton hardly flinched. Crime of this sort is not new to Lumberton. Unfortunately, neither of the youths, nor this area of North Carolina, is a stranger to violence. Shortly before the crime, Green had been released from youth prison, where he had served two years for splitting open a friend's head with an ax. Demery was awaiting trial on charges of bashing a woman's head with a cinder block during a robbery.

Robeson County, which cradles Lumberton, suffers from a per-capita murder rate that is twice the state's average, according to the North Carolina Bureau of Investigation's 1994 statistics. Nearly a quarter of its residents live in poverty. The county's teen pregnancy and child abuse rates rank among the state's highest. The N.C. Department of Public Instruction ranks its school system among the worst in the state.

Robeson County fares no better in the media than in the statistical rankings. It has been described as "hell's backyard" and a "cesspool of violence," and a March 1993 issue of *GQ* magazine called it a "snake pit" where "an endless supply of blank born violent minority youths" live alongside "genial bumpkins." In a letter to readers, a *GQ* editor went so far as to suggest that anyone driving on Interstate 95 "put the pedal to the metal" when driving through Lumberton and the surrounding county.

Jamie Everette and other native Lumbertonians squirm when they hear such descriptions by outsiders. For years the state, and recently the country, have focused on Lumberton as a microcosm of the nation's social problems. "They pick on us. But it is kind of true," Jamie says during the one-and-a-half-hour drive on flat, barren highway from Raleigh to her hometown hidden in the southeast corner of the state. Her long, straight platinum blond hair streams in the wind passing through her window. She nestles a huge-sized Coke cup from Biscuitville between her blue-jeaned thighs, wipes her hand on her brown plaid shirt, and reaches for a cigarette. Wispy bangs sweep over her green eyes, which appear innocent and gentle. Strangers smile at her sweet country looks. She doesn't understand the smiles, though, or why people turn to look at her. She suspects she looks as if she doesn't fit in, that it's apparent she was raised in a children's home.

"You have to escape Lumberton. If you stay, there's no place to go but down," she says, exhaling blue-gray smoke through the window.

Along the highway, little breaks up the monotony of dull shrubs, weeds, and pines that rise from tired sandy soil. Occasionally there are fields of tobacco plants sprouting large yellowing leaves, but more often the land is dry and spartan. Some plots seem lightly dusted by snow. It is only early autumn, and even in deep winter snows are rare here. But small cotton plants give that virgin white illusion. Cotton is making a comeback in this area. Last year's crop brought some of the highest prices since the Civil War. But heavy rains in June and a dry August have ruined most of the crop this year, along with many of the farmers who bet on them.

Beyond crime and poverty, Robeson County is a sociological hotbed for another reason, one rooted in the colonization of America. It is the home of the Lumbee Indians, who some authorities believe are the remnants of the Lost Colony of Virginia.

Robeson is the most racially diverse county in North Carolina. It is the only place in the state where everyone is a minority. Of its 105,000 residents, almost 40 percent are Lumbee Indian, 35 percent are white, and 25 percent black. The races divide in everyday life into three very separate social tiers. It was that way during Jamie's life here, and it was even more so during the childhood of her mother, Pam.

"It was like you were always making somebody unhappy," Pam remembers. "If you had a black friend, the whites and the Indians were unhappy with you. If you had an Indian friend, the whites and the blacks were unhappy with you. It was being pulled and tugged all the time. I didn't want Jamie to grow up with those same ideas that I had grown up with."

Racial tensions are never far from the surface. "Anytime you look down the street and you see a black and an Indian guy, you've got crime," the former Robeson County sheriff Hubert Stone was quoted as saying in GQ. He later denied saying it. He never had "any racial thoughts in my mind whatsoever," he told Ben Stocking of the News & Observer.

The Lumbees are the largest Indian tribe east of the Mississippi River, according to Adolph Lorenzo Dial, the tribe's late historian. He estimated that 90 percent of the original tribe never left the banks of a thin streamlike river once called the Lumbee but now anglified as the Lumber River.

"They are a people in which the Indian strain is still very strong. Yet they so thoroughly adopted the white man's lifestyle several centuries ago that they can point to no extensive remaining Indian culture," Dial wrote.

The Lumbees were once recognized by the federal government as a bona fide American Indian tribe, but no longer. The Cherokee Nation and U.S. senator Jesse Helms have opposed their recent petitions to regain that status, a recognition that can be granted only by Congress. The Cherokees deny that the Lumbees are related. The Lumbees accuse the Cherokees of snobbery and suspect they oppose recognition for fear they would receive a smaller share of federal funds distributed to Native Americans if they had to share with the Lumbees.

But Lumbee features remain too distinctive to be denied by changes in tribal names or congressional inaction. Jamie's former stepfather has the look of a Cherokee, with a long straight nose, thick black hair, and the burnished skin tone of a rich sunset. Many Lumbees have an olive cast to their skin, with the dark curly hair and the smooth, flat noses associated with West Africans. Still others appear almost white, claiming their Indian blood is mixed with that of the first white settlers in the New World.

Dial maintains the centuries-old belief that he and his people are the remnants of English settlers from the famous Lost Colony and of various Indian tribes, particularly the Cherokee, although several historians treat his claim as fanciful. According to Dial, their story begins in 1584, when Elizabeth I granted Sir Walter Raleigh, one of her favorites, rights to all land in the New World not already under Christian control. Sir Walter's scouts, seeking a suitable region to colonize, chose Roanoke Island, along the coast of what is now North Carolina.

The first settlers arrived in 1585, but their colony quickly collapsed due to internal dissension, supply shortages, and hostile natives. The original settlers set sail for England, but within a month of their departure, three ships arrived with the needed supplies and additional colonists. Of them, fifteen men chose to stay on Roanoke Island to maintain England's claim on the region. None of them could be found the next year when a third wave, of 117 settlers, came, led by Gov. John White.

The White colony was built on the mainland but also foundered. White returned to England in 1587 for new supplies, promising colonists he would soon return. But because of the Spanish naval threat, it was three years before he came back. Again, none of the colonists or even their remains could be found. There was no evidence that disease or violence had killed them off.

White believed the colony had moved inland fifty miles, an option discussed before his departure. If they did move, the settlers were to mark their trail, and if in danger signify it with a cross. White found no crosses but he did find, carved in a tree, the letters c.r.o. and, carved in a gatepost, the word CROATOAN.

A Hatteras Indian named Manteo, befriended by White in 1584, was born in a place called Croatoan. White was confident that the settlers had gone to live with Manteo's tribe. But because of bad weather and the sailing master's insistence on moving on to the West Indies, only a perfunctory search was made for the settlers, who became the first Europeans lost in colonizing North America.

Two other bits of information support the view that the Englishmen moved in with the Indians. First, Capt. John Smith of the Jamestown Colony reported in his 1607 book, *True Relation*, that local Indians told about men in the Chowan-Roanoke River area of North Carolina who dressed like Englishmen. Second, William Starchy, secretary of Virginia Colony, wrote in his *Historie of Travaile* (c. 1613) that White's colonists did move inland, where they lived with the Indians for twenty years.

OVER the centuries, Lumberton residents accepted the Lumbees as a mostly assimilated Indian tribe that had mixed with white settlers and black slaves. So well integrated were the Lumbees that they were allowed to remain in the region, unlike the Cherokees and other tribes who were forced westward along the tragic Trail of Tears.

In 1914 Congress recognized the legitimacy of the Lumbee belief in their ancestry after an Interior Department investigation concluded that the view that the Indians, then called Croatoans, were an amalgamation of the Lost Colony and a local tribe "is supported by their looks, their complexion, color of skin, hair and eyes, by their manners, customs and habits, and by the fact that while they are, in part, of undoubted Indian origin, they have no Indian names and no Indian language."

They lost their status as Indians when they changed their name. Locally, "Croatoan" had become a pejorative term. The Lumbees persuaded the state legislature to rename them "Cherokee Indians of Robeson County." But in 1953, the Cherokee Nation rejected the Lumbees as relatives and Congress withdrew its recognition; and today, the Lumbee Indians are officially regarded as Native Americans only in Lumberton.

It is from Lumberton—a place of violence, uneasy racial tones, and uncertain origin—that Pam Allen says she was trying to escape with her daughter, Jamie. But their escape became its own trail of tears.

2
Pam's Life

▨

NONE of the Allens was happy when Pam announced she was going to marry Wilbert Everette. Not one of them could see any value in him. Not even her fourteen-year-old sister could look past his conceit and unsteady nature to his good looks and charm. Even to Pam's friends, the pair seemed unlikely. Pam was quiet and sweet natured, in her own fashion. Wilbert was slick and loud, a salesman before he ever went into sales. Pam was a Vietnam-era flower child with good grades, disgusted with Lumberton's racism. Wilbert never thought of school or politics and was unfazed by Lumberton's racial divisions.

To the Allens, the differences ran much deeper. Wilbert was from the wrong side of the tracks, "below her station," in Pam's mother's words. The Allens did not have money, but they were from "good stock." Both of Pam's great-grandparents had been prominent North Carolinians. Her father's family had been rich, but that was centuries ago. From his great-great-grandfather (a minister during the first Great Awakening, in the 1730s) and his great-great-grandmother (the daughter of English landed gentry) sprang doctors, ministers, and scholars. But as their property holdings diminished, each generation grew more impoverished and was less educated.

Pam's mother's ancestors arrived from England in Charleston, South Carolina, in 1670. Her great-great-grandfather had been knighted, and with land granted by King George, he established a large plantation. For generations it grew tobacco, corn, and cotton. The Civil War destroyed the family's fortune, ravaging the fields and freeing the slaves, leaving nothing but burned land. One former slave stayed on and is cited in the family Bible. After the war, they say, the Yankees took the land, piece by piece. Throughout the twentieth century the land and its profit continued to dwindle. After Pam's grandfather died, its acres were divided among the children. By the time Pam's mother, Mrs. Gaynelle Allen, was born her parents lived in a three-bedroom house on a small parcel of the land and rented the rest to sharecroppers.

Mrs. Allen grew up in Robeson County, on the same land granted to her ancestors by King George, eighteen miles from her present, two-bedroom house in Lumberton. Before she married, she left Lumberton only once, to attend business school in Columbia, South Carolina. She grew homesick after a year, and when her mother became ill, she was happy to return and take up her mother's chores. Since she wouldn't be finishing business school, it was time to marry. At a local dance James Allen walked up to her, hat in hand, and with a slight bow asked her to dance. He had class, she remembers, and also the support of her brother, his friend. She soon fell in love.

When they met, Mr. Allen was ambitious. He intended to become a doctor. By all accounts he was smart enough. But after the Allens wed, World War II derailed his plans. Mrs. Allen followed him to virtually every army post in the United States, even after their first baby, a boy, was born. After the war, Mr. Allen worked at small jobs. Then a daughter came, then another daughter, and finally a third daughter. With four children, Mr. Allen gave up his plans for school, but he never gave up resenting his children for eclipsing his dreams. At the same time, he was proud that there were so many in his family. None of them would ever be an only child as he was. But he and his wife grew apart under financial pressures and the pressures of a growing family, and they became distant from their children as well.

Mr. Allen belt-whipped and slapped the children, particularly during the lean times when Mrs. Allen, not he, was bringing home the paycheck. But while the infrastructure of the family was crumbling, its members took care to hide their troubles from outsiders.

In town, they were thought of as "good people." They went to the Baptist church regularly. Their children remember that their parents put religion and church ahead of them.

"The basic needs were met," Pam says of her childhood. "But the emotional ones weren't even approached."

Their father's fury made all the children fearful of him. Though he sometimes lavished love on them, he could and often did suddenly turn on them with anger and even, they thought, with hatred. They learned to acquiesce, to follow the lead of their mother, to avoid any provocation that might incite his rage.

All except Pam, the second-to-youngest. If curfew was set at midnight, she would slip in at twelve-fifteen. If her mother told her to do a chore, she'd ask why. Pam took out her anger and resentment on her mother, much as her father did.

"I was a rebel," Pam admits at age forty. "But without a cause." She laughs.

"Pam was the most difficult of Mom and Dad's children," says her older sister, Kay. "Pam would question and fight back. She couldn't accept that anyone had authority over her, especially if she thought that the somebody was less intelligent."

The best thing the family thought it could hope for from Wilbert and Pam's marriage was that it might tame Pam. A husband and some responsibility would make her outgrow her past. For young as she was, she already had a past to forget.

Plenty of young men had been smitten with her in high school. Most of them, Mrs. Allen thought, were suitable. There was Brad Biggs, for example, the same Biggs who now owns much of Lumberton. And there was Willie Hayes, now a prominent lawyer, who later handled Pam's divorce.

But Pam was headstrong. She intended to marry Wilbert. As she saw it, he came into her life just when she needed him, and he understood her in ways no one else seemed to understand. She didn't exactly understand it herself. Part of her was unreachable, she thought, but somehow Wilbert reached it. He could know her and love her. Wilbert was strong. He wasn't afraid of life; he lived it. He had her same anger, and like hers, it sometimes erupted into violence.

Pam's anger was evident early on. Her older sister, Kay, looked after her and her younger sister, Teri, while Mrs. Allen worked. Kay was more like their mother, it seemed, than their mother. When Kay left home for college, Pam became unmanageable. When her mother slapped her, she slapped back. She couldn't talk to her mother, Pam complained. It was as if they were from different planets. As Mrs. Allen required increasing doses of medication for "nerves," Pam felt the family blamed her for her mother's condition. She taught herself not to care. She sometimes hated her father, but she respected him. Not her mother.

Pam's behavior grew worse. At fifteen, she took a relative's car, fell in love, and ran away to Florida. Her mother had a nervous breakdown. Her father, eleven-year-old Teri, and a man from church drove to Florida to find her. Teri convinced her to return home.

Soon afterward, Pam overdosed on Valium. She said she wanted to kill herself because her heart was broken over a young man she lost to another girl. Now she recognizes that her motives were far more complicated.

When a social worker visited her in the hospital, Pam asked to be put in a children's home.

The Allens were opposed at first. But with the social worker's urging, they agreed. So at sixteen, Pam was placed in Falcon Children's Home, in Cumberland County.

At that time, most children at Falcon were orphans. But some, like Pam, were "problem children." Her memories of the home are far from pleasant. She shivers at the memory of its cold, dormitorylike living quarters. Burns from electric heaters she put in her bed for warmth still scar her legs. At night, she often lay awake, frightened that one of the girls would carry out a threat to cut off all her long blond hair as she slept.

(A generation later, Pam apparently would visit her fears on her only child. Jamie remembers her mother crept into her room one night with a pair of scissors. Jamie woke up with her mother standing over her, intending to shear her. In the aftermath of that trauma, Pam checked herself into a hospital. But that is part of Jamie's story.)

After a year at the children's home, Pam asked to return to her family. She was less difficult than before. And Wilbert entered her life on a blind date during her senior year of high school, a time of hope. She was graduated with good grades, better than her older sister's, but she chose not to follow her to college. Instead she began training as a bank teller and rented an apartment in Lumberton with a girlfriend.

Wilbert began work as an insurance collector. Their courtship was short and sweet. But while Wilbert occasionally brought home flowers, he also brought abuse. In too many ways, he took after his father, a bully, who had regularly beat the boy as well as his wife and four daughters. Wilbert treated Pam relatively gently at first. He knocked her to the floor but then he fell on his knees and cried, asking her forgiveness. To Pam, this vulnerable side of Wilbert meant he had a "truly gentle nature."

They married on a sunny day at the Baptist church, where not long afterward Pam would faint during her pregnancy and be carried to the front lawn so as not to interrupt the sermon. Later Jamie would be baptized there.

Too soon after they married, Pam says, she became pregnant. Her frustration with Wilbert increased as she grew large with Jamie. She did not think it fair that Wilbert went out and had fun while she sat alone at home growing fatter. She worried that Wilbert did not find her attractive anymore. She began to resent the child inside her. She had not planned on getting pregnant so soon. She missed out on too much fun. Maybe even college, or a career —neither of which she attempted before getting pregnant—was what she sacrificed for this baby, she thought.

According to Pam, Wilbert became more violent. So did Pam. She hit Wilbert over the head with a Coke bottle, and he socked her. Typically, after a softball game, Wilbert would stay out late drinking and "just shooting the shit" with his old high school buddies, who worked in a local factory. Pam would question him, first because she felt excluded, then because she suspected infidelity. It excited her to see him angry. That was a measure of how much he cared. And making up after she was bruised from his blows somehow warmed her heart.

But Pam's questioning apparently became tiresome to Wilbert. He moved more quickly to shut her up with his fist, and more avidly to make it up, Pam says. At the bank, her fellow tellers and friends, not fooled by the dark glasses and pancake makeup she used to hide the purple bruises and welts, urged her to leave Wilbert. Instead, she left the job.

She was making dinner when her water broke. Wilbert dropped her off at Southeastern General Hospital.

"It sounds like a soap opera name," her daughter, Jamie, now says, laughing while driving by the hospital. "I think now I was born into a soap opera."

After Wilbert dropped his wife off, he went for a beer.

"He just didn't seem concerned," Pam remembers.

At age twenty, Pam gave birth after twenty-four hours to Jamie Allison Everette, named after Pam's father, James Allen. The next day, Pam's father drove her home. Her younger sister, Teri, spent the night with Pam and the baby. Wilbert never came home that night.

Pam and Wilbert separated three months after Jamie was born, although the marriage did not officially end for another three years, a period during which reconciliations, beatings, and disappearances punctuated Jamie's young life.

"That's the window my mom threw her wedding ring out of," Jamie says, smiling at her mom's spunk. "She said she didn't want me growing up with that violence. I believe she meant that."

After Jamie's birth, Pam seemed perpetually angry and impatient. Her emotions affected the baby. When she held Jamie to stop her crying, Jamie cried more. But when fifteen-year-old Teri held her, she snuggled into sleep. Soon Pam turned away from the baby she couldn't comfort, leaving Teri to become Jamie's surrogate mother, much as her older sister Kay had been to Pam.

The court ordered Wilbert to pay child support, and he was allowed to visit his daughter. "You could count the number of times he came to visit on one hand," Teri remembers. Then he disappeared. Unmet child support payments stacked up along with warrants for his arrest.

Wilbert went on to marry twice more. Pam, meanwhile, drew further away from her daughter. Her parents and Teri took care of Jamie, and Jamie's grandparents often overrode Pam's parental authority. Pam focused on her own future. She decided to get an education and a career. She increasingly saw Jamie as part of her old life, a life of wasted time.

"From the very beginning Jamie was an albatross around Pam's neck," says Kay, Pam's oldest sister. A successful computer consultant at forty-seven, Kay has been married twice but has chosen not to have children.

"Out of my parents' four children, two had very high IQs but zilch common sense. The other two were B, C students but had common sense. Luckily I was one of the ones who had common sense," Kay says, half jokingly. To Jamie it's not a joke at all. Common sense, she often says, is more important than intelligence.

"Pam says she raised Jamie to be her best friend," Kay continues, "but frankly I think they were more enemies than sisters or friends or anything else. Some women aren't meant to love their children. The maternal instinct that birth is supposed to trigger isn't always there."

3

Living with the Allens

▓

As a little girl on my Granddad's knee
I remember a song he would sing to me
I love coffee,
I love tea,
I love Jamie
and Jamie loves me.
The song would make me full of cheer,
For the man who sung it was so dear.

JAMIE, 14

Pam arrived on her parents' doorstep with nothing but her baby in a bundle of white blankets. Her eyes were swollen from tears, but clear with anger and resolve.

"I've left him," she told her mother and father. And they knew that she had made up her mind. She divorced Wilbert after the required six-month separation. For the next several years, she worked to pay off the debt the couple had accumulated.

Jamie lived with her mother under her grandparents' roof until she was five. She remembers nothing of the years she spent with both her parents, though her mother says the effects of that violent period lingered afterward. When a wrestling match appeared on TV, Jamie would become terrified and hide, Pam says.

But Jamie's earliest memories of her life in her grandparents' home are safe and happy ones. They bring a warm smile to her soft face and make her green eyes shine.

"The first thing I can remember is this red T-shirt I had," she says. "It went down to my knees, and across the front it had, in white letters, 'Mmm, Mmm good!' My granddad must have gotten it from Campbell's. Anyway, when I wore it, everyone would just laugh and bend down and hug me. I loved that shirt." She smiles.

Jamie also remembers, perhaps more by family stories, crawling into her grandmother's closet and discovering a box of ribbons and bows.

"I stuck some onto my Pampers to be like a bunny rabbit and crawled out. Everyone was laughing and I felt so happy," she says, pushing aside an ashtray and sipping her sweet tea.

Most of the family also recall those days well and have fond memories of Jamie.

"She was just a really sweet kid," Jamie's aunt Kay remembers. Kay was twenty-nine at the time and living on her own in a rented trailer, but she saw Jamie on holidays and many weekends. "She was really a terrific kid. The whole family always had special feelings for Jamie over all the other nieces, nephews, and grandchildren. She was affectionate, cute, and smart, all without knowing it."

"It would have been impossible not to love Jamie," says her aunt Teri. "Just because of who she was. She was the sweetest baby."

The same love and affection, however, was not shared by mother for daughter.

PAM began a new life for herself. With so many relatives around, she didn't have to give the child much attention. She could go out at night on the spur of the moment, leaving Jamie in safe hands.

"Most of the time I felt like I was more a mother to Jamie than Pam," says Teri, now a mother of two. Pam worked full-time at Amway, and Mrs. Allen worked full-time in real estate. Jamie spent most of the day in day care and started kindergarten when she was four years old. Just as Kay had taken care of Pam and Teri, Teri took care of Jamie.

When Pam was working, Teri didn't mind baby-sitting. "But at night, Pam would just go out," Teri remembers. "And I would change my plans to be home with Jamie. I loved Jamie, but I resented Pam for this. I also felt guilty and like I owed her. When I was young, I was mean to her. Kay and I would gang up on her. Kay must have felt the same. She told Pam once, 'I'm not going to feel guilty anymore. I freed myself of that guilt.' Back then I didn't know what she was talking about. Now I do."

Pam sees the problem differently. Her authority over Jamie was undermined by her parents. Because she was living at home, her parents continued to treat her as their adolescent child. And Pam reverted back to behaving as before.

"My mother wasn't so bad. But my dad was atrocious," Pam says. "Jamie would ask me if she could have some candy and I would say, 'It's too close to dinner, you can wait until after dinner.' Then Jamie would toddle up to my mom, who was cooking dinner, and my mom would say something like, 'You heard your mother.' So then Jamie would toddle up to my dad!" she says, still angry at Jamie's audacity, "and he would smile and go get her the candy. A couple times I took it up with him. I'd say, 'Look, I told her no and you told her yes. We can't do that.' And he'd say, 'This is my house and as long as you're under my roof, we'll do what I want.' "

Teri agrees that Jamie's grandparents were the bosses in their house.

"My parents didn't let Pam discipline Jamie much," she says. "She wasn't allowed to. Pam got overruled a lot when it came to Jamie. A lot."

At the same time, Pam watched Jamie bask in the love she felt had not been offered to her. She became increasingly resentful of her daughter. Once she accused her family of loving Jamie more than they loved her, and stormed out of the house. In fights, they sided with Jamie. In good times, they cooed over the child.

"It wasn't the best of situations," Pam recalls now. "It was OK. It allowed me to get on my feet." She pauses for a deep drag of her Marlboro Light, the same cigarette brand Jamie now smokes.

"Thinking back on it, I should have toughed it out, made ends meet somehow on my own with Jamie, because there comes a time when you can't go home anymore. You shouldn't go home anymore. I got married against my parents' wishes. It wasn't fair to put them in the position of supporting me again. And Jamie had three bosses," she says with a flicker of a smile.

At a table in a coffee shop in Chapel Hill, Pam takes a sip of her vanilla latte and pushes a strand of her long straight blond hair behind her shoulder. Her blue eyes are young, like Jamie's, and often just as sad. She is a thinner, more put-together version of her daughter, from her blue jean shirt and jeans to her blue-ice ring; she wears it on the same finger that Jamie wears her purple-ice ring on. Both Pam's and Jamie's rings were gifts from boyfriends. Still, Jamie insists she and her mother are nothing alike, and in truth they aren't, except for their similar style.

Although Pam claims the family interfered with attempts to discipline Jamie, Pam herself tended to allow the child to do what she wished, encouraging her to be independent and to question authority.

"Ms. Allen [Pam] revealed that she hated her father growing up and was determined that Jamie would not be afraid of her" as Pam was of him, a psychologist wrote after interviewing Pam. "As a result, it seems likely that [Pam] was quite lenient with Jamie at an early age and in fact indicated that she 'raised her like a friend—on a more equal basis,' so that they were 'best buddies' until Jamie was eight or nine."

In Jamie's view, the mother-daughter relationship, already complicated, deteriorated when Pam put work, school, and dates ahead of Jamie. And just as her father had made her feel unwanted, Pam made Jamie feel unwanted too.

"I always felt like my mom saw it like there were three doors with three different babies behind them," Jamie says. "She feels she opened the wrong door and got me."

• • •

JAMIE saw her father four times in the three years she lived in her grandparents' home. "He came over once to take me riding at his brother's farm. But I don't remember him, really. Besides, I had my granddad," Jamie says.

Wilbert paid $30 a week in child support, but only for two months before giving up. He also failed to maintain a hospital and medical insurance policy for his daughter, as required by the court. Court records show Wilbert was found guilty of abandonment and nonsupport within the first year after the divorce, and by 1984, he owed more than $1,000 in overdue child support. Pam pressed charges.

Over the next thirteen years, Wilbert went to great lengths to avoid arrest for not paying child support. He moved periodically. His mother told police she had not seen him in years. By 1987, his debt to Pam had grown to over $5,000. By September 1992, when the court finally located him, he was $12,561 behind in child support.

Two years after he and Pam divorced, and two days after his father married for a second time, Wilbert remarried. A year and a half later, he divorced again. Wilbert's father, whose name is Wilbur, divorced his second wife a couple of years later on grounds of adultery, after she returned to her first husband.

IN early fall, Jamie's grandmother's house in Lumberton is surrounded by flowers. Gaynelle Allen is as proud of her garden as she is of the small white house that Kay bought for her. She pulls me past the hanging photos of her children, grandchildren, and grandparents to look at the stack of photos from Hawaii, where Kay has just taken her.

She has great difficulty speaking about Jamie's early life and traumas. With every mention of the children's home in which Jamie lived, her eyes well with tears. Less in sadness for Jamie, it seems, than for the conditions that sent her there. For Mrs. Allen, it is still a family shame.

Jamie is out of earshot when Mrs. Allen lays a hand on my arm.

"I want to show you something," she says earnestly, drawing me into a small room. From the middle drawer of a desk she pulls old papers, their edges beginning to yellow, and three loose-leaf notebook papers. Bold and firm bubble letters fill the pages. Mrs. Allen delicately hands them to me.

"Jamie wrote these about her granddad. He died just before she graduated from high school. He wanted to see her graduate. He wanted to make sure he was there for her through then, at least.

"Her granddad loved her very much. More than his own children probably. He wanted us to take her," she mumbles. "Each time they sent her away to another home, he wanted us to take her. But I said no. I knew I'd be the one to take care of her, and I just couldn't go through those teenage years again with another girl. I don't know that either my husband or Jamie ever forgave me. But I just wouldn't allow it. I was tired. I wanted a rest. I had raised my own family."

I open one of the folded, blue-lined papers gingerly. As an introduction to the poem, Jamie has scribbled: "As a little girl with no daddy in my life, he took me upon himself as the apple in his eye. He knew not how much he meant to me, how often he'd filled my heart with glee."

And then a poem titled "Papa":

> Through the horizon, in the mountains at dawn
>   the love for my granddad will always live on,
> As a mountain his strength was a refuge to me
>   in the height of his stature, my future I see,
> My granddad in truth was gentle and wise,
>   his memories are carried through the winds of the skies
> A song through the valleys still rings in my ear
>   that through long recollection still is quite clear,
> The mountain protects the valley in the midst of a storm
>   just as granddad in his arms kept me protected and warm
> At dusk the mountains may disappear
>   but the thought of my granddad will always be near
>
> JAMIE, 15

Backing out of the driveway, beyond her grandmother's sight, Jamie lights a cigarette. She is lost in her own thoughts as we leave Lumberton. The morning haze begins to lift from the dirt road. Along Interstate 95, the trees are brown and empty. She hardly speaks on the long ride back to Raleigh.

"I don't want to hurt my family by doing this," Jamie finally says, almost to herself. "I just want to know what happened. I want to know why they didn't want me. I just want to know the truth. Do you think that's selfish?"

4

On Their Own

▓

Jamie's fullest memories begin just before her fifth birthday, when Pam took over the $46-a-month rented trailer from her older sister, Kay. Pam and Jamie lived in the trailer park until Jamie was ten.

"There were a bunch of kids there. And everyone knew each other because it was so small. All the neighbors looked out for each other and all the kids," Jamie recalls.

She remembers that period in the trailer alone with her mom as the best time of her childhood.

"I'm glad," Pam says simply, without a smile.

An old black Labrador trots up the dirt road that feeds off of Highway 41 in Lumberton and leads to the trailer park. He wags his tail and lies down in the dust. Jamie goes to pet him. His pink tongue laps up Jamie's attention. On one side of the road, a browned field lies peacefully fallow. On the other, an old barn shows its age with a caving roof. Its door is boarded and chained shut.

"I used to play in there." Jamie points. "Most of the floorboards were rotten, but that made it more exciting."

An unpaved road snakes through the trailer park. Most of the two dozen mobile homes are tidy and well lived in. Site number two stands forlorn, empty but surrounded by shrubs.

"We painted our trailer cream-and-brown and planted all those bushes around it, and the fern there we planted just under my bedroom window," Jamie says, happily animated by her memories.

Only a heater stood between Jamie and her mother's room. Jamie remembers waking periodically at night to the reassuring light of her mother studying for classes at a local community college. When morning came, she could see the familiar scaly trunks of pine trees from her bedroom window, swaying to the quiet rhythm of the wind.

It was the last secure period in Jamie's life. She had friends, and her extended family lived nearby. She looked forward to school and its reliable routine. After the trailer park, she attended eight different schools in four years.

Red pine needles cushion the ground now, as soft and gentle as Jamie's mood as she walks around the trailer park. At one trailer, she pauses to watch a young woman about her age guide a little redheaded child toward the front door. The woman stares back at Jamie until an older woman comes to the door.

"Do you know who that is, Mama?" the younger woman asks excitedly. "That's Jamie, Mama. That's Jamie!"

The women wrap their arms around each other and laugh happily. They disappear into the dark trailer to catch up on the nine years since they last saw each other. Jamie glows when she emerges.

The Wests' trailer farther along is surrounded by flowers, wood ducks, and cats, just as it was almost a decade earlier. At another fragile-looking home, Jamie points to the stoop where she, at seven, received her first kiss, from six-year-old Will James.

"His parents lived here," she says, "and his grandparents lived there." She points to the neighboring trailer.

At the water hole, falling leaves—scarlet from the maples, reddish brown from the oaks—float on the still, black surface. Two trees hold the rusted nails and fragments of a blanket that shielded young girls playing dress-up from the prying eyes of little boys. Here seventeen-year-old Bobby terrified her when he exposed himself. She was six at the time, but he told her she was old enough for a boyfriend. She was afraid to tell her mother, but confided to a friend, who in turn told Pam. That evening Jamie's mom went to "have a talk" with Bobby's parents. Jamie was proud to have a mother strong enough to scare Bobby away.

WHILE Jamie remembers the years in the Highway 41 trailer park as nearly idyllic, Pam looks back on them as the beginning of serious trouble between her and her daughter.

"Jamie missed having a father around," she says. "I would tell her a lot of kids grow up in single-parent homes, that she wasn't unique. But she felt it was my fault that her father wasn't there. Jamie seemed to need him, but in truth, I was glad he was out of our lives. It made my life easier."

Pam came to recognize that the abuse she suffered from Wilbert was not normal or deserved. "I was learning that it wasn't always my fault. I've worked with battered women since that time, and like them, I would wrack my brain saying, Gee, I must have done something to deserve it," she says.

Released from the guilt, she felt free and in control of her life for the first time. She worked full-time the first two years and enrolled in evening classes at the community college. The next year, she attended Pembroke State University full-time. Her relationship with Jamie began to deteriorate as the child challenged Pam's authority and Pam became increasingly preoccupied or absent.

"I just didn't feel like Pam gave Jamie enough attention. And Jamie needed a lot of attention," Teri says.

More disturbing were Pam's frequent mood swings.

"Sometimes she would act like, I'm the mom and I'm in control. Other times, she'd simply do nothing, and Jamie was on her own, doing whatever she pleased. Pam didn't even seem concerned about where Jamie was at times. She was not that interested in her child," Teri says.

Pam's brother-in-law, Fenner Clark, puts it more bluntly. "Pam denied her responsibility as a mother. She thought only of herself and she liked her freedom," he says.

Then Dwight came along.

5
Dwight

❖

NEAR the trailer park is a golf course where Jamie's stepfather, the man she called Daddy, pulls her in a sled one snowy day. The winter air fogs with her laughter and her sides ache from giggling. After a tumble in the snow, she is swept up into her stepfather's arms. His dark mustache turns upward in a wide smile. Shivering with the cold and wet but no longer with the tumbling fear, she melts into his steady warm embrace.

PAM had met Dwight a year before she moved into the trailer park, when both were attending the local community college.

"We were competitive," Pam says with a girlish smile. "We'd get a quiz or a test back and compare grades. I did a little better, but Dwight didn't know that I studied like crazy. He would study maybe an hour and get a ninety-six on a test. I would study three hours to get a ninety-eight."

It wasn't just for Dwight's attention that Pam worked so hard and excelled, but she says that was a good part of it. In those days, with Dwight in her classes, school came first.

"I'll always remember when I found out Dwight liked me," Pam says, her eyes sparkling. "I hung out with three girls, and I thought for sure he liked one of the others. Then one of them asked me what I thought of Dwight. I thought she was asking because she was interested in him and I said, 'He's smart, he's good looking, he seems real nice.' Then she said, 'He wants to go out with you.' "

Pam puts her hand to her heart; her blue eyes grow wide.

" 'Me?' I said. 'Me?' I couldn't believe it. Why would he want to be interested in me? He was so handsome and smart and I—well, I couldn't believe it."

Pam transferred two years later to Pembroke State University, but the two continued dating. Jamie quickly cottoned to Dwight. She loved his calm nature and his sincere smile and above all his warm dark eyes. And Dwight, unlike her mother's previous boyfriends, brought little presents for Jamie when he called. Sometimes it was a magnet man, more often it was a children's book. Not long afterward, Pam and Dwight married.

"HE was a really special person. He made me feel special too. I called him Daddy because that's who I wanted him to be," Jamie says.

Before the wedding, Pam took Jamie to a psychologist.

"I was in second or third grade," Jamie remembers. "He gave me Play-Doh and a doll to play with. I didn't know what to do. I thought something was really wrong with me. I was scared. I didn't know what was going on. I don't know why she took me there. I thought it was because I wet my bed when I was six. But now I think I must have had behavioral problems. I got an F in conduct at school. I got an A in everything else—reading, math, spelling —but not conduct. I remember that teacher too. She didn't like me. She said my mother was a slut, so I decided not to listen to her much.

"It's funny, though," Jamie adds sadly. "The next school I went to I got an A in conduct but failed everything else. I figure if I'm not causing trouble I'm not learning." She smiles.

Pam says she sought help because Jamie was becoming headstrong and she wanted to alter that behavior before it interfered with the new family. But in fact, Pam admits, with Dwight on the scene, Jamie's behavior improved. The Allens were pleased to see Dwight's effect on Jamie.

"Jamie was getting a lot more attention and a lot more discipline from Dwight, and it seemed to show. She was a much happier child," Kay remembers. "I think that she really liked having that male influence. Dwight was a little tougher on her than her granddad, but she didn't seem to mind that. It seemed to be the happiest period of her life, or of her childhood, that I recall."

But Dwight is Lumbee Indian, and race soon created problems for the new family.

"In time I think my parents came to like Dwight better than me," Pam says. But Dwight's parents weren't equally accepting of their new daughter-in-law. His mother seemed particularly hostile, Pam says.

"She would say things like, 'Do you know what those white people in Lumberton did to us?' and I was like, 'No, what have I done?' But there was more to it than race. I had been married before and had a child. I guess I was too worldly, not the wife she intended for her son."

Four months after Pam and Dwight were married, they separated.

Pam complains that Dwight sided with Jamie against her. He intervened in their fights more often. Once, when Pam was about to strike Jamie, Dwight held back her arm, Jamie remembers.

"She was hysterical, I don't remember why. I must have done something, but Dwight wouldn't let her hit me," Jamie remembers. "When it was over, Dwight shook his head and walked out. I remember listening to them talk at night. He didn't think I should go to the psychologist anymore, but my mom did."

Pam told Jamie it was her fault that Dwight left.

"It was a lot of responsibility for him to have a child," Pam explains now. "It was too much for him. Jamie was a difficult child. She was always pitting me against Dwight, and me against my parents. She did that with everyone in my life—friends, family, neighbors. It was really hard."

Pam and Dwight made several unsuccessful attempts to reconcile before they divorced legally, seven years later. Pam blamed Jamie for those failed attempts, too, as she told a psychologist when she asked the state to take custody of her daughter.

"Jamie's behavior reportedly got significantly worse and she then tried to sabotage any sort of reconciliation," the psychologist wrote.

Even after the separation, Ms. Allen and her husband continued to see one another until their final divorce in 1989. Ms. Allen had told Jamie that it was her fault that her stepfather left and this has been a particularly difficult thing for Jamie to accept and for mother and daughter to deal with.

This pattern of mother ending relationships with men due to Jamie's limit testing has been repeated through the years.

Mother appears to harbor significant anger towards Jamie which apparently has not been dealt with sufficiently as it seems that she projects much of this onto Jamie.

Another psychologist later wrote that Pam blamed all of her failures on Jamie. Rather than admitting that she and Dwight were simply unable to work things out, perhaps because they had different ideas on raising children, Pam chose to blame the child.

Jamie's distrust of people who are affectionate toward her appears to date from this time, said the psychologist, who also predicted that Jamie would have difficulty with intimate relationships.

Even now, a decade later, Pam still blames Jamie for the failed marriage.

"I wish we had made it," she says. "That's something that Jamie's got to forgive herself for."

She turns away, then suddenly looks back.

"And I wish she'd forgive me for some of my mistakes, too," she adds sharply. She softens her words with a sad smile.

6
The Accident

❖

PAM graduated from Pembroke State University with a degree in accounting and a 3.98 grade point average. Her mother still harps on the fraction of a point that set her just below perfect.

"If she hadn't started dating that professor there, she would have had a four-oh," Mrs. Allen says with a mixture of pride and annoyance.

"Maybe," Pam says and laughs lightly, brushing a blond strand behind her shoulder.

After graduation, and after Dwight had moved out, Pam wanted to get out of Lumberton for good, and as soon as possible. Every day she remained, she thought about how she could be someplace else. She couldn't wait.

But Jamie was in the middle of fourth grade. She was a happy and well-adjusted child, though she often came to school disheveled, according to her teachers. Pam took the school's advice and allowed Jamie to finish the school year in Lumberton. Also, Pam had been invited to teach some math courses at the local community college for the spring semester. Flattered, she eagerly accepted.

"It would have been perfect," she says, remembering her plans for that summer. "I had interviews lined up in Raleigh and Wilmington. I liked Raleigh, but I always thought I'd live near the beach, so I had interviews in both places. I wasn't able to keep them because Jamie had the accident."

Jamie finished school on Friday. On Saturday, Pam dropped off her daughter, now nine, at her grandparents' house. Jamie spent the night with the Allens and went to the Godwin Heights Baptist Church with them on Sunday morning.

But in her Sunday school class, Jamie grew restless. She and a friend decided to look for adventure. Jamie led the way.

The church was undergoing renovations, with ladders and scaffolding about. There were plenty of choices. She climbed up one ladder and onto a beam that ran through the attic, then jumped down onto a makeshift sheet metal floor, believing it was solid. It wasn't. She fell two stories into the church sanctuary near the altar. When she woke up, the minister was staring down at her. Above him, her friend peeped down at her through the hole in the ceiling. Even before she felt shards of pain running through her, she knew she was in trouble.

Jamie had crushed two vertebrae in her lower back. While they would heal, she was told to avoid heavy lifting for the rest of her life.

Pam learned of the accident from a reporter, who found her at the trailer. The incident made the local paper, which is how Jamie's father, Wilbert, learned about it. He came to the hospital with balloons and a teddy bear. Jamie was puzzled. It was his first visit in eight years. She didn't recognize him. She hadn't so much as a photograph of him. The reunion was awkward. It would be another six years before she saw him again.

Dwight didn't visit her in the hospital. She remembers his absence. She still called him her dad.

Teri remembers the accident vividly even though she was not in church that Sunday.

"I was like, wow. She fell through the church roof," Teri says. "Who would fall through a church roof but Jamie? That is so typical of Jamie. She was so active and always exploring. Very active. Very, very active."

"She was always getting into trouble like that," Pam also remembers. "She's always been very inquisitive. I think I fostered that. She always has been independent, very headstrong. I think those were good qualities she had. She may have had a little too much. But I think that determination and being strong willed is not such a bad thing. I like that. I like that she was an independent thinker and very much her own person. She wasn't clingy in any way. She was free spirited, and I like that."

Jamie's six-month recovery, during which she lay prone in a body cast on a bed in the trailer, was as difficult for Pam as it was for Jamie. "It was the worst summer of both of our lives," Pam says flatly.

By the end of the summer, Pam decided to move to Raleigh and find a job, while Jamie finished recovering at the Allens'. It would be another six months before Jamie rejoined her mother. Jamie wishes those six months had never ended.

7
Raleigh

WHEN Pam came to take Jamie from Lumberton, Jamie did not want to leave. She wanted to stay with her grandfather, with her friends and her school. It was selfish of her mother to insist that she leave, she said. Raleigh was too big and she was afraid of being alone there.

Her mother brought Jamie to Raleigh in March, nevertheless. Because of Jamie's excellent grades in Lumberton, the Raleigh school administrators decided she did not need to attend classes for the next few months and could still enroll in the sixth grade in the fall. During those early spring months, Jamie was free from school but without neighborhood kids to play with. She felt lonely and disconnected from her new world. In Lumberton she had had family to fill in for her mother's absences. But in Raleigh there was no one. Kay lived in town, but not in the same house, as Jamie had been used to.

Pam, meanwhile, worked a very busy schedule. Her dating also became a problem. In Lumberton, Jamie would go to stay with her grandparents or aunt when her mother went out. In Raleigh, Pam thought Jamie was old enough to spend time by herself without a baby-sitter.

IN her loneliness, Jamie played with invisible friends. She created her own world and filled it with parents. Neighbors wondered about her talking to herself and being outside in all weather, day and, often, night. They criticized her young mother and the attention she gave her boyfriends instead of Jamie. Some mothers drew their children away from Jamie. Others were intrigued by the little girl.

"My husband would say, 'I just never met anybody like her.' I said, 'I haven't either,' " remembers Cathy Stephenson, who befriended Jamie that first year. "I was not sure quite how to deal with her. Really, because you know, I told my husband, she seemed to be very simple minded. To tell you the truth, we thought she was retarded. I said we had to be very careful about letting her come in our house. You know how things are these days;

you never know what a child might go tell a parent later. But then we really grew to love her."

MRS. Stephenson works as a telephone operator in a squat brick State Farm Insurance office building in downtown Raleigh. She is a religious woman, with a kind smile but noisy attentiveness to neighbors and gossip, and full of affection for Jamie, although it's been eight years since she last saw Jamie.

"My husband had seen her first. She was just singing out loud to herself. You know, weird stuff. She'd sit up beside a tree, singing out loud and really talking to herself.

"Oh, she was always very polite and gentle, but sometimes she said things that didn't make sense when she came to play with my boy, who was two years younger. Then that one day I saw her holding a balloon right in front of her and talking to it, as if she was saying, This balloon will listen to me if no one else will.

"We could tell in a very short time that she was very neglected," says Mrs. Stephenson. "Her mother was never around."

Inevitably, Jamie became friends with a girl who was trouble. Cathy was eleven, like Jamie, but dating nineteen-year-old boys with sports cars. "She dressed incredibly inappropriately," says Pam. "Her mother allowed her to do these things so Jamie wanted to as well. I said, 'No, no way.' We butted heads on that. Cathy was drinking and smoking and I just didn't like Jamie hanging out with her."

In turn, Cathy's mother talked badly about Pam to the neighbors.

"Cathy's mother would say, 'Jamie comes over to my house hungry all the time,' " Mrs. Stephenson remembers. "And then she'd say, 'Well, you know her mom's gone a lot. Did you know she leaves Jamie overnight?' I think she's even left her a couple of days at a time. She'd come over here and tell me she doesn't have anything to eat."

Out of concern for Jamie, Mrs. Stephenson says she went into Pam's apartment one day when Pam was out. "It was pitiful," she says. Feeling sorry that Jamie's room wasn't "a typical little girls' room," she brought over heart-shaped pillows and shams for Jamie's bed.

"Her mother acted weird over that. She said, 'I don't know why you did it.' That was her attitude. Then I started buying Jamie clothes, a hundred dollars' worth sometimes. I wanted her to have stuff. I thought I was going to adopt her as my child because I didn't have a little girl and I always wanted one. Her mother didn't seem to care at all."

Despite this attention, Jamie's unusual behavior grew worse.

One night, at 12.20 A.M., Mr. Stephenson came home from working the factory's second shift to find Jamie walking around the parking lot. He sent Mrs. Stephenson after her.

"It was cold. She had her coat on and she was just walking around, looking at the sky. 'Hey, Ms. Stephenson,' she said with this grin. I said, 'Jamie, what are you doing? It's midnight.' She said, 'I can't sleep, I just wanted to walk around.' I said 'Jamie, that's dangerous.' She said, 'Well, I'm going in in a little bit.' I said, 'No, you need to go in now.

" 'Is your mother home?'

" 'Yeah she's up there with . . . ,' and she said her mother's boyfriend's name.

"I walked her home and I said, 'Jamie, we'd cry if something happened to you.' "

Neighbors, growing more concerned, tried to tell her aunt Kay, who lived on the other side of Raleigh, that Jamie wasn't well cared for. According to Mrs. Stephenson, a young woman in the housing complex also considered adopting Jamie.

"I think Jamie's mom would have let us. She really didn't care," Mrs. Stephenson says. "We just didn't have the money, though, God forgive me."

None of the neighbors called the Department of Social Services, however. "That was too scary," one said. "There's no telling what would happen to her. At least we figured all together we could look after her when her mother wasn't around."

Jamie was not such an angel as the neighbors thought, her mother says. She was lonely and sought attention, desperately, even if it was pitied attention.

"She wasn't yet twelve and she wanted to date. She wanted to dye her hair," says Pam. "She began skipping school. She'd go out and stay out all night, and I wouldn't know where she was for a couple of days. Smoking, drinking, experimenting with drugs. She just became unmanageable."

Jamie admits that she was difficult that year. She ran away from home a couple of times. But she says she did not try drugs and hadn't yet begun to smoke or drink.

"One day she asked if she could spend the night," one neighbor recalls. "I said, 'Well, sure.' Then she told me she was going up the street. A few hours later she walked in my door and she had bleached her hair. I said, 'Your mother's going to kill you!' She said, 'I don't think she'll mind.' I said, 'Where's your head?' She had had dirty blond hair and she had bleached-out Clorox hair now. I was just standing there looking; I couldn't believe she'd done this in my care." She laughs. "That girl was a trip. She sure was lively. Had to keep on your toes."

Still, Jamie learned she could win sympathy by painting her mother in the worst light.

"Her mother always had boyfriends," Stephenson says. "I remember Jamie coming to me once and saying, 'Ms. Stephenson, I know you're not going to like this.' She knew I was real straitlaced. We're religious people, we go to church. And she said, 'My mama's boyfriend is spending the night now.'

When she told me this, the chills just ran right through me. She knew I wouldn't like it."

Jamie says she does not remember any of her mother's boyfriends tucking her in bed. She thinks she may have made up that story to appeal to Mrs. Stephenson. But she does remember feeling that her mother's boyfriends were more important than she was, that she was just in her mother's way.

Mrs. Stephenson felt the same way.

"To me, her mother always had that attitude, like, I would give anything if I hadn't had you. Since you have been born, you have cramped my lifestyle.

"I thought sometimes, God, I hope Jamie is simple minded, because it would hurt her so much if she was totally on key about some of the things that were going on," Mrs. Stephenson says. "She would be even more disturbed and have more problems."

AT school, Jamie wanted to join a popular crowd. They didn't want much to do with Jamie. To get attention, Jamie told the kids that her mother abused her.

"It's the worst thing I've ever done," Jamie says now, looking down into her hands. "Well, one of the worst. I told them that my mom hit me."

That did it. Her fifth-grade teacher called social services.

"The social worker called me at work," Pam remembers. "She said she wanted to see Jamie at home and talk to her when I was there. When she came over, Jamie told her that it was not true, that she had made it up. That was pretty devastating, that I had to convince someone that I was not abusing my child.

"She wanted to move into the chic, elite crowd, which I never understood," Pam says, eyes flushed with anger. "Instead of giving it time, she tried to force her way into the group. When she told them she was abused, the teacher said, the girls all put their arms around her.

"The games she played had big consequences," Pam says, still visibly angry. "It was true what she told them, that she had run away twice. But she also said that I had broken a chair over her back. Horrible things that were not true. I didn't understand the depth of Jamie's unhappiness. I was flabbergasted. I was angry, hurt, and disappointed. Jamie's games took some very serious turns. Jamie would go to extreme lengths to get her way. I just didn't know what was going to happen next."

Both Jamie and her mother recognize that the lie Jamie told changed their relationship forever.

"I love Jamie very much, but there is a little wall I put up after that," Pam says, "a barrier. I can't love Jamie one hundred percent. I wish it wasn't there, because I have to be on guard against her manipulations and schemes. I can't tell her my feelings because she might take advantage of that. She feels the same distrust."

On the recommendation of a social worker, Jamie and her mother saw a mental health counselor for several weeks in the summer of 1986. Pam ended the visits because she said Jamie seemed to be doing better at the start of her sixth grade that fall. But a psychologist noted in Jamie's files that "Ms. Allen had made little progress in being more consistent with Jamie and also was struggling with a new relationship with a man who had moved in with the family."

The counselor recommended individual therapy for Pam, but Pam did not attend any sessions. Instead, her hostility toward Jamie intensified.

"If Jamie is to return home," another psychologist noted several years later,

it seems imperative that her mother receive individual therapy in order to help her heal from the physical abuse she suffered as a child and to understand better the dynamics that are going on between herself and her daughter. Mother appears to harbor significant anger towards Jamie which apparently has not been dealt with sufficiently as it seems that she projects much of this onto Jamie.

Both Pam and Jamie called Kay to complain about each other. Even the neighbors stopped Kay when she came to the apartment to visit, to report on the problems they were having.

"The saddest thing was that they couldn't relate on any level," Kay says. "It was so sad I would cry all night. It was driving me crazy. I didn't know what to do. Jamie would call me, crying and upset, and then Pam would get on the other line, and I was in the middle. Jamie would say, 'Mom did this,' and then Pam would say, 'It's because Jamie did this.'

"It was like, Why don't you two just admit that you hate each other? It's ridiculous to see people that are supposed to love each other act the way you do. Then it got to the point where Pam said she was afraid for her physical safety, which I never believed. I never believed Jamie was violent, but I don't know. I couldn't figure any of it out."

Pam gave up on her daughter. She threatened to leave Jamie twice. Then she sent Jamie away. Despite the threats, it came as a shock to Jamie when Pam finally gave her away.

"I'll never forget when Jamie came down here and told us that her mother was putting her in the children's home. She was about to cry, doing her hands like this," Mrs. Stephenson says, wringing her own hands and looking distraught. "She said, 'Ms. Stephenson, my mom's putting me in an orphanage.' I said, 'No she's not.' I honestly didn't believe it. She said, 'Yes she is too.' And I said, 'Why'd she want to do that, Jamie?' She said, 'Well, she says I'm getting out of control, she can't handle me.'

"I said, 'You are? I never noticed that. You must be a different person at home. I've not never noticed that around me.' 'Cuz I wanted her to know that I still thought she was the cream of the crop.

"She said, 'Well, my mama said she thinks another person would do a better job raising me because I'm causing her too many problems.' I thought, 'Yeah, you're interrupting her boyfriends and stuff like that. She's having to feed you and clothe you, so she's getting rid of you.

"She wouldn't come the day she was leaving. It was going to be too painful. I talked to her on the phone. Her mother came after that. She said, 'I guess Jamie's told you.' " Mrs. Stephenson's voice turns soft and silky. "She knew Jamie confided in us a lot. I said, 'Yeah, she did.' I said, 'I certainly wish there could have been another alternative, especially closer to here.' Then, oooh, she started turning on all this charm about how this is the nicest place she could find because she just wanted to find the best place for Jamie; it would be so good for her. And she just went on and on and I just thought, Good grief, you're ridiculous. I don't even think she went down there to visit the place before she sent her child there.

"Jamie was a sweet child. Really she was, and I was so scared. Anything could happen to her, it really could," said Stephenson. "After she left I used to pray for her like she was my own child. I said, 'Lord, look over her wherever she may be, whatever she might get into.' "

Jamie takes much of the responsibility for her mother's decision.

"I think I drove her crazy," Jamie says. "I remember one night I got her so mad she threatened to come into my room and cut off all my hair. I didn't like much about myself, but I loved my hair, and she knew it. That night she tiptoed into my room with a pair of scissors. I was so scared. She had this crazy look in her eyes. I wouldn't sleep for nights after that. It was sometime after that she checked herself into a hospital and they put her on medication. I've always thought that I pushed her to that, that it was my fault."

8

The Decision

PAM called her family together at her parents' home in mid-October, just as the leaves were changing and the afternoon temperatures grew cool, to announce the end of her relationship with her daughter. Her firm manner chilled the family more than her words. She did not speak in the tone she used to say she was no longer seeing a boyfriend. She spoke in the tone she used to say she was getting a divorce. Evenly, as if enjoying the drama, she told them that she had tried discipline, reasoning, incentives, spanking, even counseling—nothing worked. Jamie smoked, drank, stayed out late at night. And recently her behavior had gotten dangerously worse. Pam feared Jamie now, she told her family; she feared for her own safety.

The Allens sat stunned. They knew the mother-daughter relationship had always been rocky. But this they could not believe and did not want to face. They knew it would be easiest for them to accept what Pam said. But though they tried, they found it almost impossible to believe that Jamie was violent. When Jamie was around them, she was polite and well behaved— maybe a little mischievous and perhaps a little manipulative, but no more so than any other eleven-year-old. Pam swore her child was a different person when they were alone. But when the family questioned Pam, she flew into a rage.

"You always take Jamie's side," she shouted at her parents. "You love her more than your own daughter. You always have."

The guilt worked well on the Allens. All of them, even Pam's sisters, Kay and Teri, felt responsible for Pam's troubled childhood and even her suicide attempt.

"Pam says that she was the family scapegoat," Teri says now. "We don't see it that way anymore. I think we see it now that Jamie was at fault some, but Pam deserves most of the blame, if there was any blame to dish out. But then we didn't see it. We just didn't know. We wanted to say Pam's the adult, Jamie's the child. The child should never argue with an adult. It's not that simple, though."

That afternoon, the family decided to go the easiest route and accept Pam's word. Now they have regrets.

"I think all of us see now that there was something wrong with Pam, not Jamie," says one of the Allens. "It was harder to admit that than to say Jamie was just a headstrong and difficult child. No one would face up to that. That's the shame and ugliness. When we didn't say it that day, we could never say it. That would mean we made a mistake and also make us to blame."

"It was a family decision," Pam insists today, head up, with no trace of the shame or embarrassment many of the other Allens carry. "The counselor suggested she might do better in a more structured environment. Our environment wasn't so structured. Jamie and I would get up when we wanted, ate when we were hungry. The counselor suggested we do all those things that weren't so easy to do in our home environment. I obviously didn't have control over her anymore and I didn't have resources for a private school or a boarding school or anything like that."

Pam gave the family an option. One of them—either Jamie's grandparents, her two aunts, or an uncle—could take Jamie into their home. Otherwise, she was going to a children's home. She gave the family two weeks to decide.

• • •

THE Allens ran up hundreds of dollars in phone bills discussing alternatives for Jamie. Perhaps Jamie could split her time between the relatives. But Teri, Kay, and Mr. and Mrs. Allen all lived in separate towns and Jamie could attend only one school.

Teri wanted to take Jamie but her husband, Fenner, refused. Jamie was by no means a model child, he argued. If Jamie had been younger, he believed, he could whip into her the discipline she needed. But she was too old. Besides, he and Teri were starting their own family and their resources were stretched thin.

He proposed another solution. Fenner, once a difficult child himself, said military school had straightened him out. He suggested the family pool their funds and send Jamie to a military academy. But Pam, still a flower child at heart, refused.

Fenner's sister, Sara, had asked to adopt Jamie or at least take her in temporarily. Jamie got along well with Sara's daughter, who was the same age. But Fenner refused to allow his sister to become involved in the Allen family problem.

More than anyone, Jamie's grandfather, James Allen, wanted to care for her. He saw Jamie as another daughter rather than a granddaughter. They had a special relationship. He was her most vocal advocate, and she worshiped him. But his wife, Jamie's grandmother, refused.

"I know I'll be the one who has to look after her. I'll be the one who has to go through the teenage years," she said, remembering her difficulties with Pam and her nervous breakdown during that time.

If Jamie's grandfather had been ten years younger he would have insisted. In his younger days he could tell anyone what to do. But his health was failing now, and his wife called the shots.

During her last visit to her grandparents, Jamie bravely went up to her grandfather. "Don't worry about me," she said, unconvinced but putting on a brave face for him. "I'm a survivor."

As time slipped forward, Pam grew impatient. She wanted Jamie out. Desperately seeking a better solution, the family asked for more time. But by mid-November Pam felt they were no closer to a solution. Nerves frayed. Teri couldn't sleep. Kay's anger and disgust turned numb from crying so much.

"I wanted to take her myself," Kay says. "But I didn't feel at the age of forty like I could deal with those teenage years. I thought I had missed out on all the good times, the childhood years and stuff. I had made a conscious decision not to have children. I didn't think it was fair of Pam to put this choice to me. Mom and Dad and Teri went through the same agony."

Besides feeling resentment, the family became infuriated with Pam's impatience and cold tone in discussing her daughter. Perhaps they never believed she would actually send Jamie to a children's home. But in the end, they too refused to accept responsibility for the eleven-year-old.

"Basically, Pam gave up being a parent. She left it up to the family," Fenner says, "and then the county and the state."

Jamie was not angry at her relatives for declining to take her in. She was angry only that her mother had forced them to decide against her. It would have been better if Pam had decided independently, Jamie says. Instead, she was made to experience family rejection. That would be with her forever.

"I felt like a failure since I was eleven and my mother gave me to the Baptist children's home in South Carolina," she said during her last year of high school. "I've worked hard to get over that feeling, but it's always in the back of my mind that I'm not worth anything."

PAM sent her daughter to Tabernacle Children's Home in Greenville, South Carolina. It was part of a tight religious community. Pam's brother, Ron, and his wife attended a Bible college that was part of the Tabernacle community. Jamie would attend the same school as their son Eric, only three months older than Jamie, although Jamie would be boarded at the children's home.

Tabernacle's strict rules and discipline appealed to Pam. She thought the structured program and its discipline would be good for Jamie. The family favored the religious education. And Kay, a computer specialist, had a two-year contract to work in Greenville. Pam expected Kay to see Jamie on some of the hourlong weekend visits Tabernacle allowed for the children. Far away from Raleigh, Tabernacle seemed the optimum choice to Pam.

Pam now feels she made a mistake to hand over Jamie to the fundamentalist Baptist home.

"I've come to think that I was trying to rescue Jamie from herself, and I think that I perhaps just pulled her out of the frying pan and threw her into the fire," she says in a low, even tone.

"It looked so innocuous from the outside."

9

Tabernacle

❖

KAY drove Jamie to Tabernacle in South Carolina, a five-hour ride from Raleigh. Pam did not want to take Jamie to the children's home herself. She said she feared Jamie would jump out of the car at a rest stop and run away. Unaware of her mother's excuse, Jamie proved Pam wrong.

"She just sat there the whole time looking straight out the window like she was stunned," Kay remembers. "We cried all the way down there. I cried more than she did. She was acting brave for me, but I knew she was scared to death."

Once in Greenville, they drove past nestlings of trailer parks where many Tabernacle members lived, and into the Tabernacle complex. The property includes a Bible college, where Jamie's uncle, an engineer, is studying to become a preacher, as well as a primary and secondary school, a retirement home, and a children's home. Community leaders discourage members from venturing into the "ungodly" outside world. Their reigning octogenarian, Reverend Sitler, says experiences in the outside world "breed sin."

The teachings, the austere setting, and the demands of Tabernacle Children's Home differed so profoundly from Pam's free-spirited and agnostic ways that the family doubted that she had actually visited the place before she sent Jamie there.

"It was like a prison," Kay says. Her matter-of-fact demeanor crumbles and her voice grows husky. "That was my first impression when we walked in. It was old but it was clean. We went directly into the office. The boys' dorm was right next to the office and it looked like there were millions of beds to one room. They were packed in like sardines."

Tabernacle never permitted Kay to see the room where Jamie would sleep. But Kay didn't ask to see it that first day. She wanted to get away as soon as possible. It was like taking an animal to an inhumane shelter, she says. She just had to get out.

Jamie spent seventh and eighth grades at Tabernacle. At first its puritanical rules confused her. Her mother had taught her to be independent. Tabernacle taught her to obey. Her first infraction came when she recorded rock music over a tape of gospel songs. Rock music was not permitted.

It was easy to get in trouble at Tabernacle. You could get paddled for staying on the phone too long, or receiving too many phone calls, or gossiping or giggling too much, or certainly for whispering during church services. The dress code required long, full skirts. Girls weren't permitted to wear pants, jeans, and shorts, or any makeup. Movies were forbidden. Anyplace that sold alcohol was off-limits, including grocery and convenience stores.

Like the rest of the children, Jamie was taught to believe that her parents were sinful and bad. She had to atone for the sins of her parents. Otherwise she and they would be damned to hell. Staff members urged her to take notes if her relatives acted sinfully when they visited, or if they allowed her to watch television or listen to any music besides gospel.

All visitors from the outside, including relatives, were required to make an appointment to see the children. When state inspectors came, Jamie recalls, a group of the "best children" (which at that point included Jamie) were told to act surprised when they were pulled together as a "random group" for questioning. Tabernacle prepped this random group on how to answer the questions.

Because of her uncle Ron's affiliation with Tabernacle, the staff allowed Jamie to spend some extra time with her family under his supervision. But if they were not going to Ron's home for a visit, Tabernacle would send another child along as a monitor, to report back to the staff in case anybody did anything sinful.

Tabernacle was certainly a society—"a prison," as Teri also put it. But Jamie did well at first under its tutelage. She earned straight A's at school and was considered an exceptional example for other children. She found outlets for her energy and developed hobbies. And at Tabernacle she discovered singing.

"I found that I could float and soar when I sang, and I loved it," she says. She joined the children's choir. But the choir had a downside. The children performed at other churches around the state and afterward were told to ask for money. "It was like, Here are the orphan kids singing, please contribute," Jamie says. "It was awful."

On overnight trips, the children stayed in different households. Jamie was usually a very popular guest.

"She had this angelic little voice, and this blond hair, and those sweet green eyes," one hostess remembers. "She just took my breath away the moment I saw her. She was so very polite and nice too. I figured for sure her mother and father was dead and she had no surviving relatives, because surely someone would have taken this angel in."

That hostess wasn't the first to ask about adopting Jamie. But when Jamie heard about the inquiries, she would reject them immediately. Thank you very much, she would say, but I have a mother who just can't afford to keep me but who loves me and I love very much. When such an inquiry about her went directly to Tabernacle, Jamie was terrified.

"I loved my aunts and my family, and I didn't want to be separated from them. I wanted to be free so I could see them, and I wanted to say who I was, not some orphan," Jamie says. "And mostly, to be honest, I was frightened of being a part of a family again. I thought I couldn't do it. I didn't want to fail at it again."

Failure to her meant she would not be loved. At Tabernacle she quickly learned how to win affection and esteem. She handed out the most tracts when sent to the local grocery store to evangelize. Her candy-box face drew people. She became, as Tabernacle staff members said approvingly, a "holy roller." Soon she became one of the girls sent out to monitor other children's visits. But when their relatives broke rules, she never reported it, and the staff soon relieved her of those duties.

"She became more spiritual and, I guess, more ladylike," Teri says. "Tabernacle gave her a daily structure and goals. It turned her into a more structured type. But I don't really know if it turned her into a more loving child or shut her off emotionally."

The Allens worried about Tabernacle's effects on Jamie. She became unnervingly obedient and docile. And they were concerned that Jamie lived too far away from Pam. Her mother did not visit very often, and cut her monthly donation to the home from $50 to $25. The family did not think this reflected her income as much as her waning interest in her child. Now that Jamie had proven herself obedient, they pressured Pam to take her back.

Pam refused. "She either was moving in with a guy or he was moving in with her," Teri says. "Anyway, she was having a blast, and I don't think she wanted to take Jamie back."

Only after two years and the end of yet another romantic relationship did Pam relent.

10

Home Again

JAMIE began ninth grade back in Raleigh at Broughton High School—her ninth school in nine years. Broughton was a whole new world. It loomed much larger. The rules, the path to success, the kids were all different. Conformity paid off at Tabernacle, but cool rebellion paid off at Broughton.

Under its large shadow, she felt lost, and that fueled her determination to fit in.

So she went up to a cool-looking junior named Jinny Jackson. Jinny is a pretty, perky young woman with a mischievous smile. Her blond hair swings in a high, short ponytail with waterfall strands escaping around her face.

"She was in show choir, so we used to pick on her," Jinny remembers of her first talks with Jamie.

Jinny had a lot of friends. While she seemed popular to Jamie, Jinny claims she was not enormously popular. "Your parents had to be millionaires to be popular at our school," she explains.

Pam didn't like Jinny from the first. She thought she brought trouble into the house, but in truth it was more often Jamie who stirred up trouble and Jinny, although several years older, who followed. It was Jamie who suggested they drive topless around Fort Bragg, a huge army post in Fayetteville, and Jamie who snuck out at night to go dancing at clubs.

"It was like the world opened up to Jamie after Tabernacle," Teri says. "She went wild after she came out. Part of it was the action of the big city. There were things to get into. There were people who stayed up all night. But part of it too was that her mom was still not settled. Things were unscheduled, and I think she was lost without firm direction."

At first her grades, so high at Tabernacle, slipped badly. And her relationship with Pam, never easy, become hostile again. Pam complained constantly about her wayward child. Jamie didn't like overhearing her mother's exaggerations and kept Pam from meeting her friends' parents.

"Even after a long time, Jamie was very secretive about her mother," Jinny remembers. "She wouldn't talk about her to me or my parents. It was like this whole side to her she was hiding."

To ease the growing tension, Pam decided that they both needed a weekend at Myrtle Beach, South Carolina. Jamie could bring a friend. She invited Stacey, knowing full well that Jinny was unacceptable. But Stacey was grounded for some misdemeanor, so Jamie went alone with her mother. On the first evening at the beach, as Pam prepared to go out on a date, she gave Jamie $15 for carnival rides. Furious that her mother would leave her alone, Jamie stormed out into the night.

Her pout abated when a handsome young marine invited her on a head-spinning ride. He asked her age.

"Nineteen," she answered.

"No you're not," he told her.

"You're right," she laughed. "I'm seventeen."

That seemed to satisfy him, although she was just fourteen, and she believes she looked just that age.

She stayed out with the marine until 4 A.M. When she returned, she found her mother frantic. Pam had called the police. She immediately packed them up and drove back to Raleigh. Fear overtook Jamie. She thought that her mother would stop loving her again. Then she panicked. Maybe she had gotten pregnant by the marine. It had been her first sexual experience, and she hurt.

She told her mother she had been raped. Pam took her to the hospital. Not once did she doubt her daughter. She wanted to find and punish the marine. So Jamie backed down and admitted that she had consented to having sex.

Pam understood that Jamie no longer claimed rape, but instead of questioning Jamie further, she read Jamie's diary. There she learned that her daughter had gone with the marine because she was angry at her mother for leaving her alone that night. Furious, Pam questioned Jamie about every boy she had ever mentioned in her diary, wanting to know if she had slept with any of them, too.

"No," Jamie told her truthfully over and over again. "The marine was the first."

But Pam wouldn't believe it. She never forgave Jamie for her deception. Their fights escalated until one day Pam pushed Jamie down on a couch.

"She looked at me like she was going to hit me, and I looked back at her and said go ahead," Jamie remembers. "After that she was real mean."

One of Pam's boyfriends believed Jamie deserved every bit of meanness Pam gave her. Such insolence, he told Pam, needed to be beaten out of Jamie. "Hit the mess out of her," he advised.

After one argument, Pam tried to make it up by fixing breakfast.

"She had made me a really nice breakfast," Jamie remembers. "I just took it to my room. She came after me and slapped me, knocked me down. She was so mad that I hadn't sat at the table with her. I slapped her back. She was completely stunned. She went downstairs. I thought, Well, cool, if this will end her hitting me, I'll hit her."

Jamie lowers her head in embarrassment when she talks about the fight. Separately, her mother looks straight ahead, anger still chilling her eyes. The incident is one that neither Jamie nor Pam talks about much. But it was one more huge tear in their fragile relationship.

"I told my mom I would never hit her again," Jamie says. "And I haven't. I thought it would stop her from hitting me, but it just got worse."

Pam hardened to Jamie after that. "It changed our relationship forever," Pam says.

11

Back to Tabernacle

▓

AFTER one year in Raleigh, Pam sent Jamie back to Tabernacle. This time her grandparents drove her to the children's home. Kay refused to "reincarcerate" Jamie, as she put it.

"Pam didn't consult us that second time," Teri remembers. "I was really upset because I didn't think she had tried one hundred percent. She was living with or dating somebody at the time, and she wanted to build that relationship."

Pam was dating a married man, and she believed he might leave his wife and family for her. He wanted more children, and Pam wanted to give him those children. She was convinced that the problems she and her daughter had were entirely Jamie's fault. She believed then, as she does now, that a child's personality is determined entirely by genetics. Another child would not be at all like Jamie. She grew more excited about the prospect of another child each time she talked about it. The Allens worried. When it became clear that Pam was serious about getting pregnant, her mother intervened.

"You're not the mothering type," she told her daughter bluntly. It was one of the few times Mrs. Allen asserted herself into her adult children's lives. Pam told her sisters she has never been more hurt than she was by her mother's comment. She took it out on Jamie.

"She told me of all the kinds of children in the world she could have had, she got stuck with me," Jamie remembers. "Everything would have been entirely different if a different sperm had fertilized her egg. She said because of me she wouldn't have more kids. I wanted a younger brother or sister more than anything."

Her mother's words stuck in Jamie's heart. Maybe her mother was right, she thought as she rode silently back to Tabernacle. Her mother, she knew, had finally given up on her.

Tabernacle looked different this time. In her year away at public school, she had discovered jeans, rock music, dancing, boys, and makeup. After visiting the admissions office, a staff member took her to the bathroom, where she washed the makeup from Jamie's face.

Jamie lasted only three months at Tabernacle this time. She didn't intend to cause trouble there, but she could not stop questioning things they told her. She didn't think rock and roll came from the devil. And she refused to believe that the sin of parents had brought her and the other children to Tabernacle.

"There was nothing wrong with me because I was in the children's home," Jamie says. "My mom and I just didn't get along."

Before long, Jamie got caught up in trouble. First staff discovered her smoking with a girlfriend.

"I took one drag and got paddled. I didn't think that was very fair," she says, looking slightly to the heavens with a Meg Ryan smile. "I should have gotten the whole cigarette for that."

Then things got more serious. She "corrupted" other girls. Sinful ways had caught up with Jamie on the outside, staff felt, but she could be saved once again. They encouraged her to be friends with Angie, a year older and a holy roller of the first degree. Instead of lifting Jamie toward more "godly behavior," however, Angie fell into a "backsliding state." She wanted to wear slacks and go out with boys. And finally, she and Jamie were caught listening to a Prince song.

"They really came down on me hard for introducing her to worldly, sinful ways," Jamie says ruefully.

And it was not only Angie that Jamie subverted. Other girls flocked to hear of her adventures outside. Jamie encouraged them to explore and push the confines of the home.

The Tabernacle authorities complained to Jamie's mom and even her aunts that Jamie was "contaminating the entire place," Teri says. Meanwhile, the staff made an extra effort to discipline Jamie into submission.

Paddling did not work well on her. They found it increased her heresy. She even questioned the claims that Tabernacle staff were closer to God than outsiders were. The people she knew from the outside world, like Kay and Teri, smoked and drank some, but she thought they were much better people and certainly more loving than the strict and cold staff at Tabernacle. And she didn't like Tabernacle's self-righteousness.

During prayer devotions one morning, she became particularly angry. Mr. Sims, the director of the children's home, stood before its forty boys and thirty girls, sermonizing about burning the barley fields. Jamie only half paid attention. She found it hard enough to keep still and quiet during that hour-and-a-half period every morning before school without listening, too—until Sims picked on one of her classmates, Amy, almost by name. In his devotions he often alluded to children in the home and their infractions as a way to punish them further. This time he hardly tried to hide the fact he was talking about Amy.

Amy was seventeen and a few years behind in school. Her parents and her younger brother had been killed when she was five. A train had struck the family's car while it was crossing the railroad tracks. Amy's aunt escaped and pulled Amy from the car, but the others died. Amy never really understood what happened, and fleeting memories confused and preoccupied her. Did the car stall? Could she have unlocked the door for her parents to get out? Could she have unfastened her brother's seat belt?

Partly because of her preoccupation, she forgot things and made mistakes. She was terrified of Tabernacle's punishment, and even more afraid of the staff's disapproving eyes, so she would lie to cover up her mistakes. This time Mr. Sims had had enough.

"Someone in our presence, I won't say the name, but someone," he began disingenuously, and went on to describe her lies, and then, as usual, let Amy's name slip.

"He said that because Amy constantly lied, she wasn't a good testimony to God and that her parents were her barley fields to be burned because she was bad. God had taken her parents and family to punish her for lying so much," Jamie remembers.

Later she tried to tell Amy that Mr. Sims was wrong. But Amy had a hard time believing that he could be wrong. She had spent her life in the children's home and had come to accept whatever the elders told her.

"I just thought it was stupid," Jamie says. "There were so many things about the place that I thought were so stupid, but that's when it went over the limits, when it went from being dumb to devastating someone's life."

Jamie was forbidden to talk with Amy for more than a few minutes. The staff monitored the conversations. So Jamie wrote her a letter saying Mr. Sims didn't know what he was talking about. He didn't have any children of his own so he didn't know anything about kids. If anything, God was on her side, not his, she wrote. Staff confiscated the letter, but only after Amy read it and felt better.

Jamie's punishment was terrifying. A severe woman seated Jamie alone in a room dimmed by closed shades, on a stiff wooden chair, under a cross, and told her to look only at a picture of a suffering, bleeding, anguished, and crucified Jesus for three days. She could move only to go to the toilet. A staff member brought her meals. She ate alone and wasn't permitted to move more than absolutely necessary because it would interrupt her reflections and thoughts of the sins she had committed.

On the second day Mr. Sims entered the room. She could see red fury in his usually pallid checks.

"If your mother doesn't come and get you tomorrow, I'm going to call the police and they're going to take you into state foster care," he declared.

Jamie sat petrified. At least once a year the staff showed films of emaciated children, allegedly in the state foster care system, living in roach-infested rooms and regularly beaten. "If you mess up here," they said at the end of such presentations, "you're going to have to go to that foster care because your parents don't want you."

When Jamie had seen the films for the first time during her initial stay, she called her mother, crying. "Mom, please, please don't ever put me in foster care. I promise I'll be good." And her mother had promised she would not.

Now Jamie prayed under that cross that her mother would come to get her. And she waited.

On the third afternoon, Jamie left the room to go to the bathroom. From the top of the wooden staircase, she caught a glimpse of her slim, blond mother. She had never realized how beautiful her mother was or how much she loved her. All the warm feelings rose inside of her.

"Mom!" she cried and ran to the staircase.

Her mother turned on her with a furious glare.

"I think that was one of the worst feelings ever," Jamie remembers. "I felt really good about seeing her, but she had this anger on her face, like, 'You made me drive five hours to get here, why can't you be good? Why can't you just stay here, because you know I can't keep you? You're not happy at home, so why did you mess it up here?'"

Jamie heard just those words shortly afterward. She had been expelled.

"I was really at my wit's end," Pam says now. "I don't think I was angry, just very very frustrated. I just didn't know what to do. What do we try next? What do we do that we haven't already tried?"

It was a long drive home. Jamie sat quietly, frightened by her mother's anger. But she could not help enjoying the sunshine and the brightness of the free world. She would be good now, she promised. Better than ever before. And besides, whatever happened, her mother would never, never, ever put her in state foster care. She had promised. It would never happen.

She was wrong.

12

Wrenn House

THE light outside blinded Jamie. She hadn't been in sunlight for three days. She was determined to show her mother that she could be good and appreciate her now. But she never got the chance.

"There was no question about Jamie living with me," Pam says. "Our relationship had just deteriorated to that point."

And Pam was ready to start a new life with the married man, who did not want Jamie around. Pam had already quit her job and moved in with him.

"She was desperate for him," Jamie remembers. "Later she said he was a really bad thing in her life, which I could have told her."

Jamie stayed with her mother just overnight. The next morning Pam found Wrenn House, a home for runaway and homeless teenagers.

Wrenn House sits quietly in downtown Raleigh, in a neighborhood of businesses and a few residents. Little stands out about 605 West North Street except that the old two-story beige structure is tidier than the trash-strewn neighborhood engulfing it. Inside, it has the feel of a worn place struggling to maintain dignity through cleanliness. The off-white carpet is stained but well vacuumed, and fresh plaster patches mar the walls of the game room, which features a lintless green pool table. The house strives for as much of a "normal homelike environment" as possible. Its "young people" are assigned chores, transported to their schools (no matter how far), and required to study for an hour a day.

Wrenn is part of Haven House, a nonprofit child care agency founded in 1973, when the juvenile codes were revised to distinguish between delinquent children and criminal offenders. Before then, youths who skipped school were placed in the same juvenile detention center as youths who had stolen and injured their victims in the process.

Wrenn is the only facility in Raleigh's Wake County designed for teenagers who have run away and are homeless. There wasn't much need for it when it was founded, in 1981. Most runaways fled to bigger cities. In fact many of Wrenn's runaways were discovered in North Carolina while en route to Florida. But these days more parents are renouncing responsibility for their children and pushing them out of their homes. The demands on Wrenn House have increased dramatically over the last decade and a half.

"Before you may have had ten families out of a hundred that needed help. Today you have maybe twenty in a hundred," explains Wrenn's program director, Josephine Nobel. "And besides that, Raleigh has grown tremendously over the last ten years. Resources have not kept up with the population."

But the two-bedroom house can accommodate only five children at a time. Two other beds are occupied by young counselors, usually fresh out of college. "We work aggressively to get the kids out of Wrenn House as soon as possible, without returning them to a life-threatening situation," Nobel says. The average length of stay is five days, with fourteen days the maximum stay. About 150 to 200 young people pass through Wrenn House each year.

Pam told the staff that Jamie was a deeply troubled child who very well might run away. She needed somewhere to put her daughter immediately and expected Wrenn to keep Jamie the maximum fourteen days, during which time she would look for a more permanent home for her daughter. But after just two days, Wrenn discharged Jamie. It was clear to them that she didn't fit the profile of children in real need of their programs. The children at Wrenn were troubled. They included kids whose parents had thrown them out, kids on juvenile probation, and children from an abusive home environment, in which the child was often the abuser.

Jamie wasn't troubled, the staff believed, her mother simply didn't want her. Wrenn's primary mission is to reunite families. Pam wasn't looking for this solution. She refused even to take part in therapy sessions with Jamie that the Wrenn staff recommended.

"The hardest part of this job is working with parents," says Nobel. "I don't condone the bad behavior of some of these young people, but I have to say I understand it. These young people do remarkably well for the environments they come from."

There is increasing pressure on social workers not to remove young people from their homes, Nobel says, because alternative placement in group homes and children's homes is expensive for the government.

"Most of the young people who come here are reunited with their family not necessarily because it is best for them," she adds, "but because finding placement for them is so difficult. I would say there has actually been a decrease in placements of children outside their own homes over the last ten years. Ten years ago you may have been able to get some of these young people into a good foster care placement, but now that placement is reserved for the most troubled kids.

"So many times these young people just go back to a bad environment. It breaks my heart to watch some of these kids go back home"—she sighs—"because you know nothing will change for them."

Over the years, Wrenn has seen its population change. Once it was filled mostly with girls, who had a harder time making it on the street than boys because they were more likely targets of abuse. Now there is a balance of the sexes. Most of Wrenn's children are teenagers, but some are as young as ten. Some have had one or two transgressions, while others are more serious, chronic problem kids. "But about the worst change I've seen is that parents are more willing to give up on their kids. Really, the hardest part of this job is working with parents," says Nobel.

Jamie liked Wrenn House. But without her mother's participation in therapy, it refused to keep her there. Pam was put in contact with a caseworker to find Jamie a home. In the meantime Jamie was sent to Wake House,* a transitional placement that is often the last stop before a foster home, or hospitalization.

---

* Wake House is the same transitional program Damien was sent to.

13

Wake House

▓

J AMIE didn't know what to think as her mother drove her from Wrenn to Wake House, a temporary emergency shelter for children. When they were alone, the two had been getting along well, she thought. But she also knew that her mother was under relationship stress, and that made her unpredictable.

Jamie was told she would be at Wake House until things straightened out with her mom. Or maybe one of her aunts would take her. She didn't know. She tried not to think about it too much. She had been overeating compulsively in the weeks since she left Tabernacle.

Anyway, she figured, she'd meet with the man her mother had made an appointment for them to see. If things went well, she figured, she might go home for a while. If they didn't, she'd probably only have to stay overnight. In the worst case, she'd be there only a few days, as at Wrenn House.

She never expected to stay three months, or that her mother would perform as she did that day. And she'll never forget how Andrew Meyer saved her.

Meyer is the director of Wake House. Jamie found comfort in his young, direct, and cheerful manner. He was polite, and Jamie responded in kind. She could not read him, though. She was too distracted by her mother's sudden change in tone when the three sat down. At first, while her mother spoke, Jamie looked around Meyer's white-walled office trying to make sense of the place and her mother's words and behavior.

"She's just such a difficult child," Pam told Meyer. "I can't do anything. I've tried everything. I've spanked her, I've grounded her. But she never obeys me. She's just wild and there is nothing I can do about it. We can't live together."

After Pam blocked several of his suggestions, it became clear to Meyer that Pam did not want to reconcile with her daughter or even rebuild a relationship with her. Pam wanted, simply, to relinquish all her parental responsibility to the state.

Jamie couldn't believe her mother's words. But Pam pounded her point over and over so that even Jamie found it too plain to ignore. In Jamie's memory, that afternoon in Meyer's office remains excruciatingly painful. Pam wanted to sign Jamie over to state custody and divorce her child forever. She would no longer be financially responsible. She wouldn't even have to keep in contact with her daughter.

What if that meant she would never see Jamie again?

"I understand," Pam said, so cold and calm that Jamie could not even shiver. "It's just gotten to that point. We can't stand each other. I've tried everything, counseling, a boarding school. Nothing works. See, she hasn't even participated in this session."

Jamie was too stunned to say a word. She didn't know how to respond or even how to defend herself. She didn't know what, if anything, was expected of her. So she sat still, her back against the white wall, her right hand clutching her left arm so hard that she left bruised imprints of each finger.

A seething, almost unnatural anger seeped and then poured out of her mother. And then suddenly, Pam cried while Jamie remained stunned and seemingly emotionless.

"Is this what I've done?" Jamie thought to herself. "Have I destroyed my mother?"

She was told that her mother had once checked herself into a hospital and was diagnosed as manic-depressive. And Jamie believed, because she remembers her mother telling her so, that her mother's hospitalization was her fault. She also believed her mother's accusations that she had driven away her father and stepfather.

Meyer saved her that day from becoming another lost kid in state custody, Jamie says, although she doesn't recall if he sympathized with her or her mother or either of them.

"She wanted to sign me over, but he wouldn't let her," Jamie says with a sigh so deep her hands tremble. "That's all I remember except that he'd look at me every once in a while."

Meyer watched as Pam heaped blame on Jamie, occasionally on her abusive father and ex-husband, but never on herself. In the end he knew, because he had seen it all too many times before, that Pam was totally irresponsible. But he never indicated these thoughts to Jamie, because blame never helped the child. Jamie could be helped only if she recognized that she was better off some distance from her mother.

Meyer agreed to admit Jamie to Wake House and ordered a thorough psychiatric evaluation of her. He hoped that perhaps her mother would change her mind, but he didn't count on it. Before any placement, he believed Jamie needed to be assessed and, if possible, understood.

At Wake House, Jamie waited to be rescued by her aunts, her grandparents, or, she secretly dreamed, her father. She had told herself it wouldn't be long. But by her fifteenth day at Wake House, the stress became apparent.

"Jamie is a bright fourteen-year-old girl who is experiencing a significant amount of situationally induced stress creating a strong sense of helplessness and insecurity," her psychological evaluation noted.

And as each day passed, the stress wore on her optimism and extinguished her hope.

"Jamie's tendency to use intellectualizing and compulsive defenses is apparently inadequate to the task at hand as she is feeling quite unhappy, deprived of the affection and attention she needs and unable to rely or depend on an adult figure to provide the stability and predictability she requires to grow," a report stated. "Jamie voices her resignation that things will not turn out as she hopes directly in the interview and indirectly on the projective tests. There is no evidence of a thought disorder; although her perceptions may be idiosyncratic at times." Still, her "behavior at group home has been excellent."

It became clearer that Pam had more problems than Jamie and was, in fact, standing in the way of her daughter's rehabilitation. When Wake suggested that Jamie be allowed to volunteer at a day care center for children or perhaps as a candy striper at Rex Hospital, Pam refused, saying Jamie was "very irresponsible." Wake suggested Jamie might work at a veterinarian's office because she liked animals. Such work kept children occupied and increased their self-esteem. But Pam refused permission again. And when the parents of her friend Jinny inquired about taking Jamie on a weekend camping trip, Pam refused yet again, ignoring the staff's recommendation.

A committed staff saved Jamie from despair. They helped her understand her strengths and her mother's weaknesses without outwardly condemning her mother and jeopardizing a possible reconciliation. They succeeded in making her believe that she didn't need her mother and that she was in fact better off without her.

Jamie's final evaluation turned out clear and positive. Staff liked her and she proved to have good social skills, not only with adults but also with other children. She ignored the "negative behavior" of some of her peers, a critical element in a child's success in living in children's and group homes. Unlike many children tossed in the chaotic spirals of unstable parents, Jamie could make a clear connection between her behavior and the consequences of her actions. In all, she seemed not just a "normal child," but even a "good" one.

"There were no indications on this evaluation of Jamie harboring aggressive tendencies per se," one of Wake's final reports says,

although it is likely that she may become quite reactive and express her emotions intensely if sufficiently provoked. It is highly likely that mother's own unresolved rage and other issues with her abusive father and later abusive husband and/or boyfriend are being played out with her daughter who she may unconsciously provoke into repeating the pattern she is attempting to work through in her own life.

If Jamie is to return home, it seems imperative that her mother receive individual therapy as well in order to help her heal from the physical abuse she suffered as a child and to understand better the dynamics that are going on between herself and her daughter. Mother appears to harbor significant anger towards Jamie which apparently has not been dealt with sufficiently as it seems that she projects much of this on Jamie.

It was imperative, the psychologist decided in the end, that Jamie not feel abandoned again by her mother and that contacts with other family members be encouraged to give her a sense of being loved and supported. She would also benefit from therapy to deal with her issues of distrust and "likely difficulties with intimacy." While "Jamie denies suicidal idealization or intention in the past"—in fact, Jamie described the idea of suicide or dying as "gross"—the psychologist found "there are significant indicators on the Rorschach that she may be at high risk for engaging in suicidal gestures in the future." Moreover, "there are also indications that Jamie may develop psychosomatic complaints (e.g. obesity) as a way to express her internal conflicts, anxiety, and/or anger."

To the staff at Wake House, it appeared obvious the damage had been done. At fourteen, Jamie fell vulnerable to failure and to suicide, even, and had to learn to deal with her pain and distrust. Before they discharged her, they tried to make her realize she was better off without her mother. In fact, they suggested, maybe she did not even want to be with her mother.

The idea resonated with Jamie. And it worked. She stopped believing that she was a failure because her mother did not want her. Instead, she began to think that maybe she didn't want to live with her mother after all.

Jamie went to live at the Free Will Baptist Children's Home, believing she was making a fresh start. She could succeed at being whatever she chose. She had power now. She had herself, and now grown at fourteen, that was all she needed.

14
Free Will

✦

ON the last day of July 1990, Jamie officially entered state custody by way of a contract signed by her mother, a Wake County Department of Social Services caseworker, and a social worker for the Free Will Baptist Children's Home.

Only one reason is listed for the purpose of admission: "Breakdown in parent-child relationship." For teenagers entering foster care, it is the most common reason for admission.*

While Pam was giving up responsibility for raising Jamie, she was not completely severing all ties to her daughter as she had intended. Pam knew that as at Tabernacle, she would be responsible for Jamie's board costs at Free Will—only it would be far more expensive than it was at Tabernacle. If she could relinquish her role as mother, she would not be charged for Jamie's care. The Department of Social Services, however, quietly convinced Pam that while the bill might mount, no one would come after her for the money she owed, and eventually it would be forgotten. Money should not factor into such an important decision. Whether because of embarrassment or sense, the sentiment got through to Pam, who retained parental status.

Wake County, where Pam lived, agreed to take Jamie if Pam accepted six standard responsibilities, including a promise to stay in touch with Jamie at Free Will and respond to her progress and needs while in care. The county would provide the board payment of $300 per month for care and $300 a year for clothing. Half the clothing allowance would be given to Jamie in the spring and half in the fall. The county where Pam now lived would pay for medical and dental bills through Medicaid. It would also provide transportation for her weekend and holiday visits. A Free Will social worker would keep a Wake County caseworker informed about Jamie's case. And finally, a county caseworker would hold a review conference every six months "to amend, alter, or terminate this Plan Of Care."

• • •

---

* For younger children, neglect is more common.

FREE Will Baptist Children's Home is located about thirty miles west of Raleigh, less than six miles off Interstate 40, in the small farming town of Middlesex. The kids there joke it's somewhere between Foreplay and Climax. From the highway, sway-back roads rolling past abandoned barns, corn, tobacco, and occasionally cotton fields are peppered with signs pointing to the "Children's Home."

Around a sharp corner, the campus stands like a boot camp. The low brick buildings seem barrackslike in their uniformity. A large American flag flaps in full breeze above the center of campus. A sprinkling of young faces takes shape, adding color and movement to the grounds.

It was here I first met Jamie, then a seventeen-year-old with sun-gold blond hair and green eyes. She had a full figure, not well hidden by an outgrown T-shirt. The red polish on her nails flaked and cracked when she raised them to her mouth and nibbled at their ends.

June 5 was Harley Day at the home, and Jamie looked as excited about the motorcycle games as the younger children, mostly eight- and twelve-year-olds. She lined up with them to be paired with a member of the Harley gang. Her match was a large man in dark glasses and leather gloves, long thin hair, and a rolling gut. Above his jeans and boots, he wore only a black leather vest, which wasn't nearly large enough to cover his hairy belly.

Jamie got on the back of his bike and wrapped her arms around him, just as the other children did with their partners.

"Hold on tight," the director of the game called out.

The driver seemed uncomfortable with this very attractive girl on his bike, but Jamie rode with ease. At first blush, she seemed accustomed to the feel of men. But Jamie seems to know when it's safe to touch, and with a crowd around, she felt safe. She has come a long way from her younger days, when a counsellor complained that "she has trouble hugging people."

But Jamie's arms lie innocently around the Harley man this day. She concentrates only on the potato game. The motorcycles race in a circle around a pile of hay in which are hidden potatoes for every kid but one. When a whistle blows, the bikes stop, the kids jump off and scramble for a potato. Those who find one continue, always one fewer than before. Jamie is always successful, but as the game nears its climax, she quietly slips her potato to a seven-year-old boy and walks away, leaving him to compete in the final round.

Jamie is one of the good stories, a staffer tells me. She is one of the few children in the Baptist home's fifty-year history to be scheduled to go to college.

When Jamie speaks of the future, her future—which might include study abroad in France or England, she says, or a law degree or journalism or modeling—a fresh sparkle lights her eyes. When she leaves the home, she expects to feel free of her past. She will be on a level ground with the rest of the students at college.

She's not embarrassed about coming from Free Will Baptist Children's Home, but it's not information she'll volunteer, either. It's just part of the sad trail of her past, and she's ready to move on. She's thankful that of all the children's homes, she came here, close to her aunt Teri's home. She appreciates the help she got from her cottage parents, the Pattersons. And she feels that some of the people on the staff at Free Will really care, particularly the director, Mr. Johnson.

James Johnson is a young, energetic African-American man with an approachable yet distinguished manner. He wears a neat, light half mustache that is the trend now. His eyes are as bright and alert as his personality. Kids' heads turn when he walks on campus, but not just because of his good looks. Even with his hands stuffed in his pockets, they know not to mess with him when he calls them over. He's firm when he speaks adult language to them, knowing full well the language of their world. He's trying to integrate their past world of few morals or standards and horrifying experiences into the outside world that is still foreign to many of the youngsters. When he scolds lightly, they look down as they would to someone else's harsher words, and so most of them miss the gentle and understanding flicker in his eye. They trust him. He commands respect, he speaks honestly to them, and he looks sharp. Some of the girls admit to crushes on him when they first arrived, but now they think of him more like family.

He prefers that the kids not call him Dad, as many younger children do to latch on to a sense of belonging or placement, something familiar, perhaps a feeling of affection. Johnson prefers that the children accept their real fathers, even those who are not good to the child, and deal with the reality. No matter at what age and how painful it might be, he believes that the sooner the children accept their situations, the better able they will be to adjust and succeed.

"He don't always tell you what you want to hear," one boy says, shaking his head. "But he tells you the truth."

Another boy volunteers that he wants to be just like Mr. Johnson when he grows up. But Johnson doesn't want to be a role model either. He wants each of his kids to do the best they can and to be themselves.

The home's population is diverse, but has only been that way since the home integrated in 1985.

"You would be amazed at some of these kids," Johnson says, leaning over his desk eagerly. "Little six-, seven-year-olds. Beautiful, cute, wonderful children, and you wonder why would anyone, anyone not take care of this one, especially if he were your own?"

And then he explains why.

Last week a woman from a poor Southern county came with five children, wide eyed, thin, and frightened.

"Can you help us?" she asked before he even reached her hand. Her eyes were watery with exhaustion. Her husband had left months ago. She had no money, no work, no way to feed her children. For the last three months they had lived on one meal a day of beans and rice. Now with winter coming and the electricity cut off, she was desperate.

Mr. Johnson refused to consider taking the children. None of the children were victimized, troubled, or unwanted. They had no history of being difficult. Their mother displayed love and affection for them. All she wanted was Free Will to keep the children until she got on her feet.

Even in recounting the story, Johnson is furious. It does not work that way, he explained to her. Maybe during the Depression, but not in the 1990s. Today, once they're in the system, it's very difficult to get them out. It takes two years at least for a family and child to be reunited, and that is only if their problems are mild to nonexistent. The system is built on the premise that anyone willing to give up their children for a short time doesn't want them at all. More and more frequently, this is simply not the case. Poverty, refugees from shrinking AFDC, and the inability and incompetence of local government conspire to overload a system designed only for orphans and physically or emotionally dysfunctional families. What the parents and the government don't understand, according to Johnson, is just how terrible substitute child care is today.

"The counties don't want to deal with it," Johnson says, slapping the table. "Especially the smaller ones. Especially the poorer ones.

"They're almost forcing people to give up their children. They won't do anything until the child goes to school with barely any clothes and a teacher reports it, and then they're forced to take the child away. It's not neglect; it's poverty that sends many kids here."

Johnson shakes his head and moves on to another story, about a boy from the mountains who was taken into social services custody after a teacher reported that he dressed in rags. The child was polite, a good student, and well liked. The people in the town took it upon themselves to pity him. The teacher's complaint was buttressed by several churchwomen. Soon it spread throughout his small town that the boy was neglected. His family was poor and never well received by the community.

Social services swooped in and took the child. The parents didn't know how to object. They just hugged their child good-bye. They visit and call as frequently as money will allow. Today the boy walks Free Will's campus with a scowl. He has no friends at the home. He refuses to try in any of his classes. On tests and quizzes, he writes nothing but his name. He's punishing the system that took him from his family.

"They never checked to find out that his family loved him and he loves his family, or that his belly was always full," Johnson says. "Just because he didn't have what the town wanted him to have doesn't mean that they should have brought him into foster care. Sure, here he might have more clothes and the possibility of going to college, but is it worth the sacrifice? He doesn't need to be here."

If the town knew what a children's home is, they would be ashamed, Johnson says. The child has been at Free Will for a year. Johnson is still fighting to get him reunited with his family.

"He's not doing himself any favors being difficult, though," Johnson adds. "They're going to label him as troubled, and then their excuse will become a reason."

And then there was a girl at Free Will who lied. Her father, whom she considered to be strict and difficult, forbade her from dating a boy. To get back at him, she told stories about how he abused her. When the stories spiraled, she started to think that it wouldn't be such a bad thing if she was taken from under his roof. Then she could date her boyfriend. It didn't work that way. At Free Will, children are not allowed to date until they are sixteen. She was fourteen. She didn't realize how frightening it all could be. She wanted to go back home. She told Johnson of her lies soon after she arrived at Free Will. It took him two years to get her reunited with her family.

"Can you imagine what that does to a family?" he asks. "You see, even if you doubt the story, you are required to do something just in case there is truth in it. You'll get severely punished for ignoring the complaints. If you take the child away and you're wrong, well, probably no one's going to do anything about it. Few people are even going to know about it or believe it."

Johnson's final story is probably more common among the children at Free Will. A child has an alcoholic father. The father beats up the mother, or the child, or both. The mother loses her self-respect and control. She says, Take my kid, you will do better for him than I can. Or the father loses his job and the mother is a wreck. They can't care for themselves, let alone their child, so they say they don't want the child anymore. It's too much responsibility.

"Most of the kids here have been abused or neglected," Johnson explains. "But all of them have something else in common. They're here because of a troubled adult and because his or her family needed help at a crucial time. If you could just go in and help that individual and that family in time, we could prevent these tragedies," Johnson says, referring to the children in his care. "We could save so many families."

15
Wilbert

JAMIE sits on the front porch of the cottage she shares with twelve girls and two houseparents and looks up into the clear blue October sky. Flaming orange leaves drift on swirling wind currents, and Jamie feels she can identify with them. The slight chill in the air makes her think of the holidays. Already the kids at Free Will are beginning to ask one another where they'll be going for Christmas, when the campus shuts down. The luckier ones are the first to ask because they already know that they are going to the homes of relatives, and they want all the other kids to know as well. Free Will won't have to find some family to take them in, as they will for the other kids, left behind. They go where they are wanted. Jamie assumed Free Will would be like Tabernacle and she wouldn't be allowed to leave for the holidays. Now she is caught off guard, with no place to go. Next time she will make her plans months ahead.

She has been at Free Will for three months now. She works hard to control everything she can to make her life right. She feels better about school, the public school in town, where she takes advanced classes. Everyone there knows that she is from the home. The information seeped out after she explained to school girlfriends why she could not sleep over or talk very long on the phone. She volunteered nothing up front. She really didn't want people to know. But it would be worse to seem ashamed. Besides, people seemed to respect the reticence in her.

While she wanted to fit in with her classmates, she wanted to be different from the kids at Free Will. She had friends at the home; she liked them and they liked her. In many ways they understood her better than her school friends, but she didn't care to admit it. To fit in best at school, she needed to feel better about herself than most of the Free Will kids felt about themselves. Otherwise she'd be like them, too shy and afraid to try.

She identifies more with the school kids in her goals. Many of her friends at Free Will are looking forward to getting out of high school, getting married, and immediately building the family they never had. They know the family they want because they have dreamed about it all their lives. That's not what Jamie wants, not now at least. Just looking at a baby makes her mad; she doesn't know why. She wants to go to college, like the best and smartest kids in her school. Besides, she is quick to point out, she already has a family. She visits her aunt Teri or Kay almost every weekend. Her mother visits sometimes, too, with her boyfriend, and they all go out to dinner and a movie. She won't take Jamie over the holidays. But Jamie feels different, better, knowing her roots. She knows the good stock from which she came. Unlike the others, she is not an offspring of some poor, abusive, neglectful losers.

But all the talk about holidays reminds her of how much she is in fact a children's home kid. And she knows, more strongly and painfully than ever, whom she has been missing all her life. She wants to find her father. Her mother had told her that Wilbert Everette wanted no part of his daughter's life. Jamie thinks about trying to find him but is afraid of how her mother would react.

That fall, Jamie can't stop wondering about him.

"I think she had in her mind that he was some knight in white shining armor that was going to save her," Pam remembers, lighting up her fourth cigarette. "She found out different." She nods in a self-satisfied way as she blows out the match.

WHEN the entire Allen family gathered in Lumberton for Thanksgiving that year, Jamie was happy to be home.

"She was still the family favorite," her uncle Fenner says. "It was obvious too. There's even a boy in the family, her older cousin. But there were always more pictures of her at the grandparents'."

She liked being with her mother's family in Lumberton, but on each visit she couldn't help wondering if her father still lived nearby. Despite the negative stories about him—stories repeated that Thanksgiving—she wanted to meet him and find out for herself if they were true. Did she get her bad nature from him, as her mother claimed? Did she really look like him? She couldn't stop wondering.

The day after Thanksgiving, she found an Everette listed in the Lumberton phone book. Her paternal grandparents. Without telling her mother, she called them. Her surprised grandmother asked Jamie to come for a visit.

Jamie told her family that she was going to see a friend, but went to the Everettes instead. Her paternal grandmother squeezed her. She could not believe the beauty Jamie had grown into. She had not known Jamie was living in a children's home now, and her eyes filled with tears. Before Jamie left, her grandmother gave her a $100 bill and asked her to come visit on Christmas. She thought it better not to give Jamie her father's phone number or address.

So on Christmas afternoon, Jamie again walked to her paternal grandparents' home. It was filled with aunts and cousins she hardly knew. They

fawned over her. They were horrified that Pam had put her in a children's
home, and stunned too that their brother had not kept up with his child. Just
before Jamie left, her father walked in the door.

It was awkward at first. They looked at each other for a while before
speaking, but after a few minutes, he introduced her to his girlfriend of eight
years and her thirteen-year-old son. Jamie liked her father's girlfriend right
off the bat. She was not as sure about her father. At the end of the day, they
asked her to visit them.

"What do you think?" she asked a Free Will social worker when she
reported what had happened over the holiday break.

"Since they invited you, they probably want to get to know you better,"
the social worker replied. "But it depends on how you feel about it."

A week later Jamie asks for Free Will's permission to visit her father for a
weekend. The staff reacts positively, but her father must pass a social worker's scrutiny first.

"Mr. Everette and his [girl]friend live in the country (Greensboro) and
don't have much (kinda poor)," the social worker reports back, "but appear
genuine in their interest in Jamie and have already fixed up a room for her.
They are planning to be married Friday because they want to make their
living situation right since Jamie is going to be a part of the family." Free Will
approves a weekend visit for Jamie.

Jamie gets along well with her father and his new family. But she keeps
her distance, fearful of the stories about his abusiveness that her mother and
aunts told. Over several visits, she notices bruises on her stepmother and
even an occasional black eye. Jamie feels guilty that the woman has married
Wilbert just so Jamie can visit them. Jamie could have visited even if they
were not married, but her father wanted his home life to look good for the
Department of Social Services. Wilbert invites Jamie to live with them. She
demurs, exaggerating how much she likes Free Will. Her instincts serve her
well. Wilbert has recently embarked on his third marriage; neither of the first
two lasted long.

At first Jamie doesn't tell her mother or any of the Allens about her visits
to her father. She fears she would lose him again if Pam took him to court for
child support payments. But eventually she blurts it out when her maternal
grandmother asks where she is going one afternoon.

. "Now, where would a child her age have gotten an idea like that?" Fenner
asks. "Only from her father. He is still more worried about his money than
about his kid."

Pam promises she will not sue Wilbert again for unpaid child support. But
she does.

"It was the worst thing in the world," Jamie remembers. "I sat there in
court. I couldn't look at my mom or dad. I didn't know why she was doing
this to me. And then, I also thought it wasn't really fair that she had to bear
the burden and cost of raising me all alone.

"I've never felt so bad, though. I couldn't stand watching my father's face as he was being judged a criminal and knowing that I helped put him there. But then he was really mean to my mom in court. The things he said to her were so cruel." Jamie remembers his words but refuses to repeat them.

Pam does not have a strong case. Jamie has not been living under her roof, and the state has paid for her upkeep. After talking to Jamie, a social worker agrees that the prosecution would hurt Jamie more than it could help the state. So the state chooses not to join Pam in prosecuting Wilbert.

The judge decides that Wilbert should pay Pam $5,200, but adds the condition that Pam must use the money to pay for Jamie's college education. Wilbert's new wife withdraws the money from her pension and it is given to Pam. Jamie is admitted to North Carolina State University in Raleigh. But scholarships supplemented by waitressing at Applebee's will be the only money available to cover tuition and living expenses. Pam will take the money, which she believed was owed to her for having raised Jamie through elementary school, and leave town.

16

Last Straw

JAMIE's friend Jinny was studying art in Wisconsin, but she returns prematurely, pregnant, during Jamie's senior year in high school. Now nineteen, Jinny, with her baby son, is living with her parents while she completes her studies at a local school. Jamie still feels part of Jinny's family and, on weekends from the children's home, likes to visit her and her new son in Raleigh, not far from Pam's apartment.

Pam still doesn't like Jinny and is angry that her daughter has maintained a friendship with Jinny's family. But she does not admit to the jealousy she feels then.

On one weekend, Jamie goes to visit Jinny, promising to return by six-thirty so she and her mother can spend some time together before Pam drives her back to Free Will before the Sunday curfew.

She knows Pam is not happy with her visits to Jinny, but she doesn't think an extra half hour will mean much. Jinny needs more diapers for her son, so the two girls drive to the store. It is past seven when they return.

Just after six-thirty, Pam is enraged. By 7 P.M., she acts on her rage. As

Jinny pulls up to the front of her parents' house, Jamie cannot believe her eyes. All of Jamie's clothes, shoes, even the pink rabbit, which her grandmother made for her, are spilled across Jinny's yard. Jamie feels naked. Her possessions look lost and lonely, in open, helpless disarray. Sensing Jamie's pain, Jinny looks away as Jamie soundlessly picks her clothes up.

Jamie quietly phones her mother. There is no answer. She calls Free Will to say she will be a little late returning. Because she cannot put Pam on the phone to confirm her story, Free Will is skeptical. They tell her she must return that night. Jinny can't take her back. It is an hour drive on dark country roads and Jinny's car is unreliable. Jinny's parents are out of town for the weekend. Jamie panics. She doesn't know what will happen to her if she doesn't make it back to Free Will that night. And as a measure of their totally bankrupt relationship, Jamie worries that her mother might tell Free Will a different story just to get Jamie in trouble.

In the end Jamie's boyfriend drives an hour from his parents' home in Rocky Mount to pick her up in Raleigh. He then takes her to Middlesex. Jamie will never forgive her mother.

"It wasn't that big a deal, I guess," Jamie says now, almost three years later. "But I guess you could call it the straw that broke the camel's back."

The pure white of her eyes turns red and her soft fingers play trembling on her face as she faces the final break in their relationship.

The next evening Jamie is called to the phone. It is one of the two calls she is permitted to accept (and she can place two more, to the outside) each day. She can stay on for only ten minutes. Those are the cottage rules. They cramp the social life of high school seniors, but with twelve girls in each cottage and only one phone, it has to be that way.

Pam is on the phone.

"I figured if you and Jinny are so tight, she could take you back to Free Will. You're always doing that to me, putting me last," her mother complains.

Jamie looks down as she remembers how Pam then told her she would be leaving for Colorado that week.

"I'll call you when I get there," she says.

"Don't bother," Jamie replies, hurt and furious.

Pam leaves with the $5,200 of Jamie's college fund to which Pam believes she is entitled. Jamie never sees the money. Her father gives her a used Honda as a high school graduation present. She does not hear from her mother for a year.

During that year, Jamie is on her own outside an institution for the first time. It is the time, social workers warn, that is most difficult for children. Free from the constraints and oversight of the home, they must adjust to the outside world, which for many is new to them. The transition is even harder because Jamie had hoped, even planned, to get closer to her mother at college. She had chosen N.C. State because it was in Raleigh, where Pam then lived.

Although she had known her daughter's reasons for choosing N.C. State —or perhaps because she knew those plans—Pam went off to begin a new life in Colorado. She had just had a major breakup with a boyfriend, Pam now says. And, she adds, she always planned to leave North Carolina after Jamie graduated from high school, anyway.

"Jamie could have gone to just about any school," Free Will's James Johnson says, shaking his head in a mixture of pride and sorrow. "She could have had a full ride to [nearby] Duke University with those grades, her SATs, and extracurricular activities, and those recommendations. Everyone loved her. That girl could do anything. But she went to State because her mother was there in Raleigh. No one could advise her differently. She'd made up her mind. She was going to State."

Like many kids in the system, Jamie was still looking for a way to be closer to her mother. Even the most abused children try over and over again to reunite with their parents.

"There is nothing stronger than that tie for a child," Johnson says. "Nothing. Even when they know it's bad for them, they keep trying."

Jamie took one lesson from the incident. She would never put anyone before herself again.

17

North Carolina State University

❖

I<small>N</small> late August, Jamie packs her belongings into the old Honda and drives away from Free Will for the last time. The road seems wide and endless. She is a little nervous, but excited too, as she anticipates her new life. She is free from her past, she thinks, including its limits and its failures. She decides to tell no one she has grown up in children's homes. Finally, she is on equal footing with the other kids of the world.

Her new home is Lee Dorm, a massive concrete structure. "A striking example of sterile ugliness," as one student describes it. The floors are concrete with linoleum, the walls whitewashed cinder block. Her suite consists of four rooms—three doubles plus a single for the residential counselor— everyone sharing a single bathroom with a shower and two toilet stalls. The elevator, which often fails, might have come from a public housing project; its floor buttons are wet with gum, spit, or worse. Jamie uses the corner of a textbook to press *four*, smiling understandingly at a girl who refuses to touch the buttons at all. After the elevator comes a half flight of stairs and a walk along a hallway balcony until she reaches her quarters.

And she loves it. Lee Dorm is her first home.

"It's cold," a girl complains during the elevator ride. "It's like an institution."

"I hadn't noticed," Jamie says, almost starry eyed.

She has an easier time adapting to campus life than many kids. She seeks out students in the cafeteria to talk to and makes friends with quick ease. The social skills with her peers learned at children's homes serves her well.

"I haven't gone through that homesick phase a lot of kids do," she says. "This is my home now. Other kids miss stuff they left at home, but all my stuff is in my room."

All too soon, however, she finds out that her dorm is not really a home. Her roommate moves out to live with high school friends. Others in the suite move out, and still others move in. And just before Christmas, she learns that everyone is expected to vacate the dorm for the holidays. The dorms are to be shut down.

"Where are we supposed to go?" she asks a dorm supervisor.

"Home," he laughs, believing she is joking.

"You don't understand. This is my home," she says.

"This isn't anyone's home," he replies impatiently. "This is just the hellhole you stay in when you're at school. Home is where you live."

Jamie calls Lisa Cauley, who was an independent living counselor at Free Will. They decide that next year Jamie should get an apartment off campus. That would be home. Then she can put some roots down. She has tried to put them down too fast in the dorm. She will spend much of the holiday with her aunt Kay, but so as not to be a burden, will distribute her time with her grandmother, Aunt Teri, and her father.

Cauley is an important person in Jamie's life during this period. Though Cauley doesn't know it, Jamie looks to the attractive young social worker as a role model and guiding figure as she struggles with her new independence. Jamie phones Cauley not only about the upcoming holidays, but also for help on mundane chores, like preparing a tax form, on occasions when Jamie feels lonely. Cauley is there for Jamie. Even after Cauley has left the county's Department of Social Services, she spends a day helping Jamie move out of the dorm and put her stuff into storage back at Free Will after Jamie's freshman year.

Jamie does well at school the first year, both academically and socially. She chooses not to join a sorority, mostly because sororities are expensive, but also because she doesn't want to be identified with a group anymore.

"I had to fight so hard from being like other kids in the home," Jamie explains. "Most of them think it's their role in life to be unhappy or to be like their parents. I had to make myself out to be entirely different from them or else I might start thinking like them. I don't want to join a group, because you don't really see how they influence you when you're into them. Being independent is safer, I think."

She spends a lot of time worried that other students will discover her past. "I feel like people look at me," she whispers in a restaurant.

"They do," I say. "You're very pretty."

She still seems entirely unaware of her appeal. From shower to the last swipe of black mascara, her getting-ready time is as low as seven minutes. But choosing what to wear brings out self-doubts. She worries that her clothes will alert others that she came from a children's home. She does not want people to look at her closely.

"That's not it," she insists. "I'm no prettier than anyone else. It's that they can see something's different with me, something's wrong with me."

She wants desperately to fit in, to find approval at State. Her first semester grades average 3.2, with difficult classes. But with her success, she decides that acceptance comes with partying, not grades. So second semester she slacks off. Too much, she admits. Her GPA sinks to 2.8.

As a final priority at State, she looks for a boyfriend. Her relatives often ask if she is dating someone. They think a good man will be her ticket to a normal life. Until now, Jamie has chosen to emphasize her independence in any relationship. Now, she looks for security and an end to loneliness.

Her mother's sudden departure for Colorado, without saying good-bye, has shaken Jamie more than she likes to admit.

Does she still care for her mother?

"No," she says after giving the matter thought. "I don't. She's my mother, so I care about where she is and if she's OK, but I don't really care about her. I don't. She was never there for me emotionally or physically. I don't care."

But her voice is thick with emotion and the whites of her eyes redden suddenly. She turns away for a moment, and when she turns back, the damage she has tried to hide is clear in the dim restaurant. A tear streaks her makeup.

She throws herself into her food like a child then, pushing aside an artichoke, a vegetable she loves, and then stabbing at it determinedly. She moves closer to her plate, meeting the food half way, almost shoveling it into her mouth, bread, salad, pasta.

Food disappeared so quickly from the tables at children's homes that she had to learn to eat quickly, she once said. But she isn't eating quickly for that reason now. She does not cry anymore.

She has begun gaining weight. The Norplant put in her arm her last year at Free Will might be to blame. She is not sexually active, but staff at Free Will encouraged birth control, a "just in case" measure. She gains forty pounds during the two years that the Norplant remains in her arm. The extra weight makes her feel unattractive, which adds to her insecurity.

18

Sophomore Year

▓

T HE summer was anything but idyllic. Jamie spent much of her spring term trying to find a place to live during the summer. She came up with a "camp" that billed itself as helping the blind, where she could both work and live. It seemed the perfect opportunity to get away from Raleigh. Jamie had served as a volunteer to care for the younger children at Free Will and also at Tabernacle, and liked that work very much. She thought the camp for the blind would be an extension of such work. Instead, it turned out to be a place that cared for elderly people incapable of helping themselves.

"It was terrible, it really was," Lisa Cauley says. "They had Jamie changing adults' diapers and emptying bedpans. The place completely misrepresented itself. I read the brochures and thought it was a good idea for Jamie to go there. But it was a really terrible place. They didn't even give her days off. I'm surprised she lasted as long as she did. I don't think many people would have."

Jamie is more stoic and practical. "I didn't have a choice," she says matter-of-factly. "I had no place to go. I knew my aunts couldn't take me over the summer; they had told me that. And my dad didn't want me to go in the first place. He thought I could make more money if I stayed and lived with him. He said he doesn't believe in 'do-good work.'

"I just tried my best to learn from everyone I met there," Jamie says of the camp. "But it just got too much." She left after a month.

Her aunts had no room for Jamie, but Kay paid the plane fare for Jamie to fly to Colorado. The two weeks she spent with her mother there were unsteady. She came away with no more understanding of her mother or their relationship than she had had when she entered Free Will almost four years earlier.

"Sometimes I think that the more distance there is between my mother and me, the better off we are," she says in her dorm one night. "We can go on with our lives and not worry about it. At least we can focus on our lives. Visiting each other just makes everything inside spin again."

She is back in the dorm for her sophomore year because her plans for a home off campus collapsed at the last minute. She intended to live in an apartment with her boyfriend, Daniel, his two friends, and two other girls. But over the summer, Daniel helped move his family to Indiana, and he didn't return. So a few days before school starts, Jamie moves back into the dorm with an assigned roommate who finger-paints the wall with slogans like "Make love not war" and hangs up Bob Marley posters. Her roommate stays away most of the time, then moves out. Ordinarily, Jamie would like the space all to herself, but she feels lonely and unwanted.

THE phone rings, and Jamie burrows for it through the clothes on the floor as books slip from her bed. She enjoys the clutter. Free Will was so strict about clutter. Even her posters had to be hung straight. Now she can keep her room as messy as she wants, and she wallows in that freedom.

On the fifth ring she answers, her voice high and hopeful. But soon it sinks, and she sits carefully on her bed. Her father is bristling with annoyance because she did not visit him in Greensboro that weekend to celebrate his birthday. Greensboro is only a two-hour drive, he reminds her. And after all, he has given her a car.

Her voice becomes embarrassed, and a frightened tone seeps into it.

"I don't have a boyfriend," she says quietly into the phone, as though admitting failure. "No sir," she says in a hushed tone and turns away.

"I don't know why, sir. They're not interested." She catches herself, not wanting her father to think she's undesirable. "Or I'm not."

"Yes sir," she says even more quietly, "maybe I do scare them away."

Her eyes fill with tears. Then her father asks her if she's taking care of the car, if she'd gotten the oil changed.

"Thank you, I don't know what I'd do without the car," she says. "I use it to go to work. Waitress at Applebee's. No sir, I try not to use it too often. I know you told me that it's not to be used too much, only when I need it. Yes sir. Thank you. Good-bye."

And gently, she hangs up, but only after making sure he has hung up first.

A few days later a friend of Jamie's boyfriend calls.

"Did you hear from Daniel?" he asks Jamie, sounding pleased.

"No," she replies quietly.

"Well," he says, excited, "he's not coming back. He's got a girlfriend. She a real beauty, too."

Jamie's eyes moisten.

"I wonder why he didn't call you," the friend says. "Everyone knows. You want to get together Thursday night?"

Jamie says she has to work. Her voice is unusually soft during the conversation. He must notice, but he seems not to. She hangs up quietly and pulls herself together.

"I wish Daniel had called me," she says. "I can understand him not coming back. I just wished he'd called me."

TOO many people have "forgotten" to call Jamie and tell her of their plans. She hears, from her aunt, that her mother broke up with her boyfriend and is driving back from Colorado for a visit. But Jamie still hasn't heard from her mother, and according to Kay, she should be in town within the week. She wonders if her mother will call her.

She has other things to worry about, Jamie reminds herself. She finished her freshman year poorly. She was partying too hard. Now she's in danger of losing her scholarship. She thinks that with real effort she could earn a 4.0. But she's having a hard time concentrating. A really hard time.

"I don't know why, but for the first time I can't stop thinking about everything that's happened," she says. Rings are growing darkly on the soft white skin under her eyes.

"No," she tries to assure me, "it's not all this talking about the past with you. I knew I would have to do it sometime. I mean I think about all this stuff. I just didn't know it would be so hard. I wish I had someone. Something. I don't even know. Maybe if I had a boyfriend. I want someone to care without feeling like they have to because I'm some sort of responsibility or burden. I want someone to love me."

WHEN Jamie decides on a goal, she is single minded. Now, she is after love. For the first time, she finds herself seeking out guys. Usually it was the reverse. Her search for a boyfriend surprises me. It seems dangerous, I say, thinking only of a broken heart and disappointment she might suffer. In her new insecurity, she seems vulnerable. But the real danger doesn't occur to me.

19

Rape

❖

JAMIE had her eye on Jake* for weeks. Every weekend he and his friend would come into Applebee's, where she waitressed. His friend was better looking, like Tom Cruise in *Top Gun*. But Jamie preferred quiet Jake, with his soft eyes and broken smile. All sorts of girls caught his friend's attention, while Jake would mind his beer.

At first Jake didn't seem interested. His friend said he had just gone through a bad time. So Jamie was patient, and her patience paid off. Each week Jake would let Jamie get closer. He would talk to her more and more. He would even call her on the phone. But still he didn't ask her on a date.

He told her he was divorced. A negative. But he had also been in the Air Force. A positive. At twenty-eight, he was pushing the limits on the age cutoff for men she would date. He was less aggressive than his friend and less arrogant. But he was sometimes rough with her. Sometimes he'd pull her close to talk, and then abruptly push her away.

Jamie thought of Jake more and more as her grades dropped and she drew further from school and career ambitions. Sophomore year continued down the same poor path she had followed the last half of her freshman year.

She started thinking about marriage for the first time. A year earlier, with things going very well, she had said she would never marry or have children. But now she wanted a family of her own. As a prerequisite, she decided any potential boyfriend had to come from a large family. Money, job, even looks paled in comparison to a large, close-knit family. She wanted her children to have lots of aunts and uncles and cousins.

Jake qualified. Both sets of his grandparents were still living, and his parents were still together. He was close to his family. But what drew her most to Jake was the way he talked about his ex-wife. Around the table at Applebee's, his gray eyes grew misty when he spoke of her. His divorce was now final. He had loved her, he said, but once on home leave he caught her in bed with another man. He couldn't take her back. There was such tenderness in his voice. Jamie longed for that tenderness. At night, she would hear

* Not his real name.

his voice, and what he said belonged to her. There was nothing she wanted more than Jake. She wanted to marry him.

Jamie saw a strength in Jake that she found attractive too. The way he handled his wife was the way she wanted to handle her mother. They shared the same kind of pain.

"Bitch," Jake once exploded suddenly, slamming his hand on the table.

The girls fluttering around the table fled. But Jamie stayed. Jamie understood his anger. She knew she could tame it if he gave her that chance. But at the end of the evening, Jake pushed her away again.

His friend invited Jamie to a party he and Jake were giving. She wished Jake had asked, but she would take any opportunity to get closer to him. His friend encouraged Jamie. He understood that she liked Jake.

Jamie took a friend, Alley. The crowd appeared slightly older, but Jamie was determined to fit in. She and Alley drank while they waited for Jake to approach. When he finally did, he seemed gentle, even tender.

"I'm glad you came," he told Jamie. "I wanted to ask you, but I was sort of, well, I'm still sort of getting over the divorce and I don't know that I'm good to be with."

Jamie's eyes glowed. She told him she would do anything to help. He was swept away by a call for more beer. He would come back, he said. An hour passed. Alley wanted to go home. Jamie wanted to stay. Alley didn't want to leave her. She sensed something wrong about the party, even something uncomfortable about Jake, and she didn't want to leave Jamie alone.

The party waned before Jake returned. "Do you want to stay and talk some?" he asked Jamie. "I'll drive you home."

Alley wanted Jamie to come with her, but Jamie wanted to stay. So finally Alley left.

Jamie waited for two more hours until everyone left. She had three drinks by then and several beers. Jake led her to a couch. He kissed her, hard and insistent.

At first the kiss awed Jamie. But even through the numbing alcohol, she recognized that his arms held her too hard and that his hands were too persistent and rough. She asked him to stop.

"Shut up, bitch," he said so deep in his throat it didn't sound like Jake at all. Panicking, she pushed him back, but he was already on top of her.

Her panic turned everything into a blur. She couldn't move her wrists. They were pinned behind her head. Her neck hurt. She thought her head was going to fall off.

She was angry, furious, but she couldn't stop him. When he laughed, she hated him. When he told her that this is what she had waited for all night, she hated herself. She wanted to scratch him, but her hands could barely claw. She felt light and worthless. The world spun around and she passed out.

In the morning, she found herself undressed on the couch. Her head hurt worse than it ever had in her life. But her head was nothing compared to her insides. Outside, her body was sore and bruised; inside it was scalded and torn.

She dressed, but as she reached the door, Jake grasped her arm.

"Let me take you home," he told her.

She stared at him then, wondering if he was the same monster she fought last night. His neck was scratched as if he had been struck by a large cat. But other than that he was unruffled.

She climbed into his red sports car but said nothing. He left her off at Alley's dorm. She must have asked to be taken there. She walked, dazed and shocked.

"Oh my God, what happened?" Alley said when she opened her door.

"I need to go to the emergency room," Jamie said. "I hurt all over."

Alley phoned Interact, a rape hotline at school. Volunteers met them at the hospital.

The experience reinforced painful lessons of the past: Don't love. Don't trust. Just pretend. You can get through all this. Just pretend to be alive.*

20

Love

ABOUT a month later, Jamie and I are driving along the Beltline around Raleigh to dinner. Fall has stolen another hour of the day, and Jamie misses the summer light. But there is more behind her dour mood.

"Do you have a title for the book yet?" she asks, one hand on the dashboard as I swerve to avoid a rolling traffic cone.

---

* There are no statistics about the number of children in foster care who have been raped subsequent to their time in the system. But I doubt that this rape was any more unique than the great numbers of youths from the system who go on to abusive relationships. Jamie was desperate for love and attention. Her needs overtook her judgment, if it was possible to judge. The same need drove Angel to the street. She needed to feel appreciated and substantial. It wasn't money Angel was looking for, and it wasn't necessarily love that Jamie was looking for. They were looking for a way out of their numbness and unhappiness and grabbed on to fairy tales. They were just looking to be real, to feel something real and see in someone's eyes that they were appreciated.

"No," I say, "not really."

"I do," she says gently. "I mean I think I have an idea."

"What?"

"Love is a four-letter word."

From Jamie, the words are jarring.

"A great title," I say. "What does it mean?"

"Well, I guess if you have to think about it too much, you shouldn't use it," she snaps, and turns away.

"I think I know what it means, but why do you say it?" I push her.

"A girl said it at the children's home once," she shrugs. "Everyone laughed, but it stuck with me. I think my mom might love me in a bad way." She continued after a moment. "Or it's bad for me. I thought that once. Now I just think that love is a four-letter word."

"Have you heard from your mother?" I ask.

"No," she says.

We talk about inconsequential things at dinner. Finally, as she lights up her fifth Marlboro Light, she tells me about the rape, although she doesn't call it that. When she turns back to face me, her eyes are clear and almost distant, as though her heart is unaware.

21

After the Rape

❊

"He's been calling me," Jamie says a week later. "Leaves messages on my answering machine asking if I want to go out. I want to call him back. I even want to forget it happened and date him. I still want him to like me."

She stares straight ahead. Dark rings circle her eyes, making them appear heavy. She hasn't worn makeup for days. Suddenly she turns challengingly, waiting to be told she is crazy.

Does she still like him?

She shakes her head vigorously. No. She remembers too well how she said no that night, how she tried to push him away, and how he pinned her down. She notices that she is rubbing her wrists where he held her and stops abruptly.

She hasn't even thought about pressing charges against Jake. "I put myself in a bad situation," she says.

"What inside me wanted his affection so much that I couldn't see it coming?" she asks. A year ago, she could hardly understand her friends from the children's homes who had gotten married, let alone those who had had children on purpose or were living with someone, especially the many who were in bad or abusive relationships. She wondered why they were so eager to sacrifice the independence that was so new to them. She thought she was different. But now she feels fragile and scared. It is a new feeling to her.

"Something big must have happened to Jamie, but I don't know what," her aunt Teri comments a few months after the rape. She looks around her home anxiously, straightening a pillow and then picking up her son. "Jamie won't tell me," she continues, absently trying to mind her children and her concern for Jamie all at once. "It must have been big, though. Jamie doesn't usually get affected like this. She's usually so resilient."

Jamie doesn't notice the changes in herself and still refuses to tell people about the rape. When pressed about how "that night," as she prefers to call it, affected her, she thinks for a while. "It makes me look at myself," she replies. "I don't like my weight. I think it might have affected my motivation too."

She refuses to see a counselor. The children's homes have made her distrust therapy. Only the crazy kids, the ones with really bad problems, needed therapy. It was a status thing not to participate in therapy. And besides, she says, she wants to get through this alone. She wants to climb back up by herself. She doesn't need to talk about it; she doesn't want to think about it. She doesn't want it to be real.

Over the weeks that follow, Jamie finds herself shying away from hugs and simple touches. She has always been interested in good-looking men. Now she finds all men distasteful. It unsettles her.

She still doesn't relate it to the rape. Nor does she connect the rape to her slide into depression, to her dwindling number of friends, and her increasing isolation. She knows she isn't her same, outgoing self, but she doesn't know why.

"I think its something like chronic fatigue or something," she suggests one night. "I haven't gone to class in two weeks, because I can't get up. I can't sleep either, and then when morning comes, I can't get up for my eleven-twenty class."

Jamie is having nightmares for the first time since Tabernacle. In the dark she feels handcuffed somewhere and she knows she can't get away. She also experiences insomnia for the first time.

"No matter what was going on around me, I always slept well," she complains, frustrated.

A few weeks later she volunteers that she's seeing a school counselor now. She looks for my approval.

"I only get five sessions. I can't afford to pay for more," she says. "I guess it's helping, I don't know. We've had three sessions and we haven't gotten through my life yet. I have to throw it out in big blocks and [the counselor] gets confused because I've been to so many places. We haven't gotten anywhere yet because we have to keep backtracking. I like her, though."

She still hasn't told the counselor about the rape.

22
Counseling

❖

"W<small>HY</small> are you here?" the psychologist asks Jamie just after they each sit down.

"Because I manipulate people," Jamie replies.

"How?"

Jamie thinks for a moment. "Like, if I sit next to someone and they have something that looks good, I might say, 'That looks good,' so that they'll say, 'Do you want a bite?' because that's what I want. So rather than saying straight up, 'Can I have a bite?' I say, 'That looks good.' "

The therapist listens and asks more questions.

Finally, the therapist pulls out Webster's.

"Do you know what 'manipulate' means?" Glancing at Jamie's blank expression, she reads aloud:

"Manipulate. One: to treat or operate with the hands or by mechanical means, especially with skill. Two-*a:* to manage or utilize skillfully."

Jamie looks confused.

"The way I see it, manipulation isn't bad," she tells Jamie. "Let's say I have white icing and I put red dye in it because I want pink icing. That's manipulating."

Jamie thinks again.

"Well, then," Jamie says finally, "maybe I'm here because of that night."

J<small>AMIE</small> phones me later.

"I'm not sure if it's helping," she says. "I don't really like talking about it." We meet to talk.

"I'm depressed about my weight," she says. "I don't have the figure I had in high school and I can't control it. That's really depressing me. I've been thinking about what would make me happier. I plan to go off the Norplant.

I think it's affecting my mood. I feel like I'm walking around in this cloud all the time, and I think it's why I can't lose weight. And then I'm thinking of transferring to Florida State. I've always liked warmer places and the beach. I'm happier in the summer.

"But before I do all that, I want to know more about my past. The counselor thinks maybe that will help me feel more in control. I'd like to look at my files from DSS. It'd make me feel better to know what's in them. I think I'm ready."

Her eyes grow round as she rolls her cigarette tip patiently until the smoldering ashes form a smooth cone and tip.

She mashes it out decisively, and then for the first time in many months, she looks me straight in the eye and gives me a genuine smile. I feel as though I can breathe again. She is back. She has a mission now. She asks my help in obtaining her records.

23
File Quest

▓

THE next day Jamie goes to all her classes, even 8:20 A.M. chemistry. She is spirited and energetic.

"I can't wait to see my files," she says.

The files probably won't put to rest all the issues she is dealing with, I tell her, and may make them worse. I had seen terrible inaccuracies in the records of other children, including wrong birth dates, varying IQ scores, and statements by their parents, perhaps driven from emotion, that were patently untrue.*

"I understand," Jamie replies. "But they've always told us that the best way to deal with our situation is to understand it."

---

* For example, in an effort to get the county to pay for Jamie's care, Jamie's mother once tried to convince social service workers that her daughter qualified as a Willie M. child. Willie M. was a severely violent and autistic youth who was thrown out of public school for his disruptive and even dangerous behavior. His parents sued the state, claiming the state had an obligation to educate their son. They won their case and the state is now obligated to provide special funds for such children if the state refuses to allow them in the classroom. The stigma of being a Willie M. child is profound.

But the more frequently Jamie calls me to learn of my progress, the more I worry that she is expecting too much from her records.

"What am I looking for?" She repeats my question. "To understand more. And to remember and to be remembered. You know, I don't even have any old report cards or old drawings, and I stopped keeping a diary after that time my mom found it and read it and then sent me away."

There are periods of Jamie's life from which she has no photographs and few memories. She tries to keep up with friends, but it has proven difficult.

"My old boyfriends think it's weird when I call them up," she says. "I don't want to get back together. But they were my family when I went out with them and I want to remember that time, who I was. I want a link."

For several weeks we have been working to retrieve Jamie's files. I meet with Alma Shelton, the director of Wake County (which includes Raleigh) Department of Social Services and one of Jamie's social workers. But she and Lisa Cauley, while polite, are hesitant to release the information, despite Jamie's written permission.

It was a reluctance I had found in other officials in other cities. Under the guise of protecting a child, some welfare officials admitted to withholding information to protect their colleagues, staffs, or themselves from being held accountable for their actions regarding a child.

In Jamie's case, officials apparently wanted to make certain it was appropriate to release the information. Shelton first checked to insure that Jamie was officially out of DSS custody and an adult. She was. At seventeen, she had signed herself out of care. Legally, her mother, who had committed her, is obliged to sign. But her mother couldn't be found at the time. I produced the release Jamie had written to give me access. Shelton asked to speak to Jamie directly. A phone call would do, she said.

For two weeks Jamie tried unsuccessfully to reach Shelton by phone through the switchboard. She left several messages for Shelton. Shelton returned the calls when Jamie was in class. Shelton does not give the number of her direct line in DSS to any children. So Jamie resorted to tactics she had learned in the system.

"First I lied about who I was to get her direct line," she explains matter-of-factly. "Then I said it was an emergency. That's the only way you get them to respond. You can tell them two months in advance that you need something and you still won't get it. The best way is to wait until the last minute and say it's an emergency."

Finally connected, Shelton asks Jamie to make an appointment to sign a request at DSS for the files. Jamie makes the first available appointment. She is told she can in fact see her files the same day she signs the request.

24

Confidential

▓

Jamie and I arrive at the Wake County DSS building on a clear mid-November day. Jamie is nervous but happy. Despite Shelton's assurances, I warn her that she may have to wait a couple of weeks. But she is certain she will see her files that day. They told her she could.

Jamie's mood changes the moment we enter the modern brass-and-glass building. She nibbles at her fingers and peers through her bangs like a child. When Shelton comes to get her, leaving me in the reception room, Jamie looks frightened. She nods bravely, like a small child.

Alone, she is received coolly. She is shown to a small room with a table. On it are loose leaf paper and a pen. She is invited to write the names of the files she wants.

She is shaken and pale when she returns. She just wants to get out of the building. She was told they will call her in a few days, when they get the files together.

"I kept asking them what files were there for me to ask for, and they wouldn't tell me," Jamie says, frustrated. "So I wrote about four pages of things I knew about, like personality tests and report cards and IQ tests and stuff. But I don't know what they have on me, and they won't tell me.

"They weren't even nice," she says. "It's like they're trying to hide my life from me. They're not going to give the files to us," she says. "They say they are, but I just know they're not. There's something wrong."

She cannot understand the state's insistence on confidentiality.

"They've got these files on me, they're about me, and I can't even see them," she repeats in a whisper, almost to herself, to see if she is missing a part of a puzzle. "I don't understand that."

I try to reassure her that they are being very careful lest some incident in Jamie's life in the system embarrass them. Mistakes are made by caseworkers and everyone else. Most social workers I met have good intentions, but because of overwork or human error, they might have made mistakes in handling Jamie. But now, in acting so protectively and officiously about Jamie's files, they willingly allow Jamie to believe something is wrong with her rather than allow themselves to be vulnerable to the discovery of any errors. It is clear that those responsible for the children in foster care are not often willing to be held accountable. The secrecy protects negligent child care workers more than the children.*

A week later, Jamie calls about her request and is told she cannot see her files. She calls me up, crying. I phone Shelton, who says it is a "family issue" and that she does not want to "jeopardize" her staff. She found nothing wrong in Jamie's files, she insists, but she is afraid I might find otherwise. There the matter rested.

A month later, Jamie calls to say she has gone to see a lawyer about getting her files. I had never thought of this course of action.

"I'm doing it for me," she says. "They're my files, my life. I have a right to them. What they're doing is wrong."

Jamie needs only a letter of consent from her mother, the lawyer tells her. So Jamie calls her mother in Colorado. Her mother agrees to write the letter. Pam also objects to the state withholding Jamie's files.

Jamie knows it will be a long fight, but she is determined to see her files one way or another, she insists.

25

Christmas

❖

CHRISTMAS approaches and Jamie is again sad that she has nothing special ahead for the holidays. She will stay with her aunts, although she isn't certain they want her.

On this late November night, she decides she wants to go to a local radio station's Christmas party. Jinny and her friend are going, and Jamie feels left out. She is visiting Jinny when she phones.

"I've been calling this radio station all day for these G-105 Christmas party tickets," she complains. "I really want to go to this party. That new guy

---

* New York is one of several cities now considering whether to lift these secrecy laws, which were originally passed to guard children's privacy. Now, however, the laws protect caseworkers and child protective service workers from being held accountable for mistakes, some of which have led to children's deaths.

on *Beverly Hills 90210* is going to be there. You know, Jamie Walters, the guy who sings, 'How do you talk to an angel . . . how do you hold her close . . .' " She sings on for a bit.

"Lisa Lopez is going to be there, too. Jinny's going and I really want to go. I've been calling Cadillac Jack all night! Should I call again? I'll call him *one* more time and that's it. I promise. What should I say? I know. I'll say, 'I'm going to be famous someday, I'm going to be someone, so you better give me those tickets." Her voice is lively now. "I'm going to get them. You watch."

Between top-forty tracks, Cadillac Jack rants on interminably, and I'm tempted to shut him off.

"You're on *Desperate and Dateless!*" the DJ begins with professional heartiness.

"Caller, you know the rules: Twenty-one or older. Our gentleman caller will ask all three of our contestants questions and then pick one lucky lady for a date, and tickets to *the G-105 Christmas party!!*"

Canned hooting cheers Cadillac Jack.

"OK, caller! What's your name?" he asks.

"Um . . . Sondra."

Jamie? She's not yet twenty-one. But then that makes me certain. It is her. She must have decided that Sondra is a sexy name. Later she swears she had just been calling for tickets and suddenly found herself on the air.

"If you were on a deserted island, what three things would you bring?" the male guest asks.

"A radio, because music is emotion to me," she answers. I am amazed at how well spoken and composed she is.

"And a book." I know she thinks this will sound good, and she admits to that later.

"And three"—she pauses amid whispers in the background—"OK, OK," she says. "A man."

The next question is more difficult for her.

"What is the most erotic food you've ever eaten?"

Over the air, Jamie whispers, "I'm not going to say that. I can't say that."

"What?" Jack urges.

Jinny wants her to say a cherry out of her boyfriend's belly button. But to Cadillac Jack she says: "Spaghetti." She was hungry at the time and wanted pasta.

"Spaghetti? Why?" The DJ is baffled.

"Because the sounds I make eating it."

"Make them now."

Jamie refuses politely.

She wins anyway, and the next day she is off for her preparty date.

"He drives a ninety-three white Cadillac," she tells me. "I know because I called him and said, 'I have a confession to make. My name isn't Sondra.' Then he asked how old I was. I said twenty. But I think it's cool."

"I told you I wanted to go to the G-105 party," she reminds me, a smile high in her voice. "Now I can look forward to Christmas."

If there's a story to tell about Jamie's tenacity, determination, and street-wise cleverness, I suppose this might be it. When she sets her mind to it, Jamie makes things happen.

26
Sliding

the less i seek my source for some definitive
the closer i am to fine

EMILY SALIERS, Indigo Girls,

"Closer to Fine"

JAMIE'S strong alto voice carries the harmony. It is clear and strong, but not overpowering for the a cappella group. She snaps her fingers to an unaccompanied beat along with nine other young women singing without percussion. They are dressed in black but call themselves Ladies in Red. The group is North Carolina State University's modern counterpart to its hundred-year-old men's glee club.

Together the Ladies convert instrumentals to vocals, to the delight of the audience. Jamie smiles bright enough to light up the stage. Their rendition of Patty Loveless's "You're All I Think About These Days" gets almost as much applause. When the concert ends, the Ladies, in various shapes and textures of black—dresses tight and loose, sequins and wool, high heels and flats—walk offstage and into the cold and rainy night.

"I chose that song," Jamie says later about "Closer to Fine." She is still sparkling from the close harmony. "It means a lot to me."

She hasn't spoken of her files recently. And tonight, at least, she seems almost happy.

I had worried that she was sliding back into a depression. She has not been attending classes. She talks about dropping out of school for a while. She is tired of struggling for money. She works four nights a week now because her car needs new brakes. Even when she isn't tired from the job, she can't concentrate on schoolwork. Now alone in a dorm room, she wants to move into an apartment with two other girls. Neither is at university. One is an aspiring model, the other a waitress at a topless bar. But Jamie decides to stay in school at least through the fall semester because she wants very much to make the coming trip to France with the choir. No one in her family has ever been out of the country. She intends to be the first.

A few days later Jamie's voice is so low I don't immediately recognize it when she phones.

"Are you OK?" I ask.

She doesn't reply for a long moment.

"I wish I could say I was," she says finally, her voice cracking. "I mean, I am. It's my car. I have to pay $458.07 for repairs. It wouldn't start. I didn't realize anything done to a car could cost so much.

"I worked so hard this summer for that money, and I'm going to France. I need the money I saved. Anyway, I was just calling to see if you'd take me to the bank and to pick the car up."

It is quarter of four, and her bank closes in fifteen minutes, when she comes out of the campus cafeteria carrying a tray from Taco Bell and trailing a young man with a *Chariots of Fire* haircut, loose jeans, and a long dark faded shirt. She is composed now, almost smiling, although her turned-up nose is still red and her eyes dark ringed.

"This is my brother Gwen." She introduces me to her music fraternity brother. He stands with her as she eats and explains the car crisis. Gwen has a check for $164 coming, which he offers her for Christmas.

"Look, Jamie, just take it as a loan," he says, hands dug in his jeans pockets.

"No, I won't," she says flatly. She is too proud to take money from friends.

The conversation shifts to an evil political science professor, whom one of the glee club members told off. "You can just wipe your butt with the bagpipe and stick the rest where it's not supposed to go," Gwen recounts the punch line.

Jamie throws her head back and laughs.

It is Veterans Day, so the state employees' credit union, where Jamie keeps some money, is closed. She can get only $200 from the ATM. She finds almost $100 in her bag from last night's tips. That leaves her with $10 for the rest of the week. She says she can make it. She will take money from no one except family.

"I have another $100 in savings at the bank," she says, "and about $400 in checking." But then she also has a $57 speeding ticket to pay, and her father has just called to say he will no longer pay the insurance bill for her car because she hasn't visited him recently.

But she refuses to be down anymore today. She will let herself think only about France. She is in survival mode.

27
France

JAMIE is very anxious on the way to the airport.

"US Air kills everyone!" she exclaims suddenly. "Nine hours over the ocean. Anything can happen. It doesn't take that much to go down."

Her friend Alley rolls her eyes in the backseat.

"Jamie," she sighs, "it's going to be fine."

Aside from almost forgetting her passport, things are going pretty well. Jamie has had her nails lengthened and coated a thick maroon, and Jinny has lightened her hair with peroxide. Jamie's teeth were cleaned that morning; she has two cavities to be filled when she returns. Now, in the car, she has only to put on makeup and comb her towel-dried hair. No more rushed than usual.

She is leaving behind a bunch of worries. Her car died again last night, driving up a hill just ahead of an eighteen-wheeler. The floor got warm and the brake, battery, and oil lights all came on at once.

"I couldn't breathe," she says about watching the truck grow larger in her mirror.

But the little Honda putted all the way into a parking lot, and there she left it. She doubts it will ever start again. She phoned Teri and then Kay after her mother refused to help. Pam recently underwent $2,000 worth of eye laser surgery to correct an astigmatism. Anyway, she wasn't part of buying the car, which already has cost more in repairs than it did to purchase, she says, so she won't be a part of repairing it. Teri has no money to spare. She called Kay just for support. She asked for no money from Kay, who has already helped her out a great deal.

She has brought along a huge cardboard cutout in the shape of a fist;

when triggered, its middle finger flips up. Jamie thinks the French might think it's cool. Alley persuades her otherwise, and she leaves it behind, along with her worries.

28

Back Again

❖

JAMIE did have fun in France. Back in Raleigh, she is brimming with wide-eyed stories.

"They have chocolate for breakfast there. In cereal!" she says, remembering that especially for me. "It's nice chocolate, too. I don't know why we don't have it here. It's made by Kellogg's."

She went to the Louvre.

"The *Mona Lisa* was small," she says leaning forward and wrinkling up her nose a bit in fun. "The museum is *so* big. We saw hundreds of thousands of statues, and you're supposed to pick out the important ones. They all look the same, but when you get to the important ones, you're supposed to say, Wow, like they're way better than all the others. They all look amazing to me.

"And we went to this palace with this huge stable. I think it was called Chantille. It was built by a guy who thought he was going to be reincarnated into a horse. That's intelligent, right there." She rolls her eyes. "We had a tour and we were so tired from drinking all that wine. We had to hit each other to keep awake. But then we were watching this horse show and this horse"—she giggles—"well, his privacy just about touched the ground. That was the best part."

Of course she got into trouble.

"Alley and I almost missed the bus one day. We had to chase it and they go like Mach seven in Paris. A bike almost ran me over. Have you seen the way they drive in Paris? I felt like Frogger on the Atari game."

The wine impressed Jamie, but not the food.

"We had wine with everything. But they also had this cheese." She wrinkles her nose more deeply now. "It smelled like changing a baby's diaper, for real. And it oozed out. This cheese was everywhere. They even had it for dessert! That wasn't impressive to me."

And finally there were the Frenchmen.

"Jean-Baptiste," she says holding her hand to her heart and looking up toward the heavens. "He was a hotty. He was twenty-two. When it was time to leave, he came up to me and said, 'I really enjoyed getting to know you,' and kissed me on both cheeks. I was, like, wow."

Jamie is back to her old, fresh, lively self.

29

DUI

▩

A T 3:12 A.M. a shaken and frightened voice drifts over the phone.

"I'm sorry I woke you . . ." Then she breaks into sobs.

"Jamie?" I ask. "Where are you?"

"The police station." Her voice is small and alone.

"What happened?" It was a month since we had last met. She had been doing well then.

Her embarrassment comes through in her silence.

"Are you OK?"

"Yes," she says finally. "Just, I think I'm going to go to jail. I don't know what to do. Do you know a lawyer or someone? I know one but her home number isn't listed. It must be under her husband's name. And I just don't know what to do. They handcuffed me."

She breaks down into tears again.

"They didn't read me my rights, though," she says, gaining strength. "I don't think they can hold me because they searched my car without my permission and they didn't read me my rights until they got me down here."

Downtown Raleigh is dark and empty at three-thirty in the morning. Only the Wake County Public Safety building is lit.

Jamie's friend Alley meets me in the police department foyer. She has attended Jamie's breathalyzer test at the station. As we wait for the results, Alley says she hasn't seen or heard much of Jamie lately.

"She seems to be pulling away from people at school."

Jamie's blood alcohol level is .04, well short of the .08 level necessary to be charged with driving drunk. But she is still underage for drinking at all.

At 4 A.M. Jamie is brought before the magistrate, a young, attractive black woman with a serious demeanor. Jamie's eyes are swollen from crying.

The magistrate assumes Jamie is from Nashville, the largest town near the Free Will Baptist Children's Home.

"No ma'am," Jamie tells her. "Originally, I'm from Lumberton."

"And you're living in Raleigh now?"

"Yes ma'am."

"What are you doing here?"

"I'm a student at North Carolina State."

"What year?"

"Second year, sophomore, or I will be next semester."

"What are you studying?"

"Political science."

"And you're in jail now?"

Jamie feels a laugh emerging, which she barely suppresses. It isn't a snicker. She doesn't know why she wants to laugh. It just comes upon her.

The magistrate sets bail at $300. Jamie has enough cash in tips to cover the necessary percentage of the bond.

While she is processing out, the arresting officers come out to the waiting area.

"She was coming along Hillsborough Street with her bright lights on and when we flashed her, she didn't lower them. One of the headlights was out altogether," one of the officers explains. "We did a U-turn and she immediately turned off Hillsborough onto one of the side streets."

She turned right, then right again, then left, then right, the officer recounted. He says he didn't turn on the flashing blue light but that Jamie knew the officers were pulling her over. Then he jokes that if she intended to outrun the police car, she should have tried driving a different car.

"She was also driving without her license, which seems to be a habit of hers," he adds. "She's due in court this Wednesday for that."

The other officer corrects him. "No, Wednesday is for that accident she wasn't insured for," he says.

"Oh, right. That's the next court date." He laughs.

"But that's the only charge now?" I ask.

"No, she needs to get her headlights fixed, and then we found drug paraphernalia."

Jamie finally emerges, eyes puffy from crying.

She recounts her latest adventure with the law over coffee at the International House of Pancakes.

"You walked a line?" Alley asks.

"They had me walk on some dirt. I didn't see any line. And then they had me recite the ABCs, but I messed up. I was scared," she says.

"You didn't do very well at all," the officer had told her. "Have you been drinking? Because I can smell it from here. Best for you now to be truthful. Have you had any drinks tonight?"

"Yes sir."

"How many?"

"A beer."

"One beer?"

"Yes sir," Jamie said and looked to the side.

"Do you have anything in the car I should know about before I look?" the officer asked.

"Just some empty beer cans," Jamie answered. "But they're bone dry."

The officer lifted his eyebrows, then looked through her car. Their flashlights noticed a pipe, the drug paraphernalia they reported.

"You mind coming downtown with us?"

"No sir." After a moment, she asked: "Could we move my car so I don't get towed?"

"Yes ma'am."

It's 6 A.M. when we finish our coffee, and Jamie's wrists are still red from the handcuffs the police evidently believed necessary.

"I've had a run of bad luck," Jamie says. But she is sure it will change now that she is moving from the dorm into an apartment with her friend Jewels, an aspiring model who also waitresses at Applebee's.

Jewels and Jamie had been out to see the movie *Bad Boys* the night of her arrest. She is hanging with Jewels mostly now, and with Jewels's friend, who waitresses at a stripper bar.

Jamie earned mostly C's last semester and she lost the full scholarship to State. But she plans to go back anyway in the fall, if she has enough money. Her half of the apartment rent will be $350 a month, expensive for her income.

"The officer thought you'd get off lightly if you bring your license and fix your headlight," I say. "But you better start carrying your license with you. Put it in your glove compartment or something."

"Usually I have it," she says defensively. "I mean, not the last time, OK, but the last two times I was pulled over."

Alley rolls her eyes.

"I had it when I had that accident," Jamie adds.

"Why do you keep getting pulled over?" I ask.

"I don't know. Bad luck I guess."

Alley rolls her eyes again. "I've told you what I think about you driving when you've been drinking," she says.

"I wasn't really drinking," Jamie snaps. "This isn't the time to be talking about it."

So we stop.

The sun is rising over the gently wooded neighborhood when we locate Jamie's car.

"I don't want to go home," Jamie says. Instead, she follows Alley to her dorm.

30

Opening the Files

WHEN James Johnson, the director of Free Will Baptist Children's Home, learned of the difficulties Jamie encountered in seeking her files, he grew quiet on the phone. So Jamie didn't dwell on it. That wasn't the point of her call. She had learned early on that child care workers are busy, so you have to get to the point first in case they get pulled away, and if there's time, then talk.

Jamie wanted to apply to a North Carolina congressman for a summer internship in Washington, D.C., and she wanted a recommendation from Johnson. He was eager to give one, and happy to hear from her. But he was upset by the sad tone of her voice when she talked about the files beyond her reach. Without telling Jamie, he phoned Alma Shelton directly. Not happy with her response, he called Jamie back and invited her to go through her files with him at Free Will.

"We looked up my case number together. I was case number nine hundred exactly," Jamie says proudly, her eyes alight, as though it was a lucky number.

Jamie's large file contained psychological, behavioral, and academic evaluations, school reports, report cards, residential counselors' reports—just about everything. If Jamie hadn't done her chores one evening, it was recorded. If her mother called Free Will administration, a social worker wrote up a summary of the conversation for the file. To Jamie, the thick files were a gold mine of information.

Most of her behavior reports were positive. Prompt at her chores but tardy waking up. Respectful, helpful, and friendly. One counselor complained that Jamie might think she is better than the other kids at the home. Another male counselor suggested she was stingy with her hugs (which was OK by her). But generally she was credited as an example to the other children.

Only the reports of her mother's calls annoyed her. Once, while Jamie was staying with her mother over spring break, her mother phoned Free Will to report that Jamie had been gone for two nights, she didn't know where.

"She knew where I was," Jamie says angrily. It seemed a blatant attempt to try to make the home think less of Jamie, but it did not succeed. To the staff, Pam's complaint did not sound credible; it was not like Jamie to act that way. Moreover, the staff had developed a critical view of Pam over the years, although Jamie was never told.

Johnson explained that her IQ scores ranged from 135 in third grade to below 110 five years later. The stress and anxiety of her displacement from Tabernacle, and the realization that her mother was committing her to state foster care, probably explained her poor score on the second test. Besides, he cautioned, don't put too much stock on those IQ tests. Many factors in traumatized children in foster care greatly disadvantage them, making test results a dubious basis for judging true intelligence.

Other business pulled Johnson away, but he left Jamie alone with her files for most of the day. She could Xerox whatever she wanted, he said, but she could not remove papers.

Jamie left Free Will with a new ease. She felt stronger and more confident, as if she had been tumbling in a wave for a long time and was now, finally, out of the water and on firm ground.

"Most of the stuff in the files I already knew," she says later. "Some of the stuff, I don't agree with the way they saw it. But I guess we all wouldn't see things the same way."

She doesn't laugh or smile, but there is a serenity about her.

"Yes," she says with a deep sigh, "I feel a whole lot better. I feel like I can move on now. But you know, the best thing was Mr. Johnson. He really stood by me. He might get in trouble for showing me those files, I guess; he didn't say it but I bet he could. He was one of those who used to say, 'Understand your situation, accept it, and go on.' He really stood by what he said. He really cared about me and he still does. Maybe that's what I needed to know, too."

To appreciate the value of those files to Jamie, the comments of a former children's home director may be instructive. He was discussing the untoward effects that growing up within an institution can have on children.

"I had gone to a church with a couple of kids from the home to raise money, and we stopped off at a restaurant for dinner on the way back. I noticed the kids were nervous, but I couldn't figure out why. The waitress handed them the menu. They thanked her but just stared at it and then at each other. They didn't know what to do when she came back for our orders. These kids were seniors and juniors in high school and they had never ordered food at a restaurant before. They didn't even know they were supposed to. They didn't know how to live in the world.

"Some kids would go nuts if their schedules were altered. They just didn't know how to handle it if dinner was a half hour earlier or bedtime a half hour later. They were so dependent on a regimented schedule. They didn't know how to handle change."

Jamie was not that badly crippled, but she was raised in a structured system. She had difficulty adapting to her new independence, especially disciplining herself. She could function in the outside world, but she felt the void of her past. Her biological parents fluttered in and out of her life. Her relatives filled in on some weekends and vacations. But it was the system of child care workers that fed her, scolded her, encouraged her, rewarded her. When she left for college and declared herself independent, she felt freed from the stigma of being a "throwaway" in foster care. But soon that glow of freedom wore off. She missed the support and security she had felt at Free Will home. And she was nostalgic about her life there. She wondered if her memory was correct, whether the warmth and security from the home had been genuine, and if she was worthy of the support and encouragement she received there.

Now, with Johnson having put himself at some risk by giving her the files, she was reassured. Free Will had not just told her to face her situation and her past; they had helped her to do it. The reports in her files validated her memories and her life at the home. Now she felt she could get on with her life, moving on firmer ground.

31

Senator Helms

NORTH Carolina State University's legal aid to students could not help Jamie defend the charge of driving under the influence because it was a criminal case. She had passed the Breathalyzer test, but the officers complained she had failed the sobriety test. The district attorney decided to prosecute Jamie for driving while impaired. No doubt her previous parking and speeding tickets, failure to carry her license, and two accidents weighed in the decision.

Jamie was referred to an expensive Raleigh lawyer by several fellow waiters and bartenders at Applebee's. The attorney believed the charge itself could be beaten, and in fact later both charges were dropped. But at the time, he was more concerned about the marijuana pipe found in her car.

So, although happy with the files she had finally seen, Jamie was at another fork in the road. Now living in an off-campus apartment, with skidding grades and double shifts at Applebee's, she was on a slippery slope. Her friends, her school advisor, and her aunts and uncles were secretly betting she wouldn't be back to school in the fall. Even if she wanted to, she would not be able to afford tuition as well as the higher rent, car insurance payments, and now expensive legal fees.

Then the letter came. Sen. Jesse Helms had accepted her for a monthlong internship on Capitol Hill. They overlooked her dismal grade-point average and offered $100 a week for the internship in Washington.

Jamie had applied months ago, when things seemed to be going her way. Now, she was again doubting herself. She almost wished she hadn't been offered the opportunity. She wouldn't know anyone. They were of another class and would look down on her. She couldn't hack the work, whatever it was. She'd have to find a job to supplement the $100-a-week salary, and she did not know of any restaurants in Washington that might hire her.

"She's always coming to these crossroads," her uncle Fenner had said early on. "She can either go this way or that, the easy way or the hard way, the comfortable way or the challenging way. I've got to hand it to her, she's done a good job. But she's constantly coming to these forks in the road. People like you or I might come to them once or twice in our lives. With Jamie, it's all the time because she doesn't have someone she really trusts to keep her on the straight and narrow. She has to do it herself.

"If she's your success story"—he shook his head—"well, you better look for a backup."

About three weeks after the Helms letter arrived, Jamie received a call from another university student, who had seen Jamie's name along with her own on a list of North Carolina students accepted for Hill programs that summer. The young woman lived in Charlotte.

"It was so cool," Jamie bubbled the next day. "We just started talking and realized we have so much in common. She said it would be cool if we could room together in a dorm at Georgetown [University]. Do you have Senator Helms's number?"

A week past deadline, Jamie accepted the internship.

32
Washington, D.C.

◼

WASHINGTON does not begin as she expected. During her first week, the window of her Honda is smashed for the change on her dashboard. Her father agrees to wire her $50, but only if she comes home immediately. It was a harebrained idea in the first place, he says. Living above herself. She could make more money waitressing in Raleigh. Besides, it wasn't appropriate for a girl to go to a big city like Washington alone. It was dangerous. He wants her to come back to his place.

His words convinced her to stay, despite her fear. She refused her father's money and as a last resort, called her mother. Pam was receptive, even understanding.

"She doesn't like Helms's politics," Jamie explained. "But she always watches *This Week with David Brinkley* and *Inside Washington*."

Jamie asked for $100. Her mother wired her $150 and told her she need not pay back the wiring charge.

Jamie's next problem was finding a place to live. Dorm rooms were too expensive. But she soon made friends with another intern, whose father was paying her dorm fee; Jamie could stay with her for free. The two then became inseparable, except when Jamie worked nights at the Hard Rock Cafe, a job she had found her second day in Washington.

After a few weeks she was feeling more comfortable and capable. She found she could take care of herself, even in Washington. And she was learning amazing things in Helms's office.

"You know," she says, "Jesse Helms isn't the mean, nasty, brutal man people make him out to be. He's really more like a grandpa inside. He's been in office twenty-three years. That's longer than I've been alive!"

She was part of the Helms family, as they called the office. And while she didn't agree with all of Helms's politics, she was proud to be part of the family.

"Sometimes interns in other offices would say, 'How can you work for him?'" she says, rolling her eyes. "But I think it was probably the most interesting office on the Hill to work in."

Also, there were the perks.

"He comes across like some holy roller, but really his biggest supporters are tobacco companies, like R. J. Reynolds, and alcohol, like Anheuser-Busch. So they have beer right in the office fridge! And free cigarettes, too, because they give them to the office free."

So Jamie had a good time.

She also learned a bit about politics. When the debate began on the Ryan White Bill, which was to fund AIDS support groups and research on the disease, she remembered everyone in the office cringing when Helms took to the floor of the Senate. The calls are going to pour in now, a staffer complained. And they did. She didn't agree with Helms, but neither did she approve of the "radical gay rights" group that dropped, by helicopter, a giant condom over Helms's house. Sometimes, she says, politics becomes personal.

She learned something about big cities, too.

"I ran after a guy to get my money back," she says, disturbed but proud. "He came up to me in the Metro and said he needed $1.60 to get his wife and kids home. So I began to give him sixty cents, but he took a dollar right out of my hands. I thought, OK, but then I saw him go through the turnstile alone, so I ran after him. I said, 'Excuse me, but where are your kids?'

"And then he tried to sell me a necklace. I just took the dollar back. The thing is, there are a lot of people who really need help and you never know who, so in the end I was just like everyone else in Washington, people asking me for money, and I just walked by like I hadn't heard them. I even had one guy cussing me because I just walked away."

But the best part of her Washington experience was that it once again restored her self-confidence and feeling of self-worth.

Out of eight interns in Helms's office, she learned, she was the only one who had no ties to any of the staff or Helms himself. "I got there on my own," she says. "There were two hundred and fifty applicants, and I found out that I was the only one recommended by the staff intern director. Of all of them!

"Last year it was like a cloud came over me. I didn't care. I didn't fight for what I wanted. I didn't want anything bad enough. I gained all that weight. I started believing in all the negatives I'd ever heard in a children's home. This internship changed that. My confidence is back up, maybe not to a hundred percent, but way up compared to last year. It will get up further when I start doing really well in school again and drop some weight."

33
Learning How to Be Happy

JAMIE began her third year of college with a new maturity and a decision to get a political science degree, with an eye toward law or maybe journalism later.

What she found in herself while she was in Washington had helped her. She knew she could make it on her own. She could take care of herself even in a big city where she didn't know anyone. And she found out that no one was better than she, or worse, because of where they came from. She had spent the summer with kids of people with money, status, and power. She could feel comfortable with the best of them. And she came away recognizing that many of the kids she met at the children's home had strengths that they lacked.

Her sophomore year had been difficult for many reasons. Her cooperation with me in this book, the memories that surfaced in our talks, the puzzles in her past she had put aside had shaken her, she admitted.

"But I had to do it sometime," she says gently, trying to reassure me. "I feel the same way I did when we began. I thought, and I still think, that I can help some people, so kids and parents don't have to go through experiences like mine, so that they don't have to go through what my mom and me went through."

As for what Jamie wants after all this, her answer is clear and simple, though she knows the path to getting there won't be so.

"I don't want to fail in life," she says, her eyes rich in their sincerity. "I want to just be happy."

But first, she says, she'll have to find out what extended happiness is.

III

ANGEL
Los Angeles, California

1

How Najuwa Became Angel

※

ANGEL Jackson was born Najuwa Holts in Los Angeles on November 8, 1978. At seventeen she is a beautiful African-American woman, astonishingly slim and petite despite having borne five children in as many years. Her husband of three years is seventy-three. He was her foster care father.

Angel's mother doesn't know who her daughter's biological father is. She chose the surname Holts for no discernible reason. But she and her daughter believe the father is white because Angel, as she now wants to be known, has light skin. Her hair is reddish brown, but she dyes it jet black. Her wide open smile shows small, baby-sized teeth. She exudes an innocent sexuality that is attractive, particularly to men. Leaning on childlike charm and gestures to get what she wants, she can talk baby talk. But she can also spit out defiant, vicious words that, together with her flashing brown eyes, leave no doubt that Angel has attitude.

She is the product of the foster care system, a child who through resilience, courage, and ingenuity "escaped" from it, as she puts it. And one who experiences the tragic irony of fighting to prevent her own children from disappearing into the same voracious maze that society has devised for orphans of the living.

2

A Shaky Beginning

※

NAJUWA came into the world small and premature. She trembled and shook at the slightest touch. Her cry was not the full and rich cry of new life, but a harsh squall sharpened by pain and hollowed with detached confusion. When other infants began to focus, her eyes darted continually, unable to rest for even a moment on one object. The drugs she had absorbed in utero made her world too exciting. Stationary objects leapt out at her. Movements were sharp and jerky. Noise was disorienting.

The doctors called it gaze aversion, and Najuwa seemed to suffer from all its effects. She could not remain still for a nurse-timed second. But when her mother held her close, she curled herself into a tiny ball and, shaking or not, socked into a quiet place near her mother's heart. When a nurse took her, she would open her mouth to wail, but soundlessly, and flail weakly to return to her mother's warmth.

Linda Dillard saw her baby's attachment as a sign of loyalty. So she named the child Najuwa, which she heard means "queen" in an African language. Which one, she doesn't know. Through the wakening pain and sickness of cocaine withdrawal in a cold hospital ward, Dillard saw her third daughter as a fighter. She had nothing to give her daughter, not even a last name. In a world where black women get little of anything, Dillard says, she wanted her daughter to have a name to set her apart and above, to make her stand out and believe she was someone important. All she had to give was a name to christen the dignity and beauty she saw in her new child.

Within a few days, while Najuwa quaked in her crib, Dillard became convinced she was held hostage in the hospital. Social workers swarmed around, urging her to relinquish her rights to the baby and begging for the father's name. Holts, she finally told them, because she liked the sound of it. Najuwa Holts. Still, Dillard refused to give up her baby, though she resented the child for the unwanted attention she drew from the California Department of Social Services. But by then it was too late. Dillard was forced into her fifth drug rehabilitation program.

Najuwa was a casualty of the first wave of crack cocaine. Studies would call her a "crack baby." Initially, it was feared that these children would grow up incapable of remorse, unable to love, hyperactive, and hard to control. But those symptoms are now believed to be more a result of the infant's early environment than their mother's drug use. Drug-addicted infants do develop motor and cognitive skills at a much slower rate than average during their first six months of life, but longitudinal studies have found that almost all of those children raised in good, caring homes catch up to their peers.

Najuwa says she was a lucky one. Her IQ is within the medium range of children in foster care, between 85 and 95. And in terms of real life, she says an extra ten to twenty points should be added to her score for street smarts. Mr. Brown, her foster father and the man who later became her husband, nods in agreement. In all of her seventeen years, she claims, she has never been prone to violence or unable to love. She insists that she has outgrown the anger that dominated her childhood, and established a normal adult life for herself.

The California Department of Children and Family Services has reason to be skeptical. At age fourteen, two years after her foster mother died, Najuwa legally married (with a consent form signed by her biological mother) her sixty-nine-year-old foster father, Marrion Brown. A year earlier, when she was thirteen, the couple says, she bore their first child. She changed her name then, unofficially, to Angel Jackson, in an effort to shed her past and reform her behavior for her child's sake. She has since had four more children, one for each of her teenage years.

Despite the childbearing, she looks like a teenage model, although she complains that at five feet four she's not tall enough to be one. She no longer wants to go into modeling, because she thinks she's too old. But she likes to be watched. In public, Angel is always well put together. The look, her husband complains, costs him a small fortune and her several hours in the bathroom each morning. Her nails are long, manicured, and coated with red polish—always red, she says. She has a soft, café au lait skin tone, with faint freckles that only she seems to be able to see clearly. Her mother and three sisters are all a darker shade of brown, she points out. With makeup drowning the freckles and her favorite purple-pink lipstick covering her lips, she can carry off looking seventeen or eighteen years old. But without makeup, she looks a precocious fourteen or fifteen. She hides then. "I look like a baby," she complains about her fresh, unsophisticated look.

All of Angel's four children are now in foster care, allegedly sexually abused by her husband, whom she refers to as Daddy. The children were taken by Children and Family Services (the same agency that took her from her mother and, she claims, messed her up for life) three months before our first conversation. Angel acts light spirited and happy at first, but later admits to a great hollowness inside since the children left. At night she hears the voice of her eldest, Angelica, asking when she can come home. In a flash of anger, Angel swears that she will never let her children go through foster care, not the system she fought so hard to escape, the one that pushed her through fifteen foster care placements and four social workers in barely a year and a half.

She is convinced that the Family Court will order her children returned to her at the next scheduled session, which is two months away—the first available time on the court docket. Angel is anxious to get them back as soon as possible. Angelica is due to start preschool in September. She tells Angel that she's frightened and that her heart aches at night.*

---

* Angel and Mr. Brown are permitted to see their children once every other Monday, from two to four in the afternoon, in the home and under the supervision of the children's foster mother.

As for her own heart, Angel says: "Don't let anyone tell you you can't live without a heart. I'm walking proof you can. My heart is in some stranger's house with my kids. I'm just walking around pretending they'll be back soon." She breaks off then; her voice trembles.

Then she talks about the court-ordered parenting course that she and her husband have just completed with the highest grades. Suddenly, there is sunshine in her voice again. And then a pause as she comes back to a reality in which she believes she has little control.

"Sometimes I feel like I'm in Oz," she says, weary and bewildered. "I'm the Tin Man, and the judge is the Wizard."

3

Angel's Mom

MOST of her life was over, Linda Dillard believes, by the time she gave birth to Angel. At age twenty-four, Dillard had been in and out of several juvenile detention centers and foster care placements, borne three children, committed several burglaries, and been charged with murder. She had passed through numerous hospitals and drug detox centers—and just about as many abusive men. Now forty-two, she's on the streets of Los Angeles, living much the same life as always, but at a slower pace.

"When Angel was born, I knew it was over for me," she says. "I was going to make a go of it off of drugs, but I knew in the back of my mind that my life was already over and I'd go back to drugs again. But when I held my baby, I felt her life was going to be different from mine. I wasn't going to let her start in the [welfare] systems that I was deep into. There was no way I was going to give her up. I was going to set that hospital on fire before they took my child," she insists, pounding the table. "I didn't know much about what was going on with me or what would happen, but I knew that. I was going to give my baby a chance, start her off free, out of that system."

Then she laughs.

"It was easier then than it is now," she says. "They weren't as quick at taking kids away back then. I agreed to go through detox and they let my mama keep her."

Dillard is an articulate woman, and surprisingly soft. The street has weathered her and the drugs have aged her, but in her eyes there is still a hint of a vivacious beauty she had in more innocent times, and passed on to Angel. She relates to her four daughters far more as a sister than as their mother, she says. Her daughters still vie to be her favorite, sometimes nastily. And while all say that drugs ruined their mother's mind and rendered her useless, they show little anger or resentment toward her. They give her even less respect.

"Even before we were born, she messed us up," one of her children says. "All of us but the baby, Tametha, was born addicted. And she was never there for any of us. But she's still our mom, I guess."

When she was still a child living with Dillard's mother, Angel remembers, she would search neighborhood alleys for her mother, to give her food and money. As Angel grew older and saw drugs destroying her mother, she gave her mother less money and more food.

Angel also remembers that Maria, her oldest sister, took care of their mother when Maria was merely eight years old. Once when Dillard was very sick from heroin withdrawal, Maria carried Angel with her to a drug dealer.

The two children came to his door, recalls the dealer, now a slow, red-eyed, and weathered man. "They stood there, their eyes real big. And the bigger one said, 'My mama's sick real bad and I know you know how to make her better. Come take care of her.' "

Dillard revived with the dealer standing over her, shooting her a fix.

"Your daughters came to my apartment and told me to come," he said.

"I ain't doing this again," he went on. "I don't want to look into those kids' eyes again while you kill yourself." He says he refused to sell to her again.

Dillard confirms the story with pride in her kids but without noticeable shame.

"Angel and I were particularly close," she recalls. "She was so little when she would get strangers to bring her to jail to visit me and bring me money." Angel was then only nine and living with her grandmother.

"I'd say, 'How'd you get up here?' " Dillard says, her eyes twinkling at the memory of her child. "And she'd say, 'That lady bring me,' and point to someone waiting for her, or she'd say she hitched a ride."

Angel remembers, too, trying to distance herself from Dillard. "At night I would wonder where she was, if she was hungry or cold. And when there were thunderstorms—woooh, I was scared for my mama. But I didn't get close to her. She was in and out of prison. She'd come out three months, go back in."

No one in the family expected Dillard to take care of her children. When Angel's grandmother found herself terminally ill, she searched for foster parents for her grandchildren. She hardly even asked Dillard's permission to find them another home.

• • •

DILLARD'S story did not begin much differently than her four daughters. She had been born in Santa Monica, California, an only child. Her father died of a stroke when she was nine, and then she and her mother moved to Venice Beach. She describes her mother as loving and caring, so much so that she took in other troubled children in the neighborhood.

"She took in two of my best friends," Dillard remembers, her face sagging with years only the street could weigh on her. One of her friend's "mom tried to kill her all the time, and the other's dad beat her. We didn't have a lot, but my mom was a religious woman, a good-hearted woman."

In 1965, when Dillard was twelve, she began smoking pot and drinking wine.

"If you weren't using something, it was abnormal in my neighborhood," she says.

But she had been walking on the wild side even earlier. She had already run away from home several times.

"I had no reason to run away," she says. "I don't know why I did it again and again. My mom was good to me, like she was good to all the neighborhood kids. Maybe the more trouble they got into, the more attention they got, so I ran away too," with her best friends.

The last time she ran away, she was caught smoking and drinking and was placed in MacLaren Hall, a center for troubled youths in Los Angeles. In one of the many overlapping aspects of her life and her daughter's life, Angel would later be sent to the same home several times.*

At MacLaren, Dillard was surrounded by tough girls who taught her how to pick locks and rob stores—"how to survive," Dillard says. They also introduced her to what she calls the popular pills of the sixties, barbiturates, known on the street as red devils. At MacLaren, too, she says, she was raped by a staff member.

"There were two men who used to come into the rooms and hold you down and say you were bad and that this was your punishment," Dillard remembers. "I wasn't the first girl or the last to get raped there. We were in a room with lots of beds, and you could hear them get on the girls at night and them whimper or cry. The bolder ones cursed a little. But we were all scared and embarrassed more than anything. We learned we were nothing, just black girls, and we had nothing. Anything could be done with us and no one cared. So I learned everything I could from those girls so that I could protect myself."

After her release, she fell in with a crowd that was heavily into drugs.

---

* The facility's name was changed about fifteen years ago to MacLaren Children's Center, but Angel still calls it MacLaren Hall, which is still its street name and the name it had when her mother was placed there. Angel and her mother say the facility holds troubled youths, but MacLaren's director says it is simply a shelter for abused, abandoned, and neglected children.

"I was staying with Gary and Louie when I first got into big trouble with the law," she says. "They're both dead now. What happened was the police busted the house and found Gary had overdosed. They tried to wake him up but they couldn't. They said he had been dead for days. Louie and I were accused of murder. They said I tied Gary up while Louie shot him up. It didn't happen, but they said I was guilty, and they sent me up to youth authority for three years."

Released from juvenile detention, she soon found more trouble. One night, walking home from a friend's house, she was pulled into an alley. She fought hard, hard enough to get her nose broken, but was overpowered and raped by a young man she knew. "Some neighbors found me and took me to the hospital," she says. "They stitched my vagina, because he had ripped it." She was fourteen then, and now, almost thirty years later, she spits out his name as if it happened yesterday. She is still angry and, she says, she'd do just about anything to punish him.

Dillard went home and got her father's old shotgun.

"I went to where he lived and tried to shoot him and his friend," she says calmly now. "Then the police arrested me for attempted murder."

She was found guilty and spent the next year and a half in a prison for girls.

"When you're young like that you don't know how to stand up for yourself," she says. "You don't know how to talk the talk in court. All you can do is feel that anger, and it takes hold of you and everything you do. I think that's why Angel and I are close. I understand that in her. I don't like it. It makes me sad. But I recognize it. I know how you can't get no one to understand you or what happened. And you blame them because they just don't know. You can't tell them; it's like a different language or something. They just see you as nothing but wrong, nothing but guilty."

Dillard returned to her mother's home after prison. She went back to school and tried to fit in "with the good girls," she says.

But she returned to drugging. Soon she became pregnant, and at sixteen gave birth to her first child, Maria. A year later, in 1969, she began shooting heroin and committing crimes regularly—robbing and burglarizing to support her habit.

"It pretty much kept me in jail," she says. "In and out."

She bore her second child, Latachee, when she was eighteen, and then Angel. Tametha, the youngest, was born in prison.

"All my kids had different fathers," she says. "And all of them were born addicted, except for Tametha, the youngest. I had to stay straight because I was in custody for something or other, and they pumped me with vitamins. And you know, she was the sickliest. She was only three pounds when she was born."

Only her oldest and her youngest, Maria and Tametha, know who their fathers are. Maria's father, Dillard admits, was her favorite man, even though she says she knew he molested her daughters. He drifted in and out of her life for twenty years until he disappeared.

"I was blind to his faults," she mumbles. "I didn't want to believe he was sexually molesting my girls, but deep down I knew it. I knew they were getting money from somewhere."

After the state learned of the abuse, Dillard's four children were sent to live with her mother. Dillard continued to live with the man nonetheless.

"I always let my men abuse me," she admits. "I never wanted to admit that I let them abuse my babies." And then she cries.

She met one good man, she says, in rehab, and she married him. But they divorced when she went back into drugs. Last year, he died of AIDS. Neither had known he was HIV-positive.

"My last husband died of cancer of the brain a couple of months later," she says without apparent sadness.

Since then, Dillard has lived on the street. Sometimes she stays with Angel and her husband, sometimes at Maria's, but only occasionally with her second daughter, Latachee. Tametha, a young teenager, is in foster care.

"Latachee will rent a room for me in the most expensive hotel in California before she let me stay with her." Dillard laughs. "She's sort of disconnected from the family."

Dillard had just gotten out of rehab when we spoke. Her mind seemed crisp and alert. She had been clean for three months, she said, and was looking to get back her old job—ironically, as a rehabilitation counselor.

"All my kids have the isms," Dillard says, dismissing such faults—alcoholism and drug abuse—as symptoms of the layered problem of addiction. "Angel, too, but she's not on anything. I tell her if she ever take a pill or raise a glass to her lips, she be gone. She be an addict. She has to watch herself. All my kids have the isms, like me."

4

Starting Out

ANGEL and her two sisters went to live with their mother the day Dillard was released from drug rehab. Angel doesn't remember much of her first six years. But she does remember her mother's boyfriend.

"I remember he was my mom's love of her life and he would give me money for ice cream. I didn't think there was anything big deal about it," she says. Then she turns away abruptly. "I don't remember anything else."

A doctor's report in Angel's files notes physical damage from sexual abuse when, the doctor estimates, she was "four or five years old or very possibly younger."

Shutting off a topic is unusual for Angel. She can speak about her hooking, running away, beating people up—sometimes with regret, but never with the abrupt discomfort and embarrassment she shows about living with her mother and sisters.

She jumps ahead to the time she spent as a foster child with Naomi and Marrion Brown. Angel's terminally ill grandmother had placed her in the Browns' home. Angel got along with Mrs. Brown, but it was a long time before she would go anywhere near Mr. Brown.

"He'd be sitting on the couch and I would try to take the longest way around so that I wouldn't come near him." Angel giggles.

"Sometimes kids who have been abused or molested behave that way," I say carefully.

In the silence, Angel looks down at her hands, which for the moment are still. Then she looks into my eyes.

"Had you been molested before that?" I ask.

"Yep," she says almost cheerfully, and pauses. Then she flicks the underside of her long red fingernails with the back of her thumbnail. "By my sister's father. My oldest sister's father was living in the neighborhood. I remember him giving me money for ice cream. I remember him kissing me, but that's all. I didn't think there was anything big deal about it. I don't remember anything else."

She turns away, but after a moment turns back and continues in a low, smoother voice.

"But I remember when I was little and went to the doctor. They found out I was messed with." She adds quickly: "But I don't remember."

Mr. Brown looks at her as she picks barely visible lint off her red tank top, concern wrinkling his face. His thinning hair is black and slicked back straight with oil. He is a large man, with a soft but imposing structure. He speaks low, his voice almost a mumble. His eyes are tired, and he often appears hesitant and lonely.

"It's impossible for her to recall or know," he says.

"I think I chose not to know," she says. "I don't want to. I really don't. I got too much feeling left in me to think about that. I don't really care about it anymore. If he did, he did. It's over. I mean, get over it," she says, flicking her nails harder now.

Mr. Brown looks at me.

"They didn't do anything about it," he says about her molestation. "They picked him up, but they didn't press any charges. Her mother didn't want to get him in trouble." The abuser was her favorite man.

He shakes his head.

Angel looks from her red nails to the floor.

"I didn't want it either," she says. "I had enough of going to the doctor and questioning me, questioning me, questioning me." Her voice rises to a whine. "I was tired of that. I didn't want to go through it no more. And I thought that it was best that it was dropped," she ends firmly, suddenly more grave and mature.

I was struck by her transformation from a young, impatient, angry child one moment to a serious adult the next, one who had dismissed her troubled past and had gone beyond it. The struggle seems constant in her, as it is in many children in foster care who have lost their childhoods to neglect, abuse, and distrust. Most often, especially in times of stress, the younger Angel, the child, dominates.

"The people who asked you the questions—did you feel like they were there to help you?" I ask.

She looks at me, surprised.

"I think that they is nosy," she flares, speaking like an agitated child. "I think they perverts, and they get off listening to it."

Then she looks down, and when she continues, she is again calmly mature. "I didn't like it at all. I thought they were nasty people who wanted to hear it over and over so they could criticize me like a judge.*

"When I think about it now, I think it's not what happened that messes you up. It's just all the time you're questioned. First you're questioned by your parents, then you're questioned by police, then you're questioned by the judge, then you're questioned by the doctors and the judge. That's what makes kids angry. It's not the sexual molestation, but they have to keep telling it. That makes them all messed up. All crazy. I know it did for me. I'm tired of talking about those things. I don't want to hear it anymore; it's over with. I don't care."

Suddenly she is caught between being a child in foster care and a mother of children in foster care. "But if something going to happen to my kids like that, I'm gonna want to hear about it," she says. "The way I am, if I hear about it, that's going to make me madder, madder, madder, and it might make me mad enough to do something. I mean something serious like I might be sitting like O.J. [Simpson] now."

Mr. Brown laughs at her outburst. Angel looks surprised at first, then laughs too, almost uncontrollably.

---

* This reaction is not uncommon among children pressed to recall their abuse in detail. Some children remember the questioning as invasive, others as cold and mean-spirited. Still others are confused and frightened. When forced to describe the molestation, they become angry at the questioners, as if the abuse could be forgotten sooner without the interrogation, which made them feel dirty and in some way guilty.

The next day Mr. Brown meets me with some files that deal with Angel's abuse.

"When they came to our house as foster children, we had the results of physicals on each of the three girls," he says. "It was all true. This molestation happened when Angel was living with her mother. Her grandmother had been threatened by the man, too. She told us to just let that mess go. Don't push it any farther. So we didn't.

"There are a lot of things in Angel's mind that have her so bumfuckled," he says, wiping sweat from his brow. "That's one reason I go along with her so. I try to make her happy. But still she has things she has to deal with, things on her personal side. Her little mind is so distorted, she just has to find herself, and she needs time. I know that she do really love me. I know this as a fact."

This same man, a postal worker old enough to be her great-grandfather, married his fourteen-year-old foster daughter and was intimate with her when she was thirteen. But his concern somehow seems genuine when he speaks about the difficulties of being married to this woman who is little more than a child in age.

He complains that she has affairs with other men. "The things that I put up with, nobody else would. Nobody else would," he mutters darkly. "She'd either be six feet under or disfigured or put on the streets somewhere to be used. I try to protect her as much as I can."

Most of the time, he still treats her as his child rather than his wife. It's a relationship even he and Angel have a difficult time understanding.

Angel's grandmother had searched hard for foster parents for her grandchildren, rejecting those that social workers proposed, before settling on the Browns. She had heard of Naomi and Marrion Brown through friends of hers at church. She went alone to see Mrs. Brown and asked her to take in her grandchildren. She had ovarian cancer, she explained, and the girls were more than she could handle.

"She wanted to set the kids up before she died. She and my wife talked together. They hit it off real good, and she said this was a place she'd like them to come," Mr. Brown recalls.

Mrs. Brown was reluctant. She explained that they were licensed only to care for young boys. They had seen three boys through the foster care system and raised four children of their own. Their two biological sons had been killed, in connection with drugs or thefts, but somehow they believed girls would be more difficult to raise. Angel's grandmother persisted, and persuaded the children's social worker to reassure the Browns and promise them a license to care for girls. Still, Mr. Brown was dubious. He wanted to relax now that he was retired, not care for more young children.

"If it were up to him, we wouldn't have gone there," Angel laughs. "He

didn't want us. It was only because my grandmother and his wife hit it off."
In the end, he gave in.

Angel's grandmother went into a nursing home soon after the girls moved
in with the Browns.

5

The Browns

❖

THE Browns lived in a comfortable four-bedroom house on the outskirts
of Compton, a mostly black middle-class suburban community, where housing prices were slightly lower because of the roar of planes taking off and
landing at nearby Los Angeles International Airport.

Angel and her sisters were awed by the house. "I had never been in
anything like it. It had an upstairs, downstairs, dining room, living room,
kitchen, patio. It was huge. That house was so big. And every room was like
a different color. You had a blue room, then you had an eggshell white room,
then you had a hot pink room." Angel giggles and Mr. Brown smiles proudly.
"It was pretty. Real pretty."

So she liked her new home?

"Oh noooo," she says. "I didn't like it at all, not one bit, at first. I liked it
because it was a new place and a nice house, but I didn't like you, Daddy,"
she says, pointing at Mr. Brown, "and I didn't like your wife. I didn't like
your family cuz I wanted my grandma. I wanted the house and the neighborhood, but I just didn't want them in it." She laughs.

Mr. Brown wasn't home much. He had delayed his retirement from the
post office and began moonlighting as a security officer to support the household. Mrs. Brown took on most of the parenting role. Angel's oldest sister,
Maria, was living on her own. Her second-oldest sister, Latachee, rebelled.
But Angel grew to like the discipline and structure that was new to her life,
as did her youngest sister, Tametha.

It was the Browns' daughter, Marlo, who particularly drew Angel into the
family. Marlo was attending college and living at home. Angel admired her,
and through her, grew fond of Mrs. Brown.

"She was strict," Angel says of Mrs. Brown, "but she was a sweetheart. It
got to be fun living at the Browns' except when we got punished. But he

was the softy." She laughs, poking at Mr. Brown with childish playfullness in her voice. "We were Daddy's girls."

The honeymoon period only lasted until Gayle Brown and her two sons moved in. "His granddaughter and two great-grandkids," Angel explains, rolling her eyes toward the heavens.

Angel never got along with Gayle. Much of it appeared to be her own fault, although Gayle created tension because she insisted her children receive preferential treatment in the Brown household.

"They were his blood," Gayle says of Mr. Brown, looking back on the period. "But he was putting these wild things before his own blood great-grandchildren. They were foster kids and they were wrecking our home, causing trouble everywhere."

At one point Gayle accused Angel's older sister Latachee of having an affair with Mr. Brown, which both Mr. Brown and Angel say was untrue. Tensions increased as the house became more crowded when a relative of Mr. Brown's moved in. And with them came the incident that has divided the family ever since.

"[The relative] followed me into the bathroom and he was kissing me and touching me," Angel says, pouting. "I told him I didn't like it."

Then she turns to Mr. Brown with anger in her eyes.

"I told you he was doing it," she tells him accusingly. "He just says, 'Well, if he do it again, you let me know,'" she says in a singsong, rocking her head from side to side. "And he gone do it again and ain't nothing done about it," she remembers, old anger gathering like storm clouds. "Ain't nothing you did," she tells Mr. Brown directly.

"I tried to talk to him," Mr. Brown says, looking down.

"So when he did it that last time, I decided to do something about it myself," Angel says, suddenly sitting up straight and righteous with her hands on her hips. "I called a teen hot line I had seen on TV. I called on myself," she says, then adds softly: "I had no idea what I was getting myself into."

She believes that call, when she was eleven years old, ruined her life.

The police arrived just as the Browns were preparing to go out for dinner. They told Angel several times that they could take the relative out of the house and she could stay. But she chose to go with the officers.

"I hated the way his family was acting," she says. "They all said I was just mad at Mrs. Brown for something and made up the story. It wasn't true. I wasn't even mad at Mrs. Brown. I was scared then. I didn't want to go, but I was afraid of how they'd all be jumping on me when the police left. It would be hell."

From the Browns' home that night, she went on to fifteen foster placements and four social workers over the next year and a half.

"I did not know what I was getting myself into," she says, shaking her head. "I did not know. I thought it was kind of fun at first, I could go somewhere else, mess up a little bit. But it was like messing with a Pandora's box. Kind of like a can of worms. Worms was crawling all over me."

6

Police

▓

Mrs. Brown stood proud and erect at her front door, as she had taught Angel to stand and walk, but with tears in her eyes as the two officers escorted Angel to their patrol car.

"I turned back and waved," Angel says. "I knew she was caught between [her relative] and me. And I wanted her to think that I would be OK. But really I was scared."

She hoped the Browns would come for her. But for months she did not hear from them.

"I thought no one wanted me," she says like a sad child. "No one cared, so I didn't care about no one either."

"My wife, my first wife," Mr. Brown says, "was a good woman. She never gave up on Angel. We were married forty-eight years." He glances sternly at Angel. "Every day after they took Angel she would make phone calls to see how she was doing and try to get her back."

"If I had known Mrs. Brown wanted me back and she believed me even over [her relative], it might of changed things," Angel says, turning to hide her tears. "All I knew was that I was all alone and I had to take care of myself."

From the Browns' household, Angel was taken to a police station. She asked whether she would be put in jail because she was dirty. An officer said no but she remained apprehensive. When another policeman handed her a Coke, she wondered what kind of drugs might be in it to make her sleep. She only pretended to drink.

But within an hour the officers had made her laugh, and she felt comfortable enough after a while to dream of becoming an officer herself. "They're real nice to each other and they're like a family," Angel says. "No one messes with them. That's what I want."

She was sorry to leave, two hours later, when a temporary home was found for her.

"It was one of those places, you know, where they call in the middle of the night and say can you spare a bed," she remembers. She was told to be polite, that she would be a guest in this home.

The night she arrived, the family was celebrating another foster child's eighteenth birthday. Immediately, Angel felt an outsider, alone and unloved.

"It was like this," she says. "I was black, and she was white, and her foster daughter was white, and her family was white. Her son and his friends were white. I was the only black person."

Angel remembers that the family sat around the table talking and smoking. She wanted to join in.

"That lady let the other girl smoke but not me, because I was younger," Angel says. "I wanted to do the same things she did and I couldn't. It wasn't the lady treating me bad; she was OK. And her son was really nice to me, and his friends, too. It was the [foster] girl that was there. She didn't like me coming in on her territory. I stayed there about a week, and then my social worker came and got me."

7
Michael

"His name was Michael," Angel says of the social worker, looking toward the heavens with a sparkle in her eye. "He was so nice. I really liked him. He took me to a [group home] called David and Margaret's."

Then she shakes her head.

"Let me put it this way," she says. "I wouldn't want my child being put in a home like that for girls sixteen to eighteen years old when she was only eleven. You grow up fast. But I liked it."

8

David & Margaret's

▨

MICHAEL placed Angel at David & Margaret's Group Home in La Verne, a western suburb of Los Angeles, because of her history of sexual abuse. Perhaps she would respond better in a home for troubled girls that would address her abuse rather than ignore it, Michael thought. Standard foster care placements are designed primarily to provide a stable home life. David & Margaret's was designed to counsel girls who have been traumatized by abuse and neglect. The aim is to instill trust as a first step toward placing the child in a stable home and then toward independence when the child reaches legal age. Angel was young for the program. But Michael argued successfully that her experiences had aged her more than time.

The first thing Angel noticed about the group home was space. There were seven cottages spread widely across a seventeen-acre campus.

"It was a beautiful place," Angel says. "The cottages were like houses. Each had a name. I was in Tar Cottage. They were placed miles apart. Little houses with big backyards. They had a pool and school, but I got to go off campus for school because I was too young."

Like the others, Tar Cottage was filled to capacity with ten girls and four counselors. The counselors worked in teams of two, living in the cottage on three-day (seventy-two-hour) alternating shifts.

Angel was put in a therapy program conducted by ten social workers, each with a master's degree, assisted by residential counselors. Group therapy was scheduled four times a week and individual therapy once a week. There was also substance abuse counseling, psychiatric and psychological services, as well as art therapy, play therapy, and recreation therapy.

David & Margaret's began almost ninety years ago as a Methodist orphanage. In 1910, Mr. and Mrs. Henry Kuns donated a sixty-room hotel and adjoining land to the Women's Home Missionary Society of the Methodist Episcopal church. In its first year, it housed ninety-two boys and girls between the ages of two and twelve. When children reached twelve, they were discharged and sent to work. Over the years, however, the orphanage gradually extended its care to children until they reached adulthood.

Around 1950, the home began to accept more teenagers and fewer infants and young children. It acquired a few more acres of land, and like many orphanages, used the children to farm it. In 1958, the home harvested one thousand pounds of dressed beef, twelve tons of hay, sixty gallons of berries, and two thousand ears of corn.

Since then, children's labor has become less socially acceptable as well as less practical. The home focused on helping the children overcome traumatic pasts rather than simply providing shelter and food. Because more state programs existed for troubled boys than for girls, the home became a treatment center solely for adolescent girls in 1967. Today it provides one of the most extensive programs of its kind in California. As a measure of its success and the shortage of similar programs, it receives about seventeen hundred requests each year for its seventy spaces.

Angel was one of the seventy lucky ones.

The home imposes rules, discipline, and structure on the girls, but they are allowed relatively more freedom than in other foster homes. As one social worker explains, "These kids have been through a lot. Most have been sexually abused, many have been beaten, lots have done drugs. They've been on their own, parentally speaking. They've had adult experiences. So you don't want to throw them into a nursery again. You want to say, I respect you and what you've been through, and then help them deal with it and become responsible."

While Angel enjoyed the freedom to go on dates and even smoke, she says now that she was "still a baby" when she was there. Most of the girls were in their late teens. Angel was eleven.

The older girls seemed mean and tough. Sophie, a seventeen-year-old, took Angel under her wing, showing her the ropes. Angel soon fell in with boys doing drugs. She says she was never addicted to drugs, although she experimented with alcohol and smoking. As for school, the counselors trusted her to walk there alone. She had no qualms about violating that trust.

"I was supposed to walk there myself," she says, smiling. "But there were some cute boys that lived in a house off campus. I figured all the girls were going over there, so I went over there, and I was welcomed with open arms. Party, party, party."

She wiggles around and giggles.

Angel's residential counselor turned to Mr. Brown for help in persuading Angel to go to school and obey rules. She did not respond when they warned her.

"I didn't care about the future," she says. "I cared about Sophie and fitting in. There weren't anyone who cared about me, so I didn't care about no one. Not myself either."

She began to get into fights.

"I was very violent," she says. "I started beating up on people. I would suddenly get angry at something, or nothing, and I was like a tornado. I just wouldn't stop. But the kids were all bigger than me, thank God, so I didn't hurt no one too bad—at first."

One day, Angel was called to the phone. It was one of the few calls she got from her family.

"My grandmother called and said, 'Your mom died,' " Angel remembers, speaking softly.

"I said, 'Who? Linda?' " Angel was referring to Dillard, her biological mother.

"No," her grandmother said. "Naomi, Mrs. Brown."

Angel recalls being sad at the the news, but also a little bitter. "I figured, Oh well, they weren't doing nothing to get me back, so I didn't care."

Angel was permitted to attend Mrs. Brown's funeral, under supervision. It was the first time she had seen her sisters and the Browns since she had been taken away a year before. A residential counselor accompanied her everywhere.

"I was like a criminal to them," Angel says. "They thought I was going to try to run away. I couldn't go anywhere without this lady. I couldn't go to the bathroom, this lady had to go with me. I felt like the president of the United States. She was always there. But I could whup her anyway. I told her, 'If I wanted to get away from you, I really can. But let me be with the family some.' "

The Brown children refused to allow her to sit up front with the rest of the family during the funeral. They blamed her for their mother's death, even though the cause was stomach cancer. They felt Angel had caused Mrs. Brown so much worry and sadness that it killed her prematurely.

After the service, Angel was allowed to return to the Brown house rather than go to the cemetery for the interment. She was hoping her sisters would also skip the graveside service so they could spend time together before she had to return to the group home.

But Slim, the Browns' son-in-law, was at the house.

"What are you doing here?" he demanded. "This ain't your house. You can't stay here. They don't want you here." He barred her from the kitchen, where neighbors were preparing food.

The supervisor was shocked and frightened at Slim's hostility. Angel began to cry, and she and the supervisor left.

But when Angel and her supervisor came back, the family still had not returned, so they ended the visit.

"I didn't care," Angel says unconvincingly. "I knew nobody cared about me. I just didn't know why they hated me."

When Mr. Brown learned of Slim's confrontation with Angel, he was irate. "I raised sam with Slim and told him, 'You don't come into my house and try to rule my house when I'm not here. Because she has more right here than you.' "

Back at the group home, Angel found that her friend Sophie was leaving because she had turned eighteen. Angel attributes her behavior that followed to "everything bad inside me building up and exploding. I don't know what happened next," she says. "I really don't. It's just like red and then black and then handcuffs."

Tar Cottage was having a barbecue that night. Angel stood quietly to the side, thinking of nothing in particular but feeling sad. When a group of girls mocked her for being alone, she picked up a pitchfork from a nearby pile of hay.

"I know I stuck at least three people." She giggles.

Mr. Brown looks sternly at her.

"They weren't seriously hurt," she adds quickly.

Mr. Brown shifts, his body stiff with anger. "Then why did they tell me the lady was seriously crippled?" he demands angrily.

"That wasn't there," Angel lashes back. "That was later."

9

MacLaren

THE police charged Angel with "acts against persons,"* and took her in handcuffs to MacLaren Children's Center in El Monte. Angel calls it MacLaren Hall, because that's what her mother called it when she was there. It is both an emergency shelter and a home for troubled youths.

"People told me how wonderful it was there," Angel mumbles. "It wasn't great there at all. It was terrible there. It was the scariest place I've ever been. Even scarier than my pimp. All I cared about was getting away," she says. She followed the advice of her social worker, Michael, to be on her best behavior and to curb her anger. She trusted Michael more than she trusted anyone else at that age, when she was twelve.

---

* The charge covers acts ranging from striking to shooting another person. The number of girls who commit such crimes is growing nationwide, even as some cities report a drop in the rate of these crimes committed by boys. Girls are less likely than boys to commit crimes for material gain, court statistics suggest. Crime for girls is more likely to be personal. Forty percent of cases involving girls in the juvenile system are categorized as "acts against persons"; many of the victims were a neighborhood nemesis, a rival for a boy, or (often) a member of the family.

"He understood things like they really were, not how they should be," Angel says. "And he really cared. He really did."

She pauses for a moment, her eyes soft and moist. It is a side that Angel rarely shows. "I'll never forget when I was at MacLaren. There was a phone call for me one time. And I *never* got phone calls. I don't know if anyone even knew where I was. Michael called up and asked me if I wanted to go to lunch with him and his wife the next day. I was so excited. He even brought his son. He was just really nice and he cared, so I listened to him.

"He gave me respect too. Most of the social workers don't want to even tell you if they have kids or are married, nothing, cuz they don't trust you and cuz you beneath them. But not Michael." She smiles. "I was good enough to meet his family. It made me feel, well, like I was a person like them. No different."

Each week, representatives of group homes and foster parents visited MacLaren to interview the children as potential new members of their homes. Angel was passed over several times. But she persisted in working to improve her attitude and manners, and after two months, a woman accepted her.

"If she had really knowed what kind of child I was, I wouldn't have gotten out of the door of MacLaren Hall." Angel laughs. "It was easy, though. It was just a couple hours to spend with her before she accepted me. She thought I was just misguided, being a religious woman. But I was way more than that. I was a handful."

Angel got along well with her new foster mother until she was caught smoking. That night, the woman entered Angel's room and said she was going to exorcise the demons from Angel.

"She told me to hold still, then she brought in candles and a knife, turned off all the lights, and then she squeezed my head!" Angel exclaims. "I was so scared. She was a nice woman, but she was strong, and you never know what those real religious types are going to do."

Angel ran away when her foster mother went for more matches. She called Mr. Brown, crying, and then went to the police station as he told her to. She was returned to MacLaren. But within a few days, she was placed out again, this time to Maryvale.

10

Maryvale

❖

"MARYVALE was this orphanage full of nuns," Angel says, raising her eyebrows. "All sorts of nuns.

"They had nuns in blue-and-white, nuns in black-and-white, nuns in all blue," she continues in mock breathlessness while fluttering her long, fine fingers. "You never seen so many different types of nuns. And their names was, you know, Saint Joseph, Saint Stephen, Saint Maria. It was all very religious."

MARYVALE is run by the same religious order that founded it almost a century and a half ago, the Daughters of Charity of Saint Vincent de Paul,* but it is open to girls of all faiths. Most girls come from families like Angel's, where little attention was given to religion, although, like Angel, most describe their faith as Christian. Angel does not distinguish between denominations, but supposes Baptist will do because the only church she went to regularly was the Baptist church where Mr. Brown was a deacon.

As in many children's homes run by religious orders or specific persuasions, religion has little to do with Maryvale's day-to-day functioning. The campus occupies fourteen acres, its buildings surrounded by tall palm trees and short dry grass. It is a gentle place for eighty-five girls between the ages

---

* Saint Vincent de Paul was born in the latter half of the sixteenth century to a poor family in southwest France. At nineteen, he became a priest to escape poverty. He was canonized for his work with the poor and orphaned. In 1850, his order was united with a mission established by Saint Elizabeth Ann Seton, the first American-born saint. Six years later, at the request of the bishop of Los Angeles, five nuns journeyed from Seton's community in Maryland to Pueblo, California, to establish an orphanage for abandoned children. Today it is one of the country's more successful programs. And it is expensive. The federal and state governments pay 65 percent of expenses. To make up the rest, Maryvale depends on donations, primarily through a guild formed in the early 1950s called Friends of the Orphanage. Most of the contributions come from an advertising supplement run in the *Los Angeles Times* every year on Mother's Day.

of two and eighteen, many with psychiatric and behavioral problems due to abuse, neglect, and simply bad parenting.

Angel was placed in Maryvale's twenty-four-hour residential treatment program with a 150-person staff that included psychiatrists, psychologists, social workers, recreation therapists, and counselors.* To Maryvale's credit, Angel remembers the people, not the programs or treatments.

She was housed in one of the six groups, fourteen girls in each. Each group had a designated activity area, a television room, recreation room, a dining room/kitchen, and bedrooms. Each bedroom accommodated two girls. It was a pleasant arrangement, as even Angel admits. But her attitude came with her to Maryvale.

"I didn't get along with them girls neither," Angel says. "Cuz theys was very stuck up, to be in the same place that I am. They ain't no better, they're in an orphanage too."

When Angel is being careful, she speaks, she says, as if she is on television. When she is swept back into her childhood experiences, her TV English loses out to angry street talk.

Angel had learned at David & Margaret's, and then at MacLaren, the importance of being tough, or seeming tough, when dealing with other kids.

"They check you out all the time and you have to show you're cool or you get picked on," she says.

"I tried to show them. There were some girls that was being nice and I said to them, to show the others, I don't like school. Let's not go to school, let's ditch. That's when a lot of stuff started happening."

Here, Angel shows one of her recurring and most troublesome features. She is a "runner." At just about every opportunity, whether happy or not, she tries to run away. It prevents her from establishing meaningful ties that could anchor her to a more secure and normal world.

Most runners are, like her, impatient and energetic. Many try to gain the respect of their peers by adopting a lofty independence toward authority. Runners are a major problem in children's homes, not only because the homes are responsible for the children at all times, but because running is contagious. Runners take other children along in their wake. Usually the runner is not satisfied with one attempt, successful or not. She or he tries it again and again.

"You get one kid who wants to run to his aunt's in the city," explains the director of one children's home. "He tries it with his two buddies, then you got eight more trying to run. We had a whole cottage run once. It's like a disease. It catches like wildfire."

---

* The program offers a structured group living situation; an individualized psychotherapeutic treatment plan; individual, group, and family therapy; psychiatric, neurological, and psychological service; an educational plan; independent living skills and vocational training programs; and family reunification services.

Applicants are often refused admittance into a home because they have a history of running. Many children are also expelled from homes for the same reason.

At Maryvale, Angel is not a successful runner. She does not know the area at all and cannot read a map. Even worse, she acts on emotion and impulse, without considering the next step or the consequences. Rarely does she have plans, or if she does, she almost never sticks to them. So when she tries, on the spur of a moment, to lead a pack of girls from Maryvale, she only gets into more trouble.

After the girls skipped school at her urging, they did not know what to do, where to go, or how to get there. By early evening, after just a few hours on the lam, they were tired and out of money.

"We ran out of having fun so we decided to go back," Angel says. "We didn't know where we was, so we called the police. We called the police!" She laughs and slaps her knee. "When I think back, we did the most stupidest stuff. There were six of us. We didn't call the police from a phone booth. We were lost in a residential area so we went up to the lady who opened the door; she had a beautiful home and we explained to her what happened and asked could we use the phone."

While calling the police seemed a wise move then, Angel has since decided that only as a last resort should she phone the police. "It goes on your record when you call them, whatever you call them for," she explains. "They put in my files that I led a group to run away. That didn't do me no favors."

Back at Maryvale, the other children ridicule the runners for their failure. So the six girls become more determined to prove themselves, and that means running away again. This time they are caught by staff just a few blocks away and herded back.

"Somebody tipped them off," Angel says. "They said, 'These girls are supposed to be in the orphanage.' See, we stand out everywhere; they can tell we different."

The second failure further intensifies their desire to escape, so three of the six girls make one final and almost fatal try.

"But theys were onto us by then," she says.

As they run through the halls, rooms, and rest areas, panic quickens with their pace and yells, then heavy footsteps, gain at their heels.

"We have all these people behind us running," Angel remembers, still frightened. "One girl goes this way, the other girl goes that way, and I'm going straight. And I can feel them [staff] behind me, coming to get me with ropes and stuff. My ears are pounding. I thought I was going to die."

Suddenly a large woman appears before her, blocking the last doorway to the outside.

"I keep telling her, Let me go. But she wants to play Mr. Big. I was scared, scareder than I've ever been. I thought they were coming to kill me, and I'm like, Please, God, I want to get by. She is like, No. And I'm thinking, They're coming, they're coming. So I reach over and grab a stick and hit her in the legs."

After a pause, she says, "She let me go then." The wide-eyed terror of reliving the event melts to embarrassment. She looks down calmly now at her hands lying in her lap.

She had struck the woman more than on her legs. At least one of her blows broke the woman's spine, leaving her crippled for life.

"I know I did it, but I don't remember it," Angel claims, picking at her fingernail. "All I could think was, They're coming, they're coming, and freedom is out this door."

11

MacLaren Again

▓

"I FEEL bad," she adds. But the guilt evaporates quickly. "Kids, you know, that's what you do.

"Oh, well," Angel sighs, dismissing another ugly part of her past with a shrug.

The consequences of violently forcing her way through that door remain with Angel throughout her years in the foster care system.

Security immediately grabs her just outside. The police take her directly back to MacLaren, in the more guarded west wing, for older troubled girls.

Angel refuses to cooperate with the staff there. She is not violent, but she often refuses to follow instructions. At school, she merely stares out the window, thinking mostly about candy and boys.

After a series of detentions and furious tantrums, she marches into a counselor's office and announces she does not want to be at MacLaren. She hates it and all the staff, she says, and she will never cooperate with any of them.

"I told her I don't care where you put me, I just don't want to stay here, I hate it," she says proudly.

The counselor looks at Angel and then looks over Angel's record.

"Well," she replies. "We've got a place to put you."

Angel laughs now as she remembers.

"It was Kedren," Angel says, "a mental hospital."

12

Kedren

▓

ANGEL spent seven months at Kedren Mental Health Facility in south-central Los Angeles and liked it. She was afraid at first, but it turned out to be her best placement, she says.

"It beat the other places. The kids were nice. Weren't nobody crazy. The children weren't, you know. There were boys' rooms and girls' rooms. It wasn't no kids crazy. It was kids who had been abused."

Mr. Brown shakes his head solemnly as he listens. He disagrees. At his first wife's request, he had continued to track Angel in the system in case she needed extra help. He had not been allowed to see her at MacLaren, nor at Kedren at first. But he convinced a Kedren staff member to allow several visits for up to a half hour each, during which he usually brought Angel candy.

His impression of Kedren was vastly different than Angel's. To him, Kedren was a mental institution for seriously disturbed people.

"The adults was really crazy," Angel admits. "They really had problems, but the children weren't. The children were normal like me. I loved it."

WHILE in Kedren, Angel began to menstruate. "I didn't know what the hell was going on," Angel says. "I'm thinking all this stuff is happening to me because I'm a bad person. My grandma died and then this happens. Am I being really bad? Is that why all this is going on? Because I didn't know anything about all of this."

Children in the system often go through a time when they believe that everything, including bad weather, is punishment because they were bad. Many, like Angel, feel that a loved one's death or a parent's divorce was their fault. No matter how much counseling they receive, many never get over the guilt.

Angel's psychiatrist at Kedren worked hard with her in this respect, while also trying to instill in her a sense of responsibility for her future and recognition that there are consequences to her actions. By the time she left, the doctor felt she had made significant progress and had somewhat greater control over her emotions. She no longer became violent, even in her most angry times. But she had not yet accepted that she had a future. Her world was still filled with single hours and single days. Her dreams had little or no connection to where she stood. She looked not to the future, but for immediate survival and pleasure.

ALTHOUGH Mr. Brown had tracked Angel after she left his house, it was his final visit to her grandmother that convinced him to persevere in watching over Angel.

"She was in a coma," Mr. Brown remembers. "All her relatives were trying to wake her up. I told them it was useless, and I said I was just going to leave.

"Her eyes popped open just as I got to the door." He smiles. "And she said, 'You come back here, boy. I'm not done with you.' She said 'You're a good man and you're all my grandkids have left, so take care of them. Get Angel out of that crazy house.' "

After that, Mr. Brown appealed to the Kedren staff to allow Angel to return to his home as a foster child.

At first Angel's caseworker was reluctant because records showed that children in his home had been molested by a relative of Mr. Brown. But he pointed out that Angel's younger sister still lived with him and was well cared for, with no signs of abuse.

As a condition for getting custody of Angel, Mr. Brown was required to attend a series of classes that prepare foster parents to handle hyperactive and emotional children.

As for Angel, she was excited at the prospect of going back to her sister and Mr. Brown. As much as she liked Kedren, there was nothing like a real home.

"I remember him coming to pick me up in a white van." She giggles and wiggles with excitement like a child. "And everything was good."

13

Vacation

❧

ANGEL was released from Kedren in time to celebrate her thirteenth birthday at home with Mr. Brown and her younger sister, Tametha. The freedom was heaven. At home she could say or do anything. Mr. Brown bought her almost anything she wanted, including the pink birthday cake she had always dreamed of. The gifts raised eyebrows in his family, but Mr. Brown claimed they were to make up for the trauma she had suffered over the past year.

To celebrate her return and bring the family closer together, he planned to take his two foster daughters to Walt Disney World, in Florida. This was forbidden under the terms of foster care. The children were not to be taken out of state. But he decided to risk it.

The trip would take all summer. He planned to drive through Texas and Mississippi, visiting relatives along the way.

Angel and her younger sister were beyond excitement. They chattered endlessly about the adventure. Inevitably, Mr. Brown's granddaughter heard about it and asked if her two sons, Mr. Brown's great-grandsons, could also go along. He agreed. He and the foster children got along well with the boys, who were their same ages. But then there was an argument. Mr. Brown asked his granddaughter for money to pay for the boys' food. "I was going to pay for gas and lodging from my pocket," Mr. Brown says, and use the state's foster care payments for the girls' food. "I didn't want to use their money for the boys."

His granddaughter refused to pay. Angel is still upset about it.

"They had money all the time," Angel says. "[The granddaughter's boyfriend] has new cars all the time. I wanted [the boys] to come. But Daddy [Mr. Brown] said no, because she won't pay."

Mr. Brown's granddaughter never forgave him.

She told her mother that Mr. Brown had simply refused to take his great-grandchildren with them. She also suggested to her mother that Mr. Brown wanted the girls alone to abuse them. Mr. Brown shakes his head at this accusation. "There was nothing sexual going on then," he says. Mr. Brown's daughter called the Department of Children and Family Services.

Two days after Mr. Brown returned from the trip, DCFS took Angel and her sister downtown for questioning.

"First they asked us, You went here? There? And we said, 'Yeah.' But we weren't supposed to be taken out of state. We should have lied but we didn't know better then," Angel says. "But we should have, because that's when they took me *and Tametha* out of the home. *My baby sister,*" she empha- sizes.

There were no foster homes with two placements available, so the sisters were separated.

"I was mad," Angel says. "I wanted to be with my sister. I didn't want her to be scared." So the first night back in DCFS custody, Angel went to find her sister. She ran—again.

14

Running Home

※

IT was dark on the street at night, and Angel realized that she had no way to find her sister. "So I went home," to Mr. Brown's house, in Compton, she says with a shrug. Angel found Mr. Brown in bed, with one of his daughters hovering over him. Shortly after she and Tametha were taken from his home, Mr. Brown had suffered a heart attack.

Mr. Brown's daughter and granddaughter were going to send Angel back, but Mr. Brown insisted they let her stay. For two weeks she slept on a cot just outside his room. She set her alarm clock every four hours to check on him and give him medicine.

"I'm what got Daddy well," Angel says proudly. "Everyone left but I stayed and I cooked and cleaned and gave him his medicine."

Mr. Brown nods. "She sure did," he agrees. "She was the only one to help me when I needed help."

That's when Angel learned to cook. Each morning she burnt eggs and bacon for him. They laugh now at some of her attempts, which filled the house with smoke and set off the fire alarms. Mr. Brown didn't believe in sticking to the doctor's diet, which pleased Angel because she says she had never seen some of the foods he was supposed to eat.

If the Department of Children and Family Services was searching for Angel, they never came to Brown's door. She did not go to school, but that was not unusual.

"Things were like normal," Angel says. "Until the jealousy started."

When Mr. Brown regained his strength, he thanked Angel with presents. He bought her an old cash register because she had always wanted one. She liked to play with money, real or fake. It kept her attention for three days, and then she sold it. Then there was a calculator and finally the piano.

The family believed Mr. Brown and Angel were sexually intimate. Both deny it, claiming they maintained strictly a father-daughter relationship. Even if they had been interested in each other, they say—and the doctor later concurred—Mr. Brown was too ill to have intercourse at the time. But when she is most angry at Mr. Brown, Angel alludes to times he touched her inappropriately when she first went to live with the family. When asked directly in calmer moments, however, she says he never acted inappropriately.

On top of the family recriminations, Mr. Brown became financially strapped.

"My first wife and I had taken a loan out to pay her mother's medical expenses. Then my wife got sick, and now there were my medical bills, too. The bank was threatening to foreclose on my house. I asked everyone who was staying in my home then to chip in $145. There was my granddaughter, and my daughter and grandson. And you know what happened? They moved out on me instead. Only Angel stayed on that little cot."

The relatives claim that they moved out because they were troubled by Angel and her relationship with Mr. Brown, not because they didn't want to pay the money. In any case, they gave no money to him and the bank gave him an eviction notice. At the same time, a family member tipped off the Department of Children and Family Services that Angel was living with Mr. Brown. The police came to the front door and asked for her. She hid in a closet until they left, but a few hours later, they caught her at the pinball arcade she frequented.

For the third time, she was taken back to MacLaren Hall.

"Prison," she calls it.

15
Crenshaw

✼

ANGEL knew the game at MacLaren this time around. She had learned it over her last three stays. This time she decided to play by the rules.

"They had recruiters come," she explains. "Like recruiters coming for basketball players. They pick out the kids they want to go to their group home. When recruiters came, I was on my best behavior," she says with a smile in her voice. Then a seriousness falls over her. "I just wanted out," she says.

Angel caught the eye of a woman who ran a group home in Crenshaw. When the woman interviewed her, Angel sat up straight, kept her hands from fidgeting by locking them together on the table before her, and spoke in her best TV English. She even threw in a few "ma'am's," which today she won't allow any of her children to use, because she says it's degrading. She wore little makeup and made little eye contact with the boys in the room. She stayed alert and happy, but not too energetic. She was honest with the facts that she knew were recorded in her files and finessed those that were not.

"Yes," she said, she had smoked a few times but was caught each time.

Yes, there are a lot of people she loves. All of them in her family.

Yes, she is very religious.

She smiled and played young, but not stupid. And she was picked right off the bat, in her very first interview.

But it did not turn out as well as she planned.

"I didn't like it [at that group home] because every night you had to go to a meeting," she says.

The Al-Anon meeting was required of all the girls. It was a group very much like Alcoholics Anonymous but dealt with dysfunctional families rather than alcoholism.

"It was like brainwashing. I didn't like it," she says.

So she called Mr. Brown.

"I said, 'Come get me, I want to go home,' " she says, giggling. "I told him, 'If you don't come get me, I'm leaving.' "

She pauses to look at Mr. Brown, smiling at the memory of her cunning.

"And *he* came and got me, him and Marlo, his daughter. They took me home."

The next day Angel was due in court for her probation update. She had been on probation since Maryvale.

"*He* took me to court," Angel says unforgivingly of Mr. Brown. "What happened? He took me and what happened?" she glares at him. "Tell her, Daddy."

Mr. Brown looks uncomfortable.

"They grabbed hold of her again," he says sheepishly.

"Like I told you they would," she says, hands hard on her hips. "Only this time it was worser, much worser, and you know why."

Mr. Brown turns away from her and searches the darkening sky.

16

MacLaren Once More

▓

Mr. Brown had expected to be thanked for keeping Angel off the streets and bringing her to court. He hoped he would be rewarded for his support of a wayward child by getting official custody of Angel. Instead, the judge sent Angel back to MacLaren and forbade Mr. Brown to see her. Angel knows why.

"They found out that he had come and got me every time I ran away from a foster home. They told him, Look, don't visit her, don't see her, nothing."

The court also took into consideration the accusations by Mr. Brown's granddaughter that he had molested Angel.

"I didn't have no evidence," his granddaughter says. "But he'd teach her to drive in these secluded areas where nobody could see."

Mr. Brown points out that it was the same place he had taught his two great-grandsons to drive.

The judge agreed with Angel's new social worker that the best course of action was the toughest one—to cut all ties to those who had helped her get out of trouble (as they saw it), or helped her in time of crisis (as Angel saw it). Angel's last social worker, Michael, had welcomed Mr. Brown's support for Angel. But Michael had taken a new job in Hawaii.

Suddenly Angel brings him back into her story. Michael has not yet left town when he phones her at MacLaren to say he has found another placement for her. He has stayed on an extra day to find the new placement.

"Why don't you tell what happened to you before that?" Mr. Brown asks Angel.

"What happened?" she asks, puzzled. And then she turns suddenly to glare at her husband.

"Oh, why do you always bring that stuff up?" She clenches her fists until her nails leave deep scarlet imprints on the palms of her hands. "Why? It makes me so mad!"

She takes a deep breath and rushes through the episode she omitted.

"One of the staff was messing with me," she says. "Kissing me, touching me. But the bad thing was, he was doing this with other girls around. Which was kind of sick. It made me feel ugly. And so I told what happened. The police came. The girls told, too. They had seen it. And other girls, too, he had messed with.

"The police separated all us girls up in different rooms. I heard these police officers say, 'Well, all these stories match.' They said, OK, we're going to file a report. But you know, I don't think they ever filed that report, because that rape was never in my files.

"I don't care, though. It's over with. But it just shows that whatever you say, whatever happens to you, no matter what, they don't hear you, they just think you lie."

It was the next night that Michael called her at MacLaren. "We just got in touch with your godmother," he said.

"What she want with me?" Angel asked skeptically.

"She wants to take you in her home. What do you think about that?"

"Okay," Angel told him in her casual, noncaring tone, when in fact her heart jumped. She was so excited she couldn't sleep.

Life at her godmother's did not turn out as well as Angel had hoped. Her godmother had another foster child, who was much younger than Angel, and Angel was jealous. And her godmother was strict. Angel interpreted her godmother's attempts to discipline her as plain "mean." After school, Angel was required to go the Veterans Administration office, where her godmother worked, to help her file and run errands. Angel saw these attempts to keep an eye on her as slave labor.

Her godmother had little faith in Angel's academic abilities. She recognized early on that Angel was street smart, if not intelligent. But she believed Angel could not settle down long enough to graduate from high school. Angel's best hope would be marriage to a stable man who would put up with her.

Angel, then thirteen, says her godmother began setting her up with men from work. They were older, but Angel could benefit from a father figure. She wasn't a virgin, after all. She had been raped at least twice.

"We got into a big mess," Angel says. "She wasn't treating me right, introducing me to friends of hers, just guys, which I still don't think was right. We kind of like went on dates, I guess you would call it. During work we'd go to the snack bar and get lunch or something to eat or whatever."

Sometimes the men would hold her hand. There was no kissing or sex involved, but looking back, Angel thinks the hand holding was inappropriate.

"Back then it was OK with her if it was OK with me," Angel says. "It wasn't like they was ugly or anything. They was cute." She giggles.

But Angel began to think of alternatives to life with her godmother and her male friends.

"The girls I hanged with would say, Why are you with them when you could do this or that?" she says. What she meant was, become a prostitute.

"I wanted to try it," she admits. "Even as a little kid I used to watch movies and see the glamour of the prostitutes and the things they got. I would say, I want to do this. And then listening to other people's mouths telling me I could do that. It would be cool." She giggles.

ANGEL loved the movie *Pretty Woman.* "Julia Roberts is who I wanted to be. I thought I'd go out there and hook Richard Gere. So I ran away from [my godmother's] house," she says.

On the street, her dream crashed into reality. But at night sometimes, Angel still imagines Richard Gere saving her.

17

Trouble

HOLLYWOOD'S Sunset Boulevard is far worse than her godmother's. As Angel stands on the corner, the glares of other hookers frighten her, and she hardly scares anymore. The guys pulling up in cars look nothing like Richard Gere.

A battered woman in tight leather comes up to her quickly. "You better run while you can, honey," she says. That is all Angel needs to get out.

She sees only one way out. Her mother is in jail again. Her sister Maria is in rehab.

"Daddy!" She calls Mr. Brown from a phone booth along the boulevard, the same corner from which Marilyn Monroe reportedly sold herself briefly.

"Daddy, I'm not going back."

"Angel, where are you?" he asks. She is crying by now. "I'll get help," he promises and hangs up.

Mr. Brown calls Angel's new social worker.

"I know where she is," he says.

"Who?" the social worker asks.

"Najuwa."

"Who's Najuwa?"

"Najuwa," Mr. Brown repeats. "She's been missing for a month; she's on your caseload."

"Hold on," the social worker says. Brown hears papers shuffled as the social worker checks through his files.

"Oh yeah," he mumbles into the phone. "Trouble."

"I know where to get her but you have to promise not to put her back in MacLaren Hall," Mr. Brown pleads.

"I can't do that. That's where she's supposed to be."

"No, she doesn't belong there. She's a good girl, at heart."

"Well, I can't do anything about it," the social worker says. "That's where she's supposed to be and that's where she'll go."

"She'll run away again," Brown warns.

"If she can," the social worker counters. "That's why she has to come to us. We can't keep going out to get her. We don't have that kind of time or resources."

"I'll bring her to you," Brown says.

"Mr. Brown," the social worker says firmly, "let me give you a piece of advice. If she wants to go and whore herself on the streets, that's her business. There's nothing we can do. If she wants help, she'll ask for it. Otherwise, we can't help her. We can't keep rounding her up. She'll just keep running away. Let her go. You should stay out of it. There's nothing going to help her now. Don't get sucked in. Let her go, she's already gone."

"What?" Brown demands, stunned. "I can't do that. She's my child."

"That's my advice," says the social worker matter-of-factly. "Bring her in if you want to, but my advice is, Stay away. She's a mess of trouble."

18

On the Lam

❖

Mr. Brown picked Angel up from Sunset Boulevard in the early morning hours. He intended to return her to MacLaren after breakfast, but he was beginning to believe that the foster care system was messing her up more each time.

"You gonna take me back to MacLaren?" she asked when they pulled onto an L.A. freeway.

"Yes."

"You really going to take me back there?" Her voice rose in panic.

"Yes. I have to or we'll both get in trouble and they'll never let you come back to me."

She sat quietly for a moment.

"Can you get my nails done first and buy me a new outfit?" she asked. "I want to go back looking good."

"I got her everything," Mr. Brown said later. "Clothes, nails, hair, the works. She cried the whole time."

When they finally headed for MacLaren, Angel cried hysterically.

"You gonna take me back after you know all that happened?" she challenged Mr. Brown. "You, Daddy, you gonna make me go back there? If you take me back there I'll tell them you raped me," she warned him, suddenly shifting gears from guilt to threats.

Exhausted from crying, Angel fell asleep in the car as Mr. Brown drove on toward MacLaren. Suddenly he caved in again and took off in a different direction.

"Let's go talk to your mom, because I don't know what to do," he told her when she awoke.

Linda Dillard was in a residential drug recovery program but she was permitted to go to the car to speak to them.

"I know MacLaren Hall," Dillard said. "I've been raped there, too." And after a moment, she added: "Just take her. Go. At least with you she's safe."

Angel was surprised.

"I'm like, OK. And he says OK. And that's what we do," she says. "We ran."

• • •

Two days after her godmother reported Angel missing, the Department of Children and Family Services called Mr. Brown. When they couldn't reach him, they suspected that he and Angel were together. Their disappearance seemed to confirm Mr. Brown's granddaughter's accusations that the two had a sexual relationship.

After a week, Children's Services notified Dillard, telling her they suspected Mr. Brown was intimate with Angel.

"I was so angry," she recalls now. "I didn't know that they were already messing around when I told him to go ahead and take her. When they [DCFS] told me that he had eyes for her, and she no more than just a child, I was furious. I wanted him castrated."

Mr. Brown rented a hotel room a few blocks from his house for Angel and himself because he was afraid DCFS would look for them. After a week they returned to his house. He expected the search for them was over, but it had just begun. No sooner had they gotten home than police cars arrived. Mr. Brown took Angel by the hand and they raced out the back door.

"They came to the house with dogs looking for me," Angel says with wide eyes and a creeping smile. "It was exciting. We was running, ducking, staying at hotels."

Mr. Brown decided that they would go to Vegas for a few days until the heat cooled. But rather than cooling, the situation burst into flames.

19
Sex

▒

It was in Las Vegas, when Angel was thirteen and Mr. Brown sixty-eight, that they admit to having sexual intercourse for the first time.

"I wanted to," Angel says. "He had been good to me, like my mom said. And he was my ticket out of MacLaren Hall and all the other places they put me through. He just said, 'Well, everyone thinks we're doing it anyway, so why don't we just do it?' "

In a separate interview, Mr. Brown shakes his head.

"It was a mistake I'll be punished for for the rest of my life," he says. "There

had been so many allegations that it was like, Jesus Christ, if everybody is
making allegations—what's that song? 'Let's give them something to talk
about'? It was a mess."

Angel and Mr. Brown agree it was a consensual act. Legally, however, it
was statutory rape.

"I was already an adult," Angel claims, brushing aside the law with a
shrug. "That time I was in MacLaren Hall, that made me an adult."

He bought her a fur coat, and the two returned to Los Angeles.

"That's when you got pregnant from that guy," Mr. Brown says.

"I didn't get pregnant from that guy. You're running it together." Angel's
tongue whips out the words. "I was pregnant in Vegas. I can remember a
few things I did."

Mr. Brown nods his head in agreement. The child, he claims now, is his.

"Yes, you were," he agrees. "She kept eating this soup. Soup, soup, soup,
soup, soup. She doesn't even like soup."

Angel nods too.

"It was tomatoes soup," she says. "I don't eat tomatoes. This soup was
made with tomatoes and I kept eating it. And this soup was like $7 and I ate
like six bowls. For some reason I just kept telling them just bring me more
soup. I guess that's a sign of pregnancy."

But there is also reason to doubt the child's paternity.

On their way back from Las Vegas, they stopped at a Best Western motel
because Mr. Brown suspected that Children and Family Services was still
searching for them. In the motel parking lot, several men stood smoking. Mr.
Brown thought they were drug dealers and told Angel to be careful. But
Angel liked the way one man looked at her. When she left Mr. Brown on the
excuse to get ice, she went to get a closer look at the man. She liked the way
he talked to her.

"He was saying how much he liked me, you know, 'Oh you're so cute'
and this and that. And I'm thinking, 'Oh wow,' cuz ain't nothing going on
between me and Daddy, yet—I mean serious."

The man invited Angel to go to the Jacuzzi with him.

Coincidentally, Angel says, she and Mr. Brown got into an argument that
night. Mr. Brown, unaware that she was going to meet anyone, did not want
her to go to the Jacuzzi alone, and Angel complained he wouldn't allow her
the space an adult should have.

So she went to the Jacuzzi for two minutes and then to the guy's room to
talk, she says. She spent the night.

In the morning Angel went back to her room to find Mr. Brown gone.
She says she wasn't upset in the least. In fact, she was more relieved than
anything.

"So he's gone," she recalls. "So I went to the guy and said, 'Well, he's
gone, I'm with you now,' and I'm thinking, What a great turn of events.

He's gone and I can stay here. It didn't turn out like that either," she says sadly.

ANGEL had breakfast with the new man. That evening, she says, things were still normal until he asked her a question that she says should have alerted her to trouble.

"Do you know what I do for a living?" he asked.

"Yeah," Angel said. She had seen a wad of $20 and $100 bills in a gym bag, so she was pretty sure of two things. First, that he was a drug dealer, and second, that she had stepped up in life.

"You're a drug dealer," she said.

"He said nope, and then he told me. I'm like, Oh God, not again."

The man was a pimp. And that night he brought two men to the room, who paid to have sex with her.

"Yeah, it was scary," Angel says. "It was. But I didn't want to call home this time and be a big crybaby and say, Come get me, guess what happened. I thought I could tough this out."

It wasn't rape, Angel says.

"No rape was going on," she says. "I had no choice, so I would rather give it away than be raped."

The next night her boyfriend/pimp took her to Sunset Boulevard.

"I ain't done nothing like that. I was real scared," she says. "I thought, What do I do? You see these cars coming and girls going up to them. But none were stopping. He slapped me and said, 'Go up to them.'

"Then I see these old pros out there," she continues. "Older women in their twenties, and I hung out with them, and they showed me. And when a bad one pulled over, they'd pull me away and tell them not to mess with me. They looked out for me, I don't know why."

IT's all a bad memory for Angel, but one that she doesn't try to hide. In fact, every once in a while she asks Mr. Brown to take her down to Sunset Boulevard at night, just to drive by and look.

"When I look I can see those women out there, and I feel so sorry for them. Now I understand," she says. "They go through hell. I only stayed there for three days and I can't believe I survived."

While her pimp was busy beating up another girl who stole some money, Angel ran into a phone booth.

"But he seen me using the phone and he pulled me into the alley and jumped me. I was beat up pretty bad."

Before Mr. Brown could find Angel, the pimp moved her to another hotel.

• • •

WHAT Angel didn't know was that from the first night she disappeared to the Jacuzzi, Mr. Brown had been looking for her. A man in the lobby had pulled him aside and told him Angel was with a pimp.

"I went right home to find my shotgun," Mr. Brown says. "And I came back. I'm glad I didn't find him when I got back that time."

Mr. Brown was carrying his shotgun and searching hotel lobbies during the day. The second call he got from Angel was from jail.

"I got arrested that night and I was so happy because I knew I could go home now. I could escape now," Angel says, her face lighting up. "The first thing I did was call him. I was so happy."

Angel was put on probation. The court did not know she was only fourteen or running from the Department of Children and Family Services. She showed the police the fabricated identity card the pimp had given her.

The pimp traced Angel on the court docket by the fake name. After the proceeding, he stood across the street waiting for her.

"He thought I was going home to him," Angel says. "I just laughed in his face. Dying was better than going back to him. Dying a hundred thousand times!"

20

Dynasty

"THAT'S about the time I decided to get my act together," Angel says.

The first thing she did was change her name, unofficially, from Najuwa Holts to Angel Jackson. She chose Angel because she wanted to be good, and she liked the name. And she chose Jackson because Mr. Brown's last name was originally Jackson. When he was adopted as a child by his aunt and her husband, he took their surname of Brown.

She believes she became a new person with the name change. She shed the bad Najuwa. But when things don't go her way and she feels used and powerless, she slips back to being the old Najuwa—a child she describes as wild and bad. When she's depressed, she calls herself Najuwa, as she did in a suicide note she wrote a year after her own children were placed in foster care.

Soon after she became Angel, she and Mr. Brown checked into the Dynasty Motel near the apartment where they now live. A few weeks later, Angel knew something was wrong. She began feeling queasy. She threw up after every meal. She was hungry all the time. Her ankles and tummy were swelling.

Mr. Brown bought a home pregnancy test.

"I thought I was going to die," Angel says. "It was supposed to turn pink if you're pregnant and it turned purple. We kept doing that test over and over again. I was like, This couldn't be right."

It was. She was in fact pregnant.

They resolved to stay in the hotel at least until Angel gave birth. But as her belly swelled, Angel grew more ill. She suffered bouts of nausea and cramps. She felt something pulling at her insides.

Mr. Brown was afraid to take Angel to a doctor. He hoped the baby could be delivered with the help of a family friend, a woman who was not a midwife but helped out in such situations. On her first examination of Angel, the woman said something was wrong and a child like Angel needed a doctor. But they refused. They believed the DCFS had alerted hospitals in the area since an overwhelming number of runaways, particularly girls, wind up the victims of violent crime.

The last day they spent at the Dynasty, Angel threw up four times, the last time spewing watermelon and red Kool-Aid all over the room. Mr. Brown was at his wits' end.

"You know what," he told Angel. "Let's just go home and get a doctor."

But Angel was afraid. She was afraid that she would get in trouble and Mr. Brown would go to jail. And she was afraid DCFS would take her baby from her when it was born. She dreaded the disapproval of outsiders, particularly doctors, nurses, and social workers.

"I couldn't stand their faces looking at me," Angel says. "I imagined how it would be, and I knew the faces. They'd look at me like I was bad or disgusting, or stupid. I didn't want to deal with that. But then I was sick, very sick, and I didn't care about nothing then."

Mr. Brown found Angel a doctor and rented an apartment nearby. They narrowly escaped being caught again at the house by police, who still sought her for crippling the woman counselor. Her discomfort turned out to be due to her pregnancy, one she believes was difficult but the doctor concluded was normal.

When she was eight and a half months pregnant, Angel had sharp pains she believed were contractions. But at the hospital, a doctor said she was not yet in labor and sent her home to rest. Back in their apartment, however, she collapsed on the kitchen floor. Mr. Brown rushed out to borrow $2 from a friend for gas. By the time they reached the hospital, Angel was in screaming labor.

"It happened pretty quick so I don't remember much," Angel says. "Except that they were mean. They kept asking me questions even in the operating room. They said they were going to have to cut me open and give me a cesarean. One nurse said, 'That's what happens when little girls like you have babies. We have to cut you open so you don't do it again. You're not ready yet.'

"And then another nurse went and named my baby before I woke up. I was so mad." Angel shifts in her seat. "When she brought the baby to me, she said, 'Here's your baby, Angelica.' I was so mad. I wanted to name my baby."

Angel did not realize that the child is not formally named until a name is recorded on the birth certificate. She believes that once the nurse called her daughter Angelica, that had to be her name. Nor did she think that perhaps the nurse may simply have gotten her own name wrong and said: "Angelica, here's your baby."

Mr. Brown posed as Angel's father, and she was released to him a few days later.

Angel remembers the next several weeks blissfully.

"We was getting along great," she said. "He kept asking me to marry him before Angelica was born but I wouldn't because, I don't know, I just wouldn't. Now I thought I would. We went to Las Vegas again. But at the last minute I got scared and wouldn't marry him."

Two more happy months passed before Angel's mother found them.

Angel and Mr. Brown were sitting in their living room watching a game show when she saw her mother and oldest sister walk by their open window.

"She was going around to all the neighbors and showing my picture like I'm a fugitive," Angel remembers. "So before she got to the manager we stuck Angelica in the bedroom and went out for her."

Angel and her mom and sister hugged and kissed. But then suddenly Angel started crying. She couldn't stop.

" 'Mom,' I said. 'You go in the bedroom, there's something I got to show you.' She's like, 'What?' I said, 'Just go.' And so she go in there and I was nervous. She said, 'Maria, come in here and look, it's a baby!' They asked whose baby I was baby-sitting, and I couldn't lie. I said it was mine."

Angel was happily shocked by their reaction. Her mother's face lit up with a smile she had never before seen.

"You just had a baby?" her mother asked, incredulous. "Why don't you got no socks on?"

Angel's sister and her boyfriend immediately went to get a congratulations card and some socks.

"Everybody was being real wonderful," Angel says with a proud smile. "I was someone. I didn't know you could get so much respect just for having a baby. So I guess maybe that's part of why I had more and more and more."

21

Emancipation

SHORTLY after the reunion, Angel's mother received a letter from the Department of Children and Family Services. She read it, and then immediately ran to Angel and Mr. Brown's apartment.

"It said, 'Dear Mrs. Dillard: Regarding Najuwa Holts,' " Angel recalls, squirming and wriggling with excitment.

"It said, 'We heard that she's with Mr. Brown. We cannot keep up with her and we really don't care anymore what happens to her. If you find her, she's yours. But we know she's OK, because we know she's with Mr. Brown. And' "—she draws out a long, happy breath—" 'from this time on we have nothing more to do with her and we release her in your custody.' "

Angel squeals and jumps, clapping her hands like a cheerleader.

"I think that was the most happiest day of my life," she says. "You know, it was like, I'm *free*. Yes!! Just like being released from jail. It was like walking through the gates of a jail door and having it clink behind you."

But then Angel lowers her head as she thinks about her children, who are now in foster care. She believes they are there because of her. Their future, she says, is held hostage by her past.

"They knew they couldn't punish me for what I did so they punishing my kids," she says of DCFS. "But I'd rather my kids be home with Daddy and they take me and do what they want to. At least I know that my kids are OK at home. I know what it's like out there with Children's Services. The kids ain't safe from nothing.

"When I go to court tomorrow," she says, her hands forming fists of resolve, "I'm going to get them back. I don't care how. I don't care what I say, if I'm supposed to or not. I'm going to, that's all."

Angel and Mr. Brown are to go to court for their third custody hearing in the seven months since their children were taken into foster care. All day Angel flutters about nervously while Mr. Brown sits solid and morose. Her emotions ping-pong from elation to tears.

"I'm nervous," she concedes. "I'm scared to death. I don't know what's going to happen. The first time I went to court I tried playing by their rules. I got a parent's certificate. I went to group [therapy]. I did everything they said. But this time, if it don't work out, I'm not going to be the nice person that I was. It's time for me to set my own rules and play by them. Because the judge know how I am because he wouldn't have made a statement in court the way he did," she says, her voice shaking with tears.

"He looked at me, when they took us to court. It was supposed to be about the kids. It was not about the kids at all. It was about me. The Department of Children and Family Services said, like, 'Let me show you her record, Your Honor. I would really like you to read her record.' And the judge said, 'We're not dealing with the minor right now, we're dealing with her kids.' They [the state] took out my file anyway, and it was thick.

"It was minor this, minor that. I said to the judge, 'Look, haven't you looked at the statistics today? There are a lot of teen pregnancies out there. Them are single moms. They don't have no money, no husbands. The father might be gone. They're on welfare. They're living with their mom. They ain't got no mom. They ain't going to school. Yeah, I'm a teenage mom, but you have to look at the difference. I got a husband. I'm not on welfare. My kids are well taken care of. We have our own place.'

"At that time we had two cars. I mean, so everything was going good for me. I'm not like a normal teenage mom. But they kept bringing up minor, minor. That ain't got nothing to do with it. It's about revenge because they could never catch up with me, never."

22

Married

ANGEL thought that her emancipation from the foster care system meant that she could start with a clean slate. She even imagined her bulging files being pulled from a black, dusty, morguelike cabinet and burned to ashes. Her past would be gone. She didn't realize that those files were not destroyed and would be used against her when she sought to regain custody of her children. While her children's social worker and the state's lawyers see her unstable past, volatile nature, and often irresponsible behavior as a cause not to trust her with her own children, Angel replies simply that it was the past. It bothers Angel to think of a file with her name on it now that she's seventeen years old and not a dependent of the state. She asks what right the state has to keep her life on paper, as if she still belonged to them.

"For a long time I tried just to fix it," she says, still not understanding the foster care system. "I did the right things and acted the right way, but they never put that down. The only thing we did right in the court's eyes was get married," she says. "But then at the time that weren't right either."

Eleven months after Angelica was born, Angel gave birth to Marrion Jr., or Squeak, as she calls him because he cries like a squeaking door. Almost immediately after that, she was pregnant with her third baby, Francina.

"I thought Angelica was so much fun we might as well keep having them because it could only get funner," Angel says.

Angel and Mr. Brown were doing well and for the first time Angel was thinking about the future—still not hers but her children's. She wanted them to have the daddy she never had.

"I was two months pregnant with Francina and I said, 'Well c'mon, we'll get married. Might as well. You put up with me this long and we're damn near married.' I thought we should do it while the kids are babies, too. They don't have to know that we weren't married when they were born. All they have to know is that they grew up with a mommy and a daddy. I would lie so I could say to them, 'Don't have babies until you're married.' "

The only hitch was that Angel was still too young to get legally married, even in Las Vegas.

So Angel and Mr. Brown went to Linda Dillard to ask for written permission to marry. Dillard was in yet another drug rehab program at the time. As before, she was allowed to leave the building and sit in the car with Angel and Mr. Brown for fifteen minutes.

"I looked at them and thought, No way," Dillard explained later. "But then I thought, I wasn't there as a mother. The best I could do for my daughter was be a friend. And I thought, At least he'll keep her safe and maybe teach her some things."

"You know what?" she told her daughter after a moment. "He's good for you. He's the only one to take care of you real well. Young guys out here only want sex."

So she wrote out permission for her fourteen-year-old daughter to marry and had a counselor sign as a witness.

In bubbling letters a little more uniform than her daughter's, she wrote:

To whom it may concern:
  I give my permission for my daughter, Najuwa Holts, to marry Marrion Brown.
I wish them a happy and restful life together. Go in peace.

> Your loving mother,
> Linda Dillard

Angel cried when she read her mother's letter. And she cried all the way to Las Vegas. In her heart, she wasn't sure she wanted to marry Mr. Brown. She wanted security, but he was so old. To make her smile, Mr. Brown promised to spend as much money as she wanted on the wedding. He wore the same black suit he had worn to his first wife's funeral and paid a $200 package for the chapel, the minister, the photographer, and the limo.

Angel bought a $400 white wedding gown glittering with sequins and pearls. It was size ten and Angel is a size four, so she had to pay $200 more to have it altered. Then there was the $200 veil, the $100 or so at the beauty salon to braid her hair, and $50 for a manicure of cotton-candy pink long nails embedded with sequins and pearls.

"Oooh, they was so pretty," Angel says, leafing through her photo album. "It's the only time I had my nails anything but red."

A child engulfed in a wedding gown smiles out from the picture. She stands, flirting with the camera, as her husband kneels, gazing up at her. Behind them, a fake waterfall stands still.

"It was like a fairy tale," Angel says with a smile captured from the past.

23

Married Life

▓

Angel and Mr. Brown were so busy with their children that they had little time to be unhappy. When they weren't changing diapers, feeding the children, or taking them to doctors, they talked about what profession the children would join when they grew up. Angel is certain she knows, as certain as she knows their personalities now. Angelica will be a power lawyer because already she can talk back in a smart way. Squeak will be an architect, because he won't fight anyone. His younger sister, Francina, even has to protect him from bullying youngsters. Francina will be an accountant, because she has a mean streak. And Roger, the baby, will be a quarterback for the Broncos because he's the biggest. Even now Angel and Mr. Brown light up when they tell stories of their children—how Angelica is so much in love with Dylan on *Beverly Hills 90210* that she will sit still only when he is on TV; how Squeak giggles and lets his younger sister, Francina, push him around; and how Francina rules the play. Roger, only a bundle of yawns and cries at a few months old, also has his story.

Roger was born at 1 A.M. on January 13, 1994, delivered via Angel's fourth cesarean. Several times before her labor, the doctor asked Angel if she wanted to stop having babies after this one.

"No," Angel said.

"It wouldn't be a problem," the doctor urged. "We'll be right in there anyway. Medicaid will gladly pay for it."

"No," Angel told him again as she was wheeled into the operating room. "No."

The last thing she remembers before her baby was born was the pissed-off look on the doctor's face.

It took four staples to clamp Angel together after Roger's birth. It was no big deal for Angel. But before dawn four days later, she awoke suddenly to a slight tremble. Before she knew it, she had climbed over her sleeping husband, grabbed her newborn from the crib, and was standing in the door frame.

The tremble grew into a powerful shaking as Mr. Brown reached their other children. Angel curled into a ball in the door frame, now terrified. Pictures fell from the wall, the crib slid across the room, furniture fell into awkward angles. Angel prayed that the earthquake would be over soon, and that if it wasn't, someone would save her baby.

"Take anyone, God," she heard herself say. "Take anyone but my baby and me."

The sound of a landslide came from the bathroom. She was sure the roof was caving in. She cradled the baby, so small and frightened, to protect it.

"Take me, God," she now heard herself saying. "Save my baby but take me."

She closed her eyes tight and put one hand over the baby's eyes so that neither of them could see what would happen next.

A few moments later the earth settled. Angel drew a breath and opened her eyes.

Mr. Brown gasped when he saw his wife. "Look," he said, aghast. "Look at yourself."

She was spurting blood. The baby's white blankets were soaked in red. She unwrapped him, terrified that he was hurt. She held him above her shoulders, looking him over thoroughly. Not a scratch. Then she remembered she was not supposed to lift her arms like that. She was not supposed to even get out of bed. And it was from the bed that the trail of blood began. She howled in the pain she expected she was feeling but didn't. The staples were hanging open from her belly. Mr. Brown rushed her back to the hospital, calling on a neighbor to look after the children.

She was young, they told Mr. Brown; she'd be fine. And as it turned out, like the other births, the incident hardly left its mark on Angel's young body.

Mr. Brown catered to Angel now more than ever. He treated her both as a wife and a favorite child. "Daddy!" she would call to him shrilly, to polish her shoes or find her curlers or fetch some tea or cocoa. And he jumped like an eager or fearful dog.

But she soon had her restless moments again. Angel had periods when, as Mr. Brown puts it, "she had to go do her thing." Her thing was visiting nightclubs, dancing, flirting, running wild, and often winding up in another man or woman's bed.

Mr. Brown would get angry, but there was little he could do. Angel was impatient with the restraints he tried to put on her. "Treating me like a baby." She sneers. "Like a child. I want my freedom, I'm seventeen now."

Mr. Brown continued to be confused about his role. "I didn't marry her because she's young and pretty so she would be some kind of trophy," he says. "I married her to keep her off the streets, so that I could take care of her."

Their relationship is difficult and often disturbing to watch. Not even they can explain it. Angel calls Mr. Brown Daddy, except in court. She is careful not to call him anything at all in court.

"The courts don't understand," Mr. Brown says. "They think I'm some kind of pervert because I married a wife so young, and then there's that thing about me being her foster father. But God in heaven knows I'm no pervert. I wouldn't touch my kids for anything in the world. Anyone who knows me knows that," he insists.

24

Talk Shows

▩

Mr. Brown attempted to bring Angel's family back together. But he now regrets those attempts. Angel gave her mother their phone card number in case she was in trouble on the streets and needed help. She used it twice to call Angel, once to ask about her and her grandchildren, the second time to ask for money. But when the phone bill arrived, the Browns owed over $5,000. They could not pay even a fraction of it, so the phone company cut off service. Dillard had been selling their number for money, all of which she spent before Mr. Brown found her. Several of the calls had been made to psychic hot lines and expensive party lines and dating services, however. Angel denies making all of those calls, but she admits to some. For almost a year, their phone was cut off.

At Mr. Brown's urging, Angel grew close to her second-oldest sister, Latachee. They spoke several times a day, mostly about soap operas and talk shows. But that also had catastrophic consequences.

"You know you could be on one of those talk shows," Latachee told Angel one day.

"You think so?" Angel asked, pleased.

"Yeah, you could," her sister told her. "A fourteen-year-old marrying a sixty-nine-year-old? Yeah. I mean, and now seventeen and seventy-three. You could do it. You could be on national TV."

Latachee phoned several talk shows. *The Jerry Springer Show,* based in Chicago, called her back. The producer wanted to talk to Angel.

Springer was interested in doing a show on older men marrying younger girls, the producer said. They wanted Angel, her husband, her mother, and her children to appear.

Latachee was furious. She wanted to be on TV, too. She had made the calls, she fumed; without her there would be no show. But the producer bluntly told Angel there was not enough room.

Latachee, it seems, would make room.

25

Mother's Day

MOTHER'S Day 1994. Angel remembers it more clearly than any other. The exact tint of the baby blue sky, the feel of the light air, the smell of her baby's diaper. Most of all, the knock at her front door in Compton and two plainclothes child protective service workers with grim faces. She thought, at first, that the Department of Children and Family Services had finally caught up with her and her husband, Mr. Brown. Probably they had forgotten that, since her marriage at age fourteen, she had been emancipated from the system. Now with four children of her own and a three-year marriage behind her, she felt safe.

"We weren't even on welfare," she says, believing welfare recipients are under exceptional scrutiny by the state. Angel feels the welfare provided by Aid to Families with Dependent Children carries stigma and disgrace. But mostly she objects to the intrusive power of the state over its recipients.

"Could I speak with your children?" one of the men asked.

"Sure," Angel said. She was in a good mood, with nothing to hide.

They gathered the four children in the single bedroom. Aside from the bathroom, the bedroom is the only room in the apartment with a door. The narrow kitchen opens into a small dining area with a round table and four chairs, and forms part of the L-shaped living room. Two cheerful, shining cribs, one white and the other cherry wood, liven the brown-and-gray main room. Pastel circus animals dangle happily over them.

Four small kids meant the apartment was in disarray almost all the time. But it was always clean. Mr. Brown insisted on it. Angel had spent the morning tidying up, and she was proud of her work. Eager to show off her neat apartment and clean children, she was almost happy they knocked on her door.

But they had not come to look for neglect. They came to investigate a report of abuse. Angel's eyes swept over the children with a smile. They wouldn't find a mark on them, she knew. Neither Angel nor Mr. Brown believes in spanking, particularly under the age of eight.

The men took the children into the bedroom and closed the door behind them. They stayed a long time. Angel became anxious. She started pacing the floor, wondering what was going on. Listening at the door, she heard them ask her eldest child, four-year-old Angelica, about her Daddy.

Just then, Mr. Brown walked in with a smile, a huge bouquet of flowers, and a brand new Gloria Vanderbilt watch—Angel's Mother's Day booty.

One look at Angel and his smile melted to confusion.

She marched up to him, arms folded, and looked him long and deep in the eye. Then she took the flowers, threw them on the floor, grabbed the watch, and did the same.

"I was just like, I didn't want it," she recalls, mumbling like an angry and pouting child. "I was mad at everyone because something was wrong."

When the social workers came out of the bedroom, the children were quiet, even solemn, until two-year-old Squeak saw his father, squeezed between the two men, and ran to him.

Angel stood with folded arms. She felt Najuwa's attitude returning and she couldn't stop it seeping across her face, setting her mouth in an angry pout and her eyebrows in a stormy frown.

One of the men addressed Angel without looking at her.

"I got to call in and ask them what to do here," he said. Angel didn't offer her phone. He went outside to find a pay phone. He returned fifteen minutes later.

"I got to go back to my office," he told Angel.

Angel shakes her head at the memory.

"I knew something was up then," she says. "I knew something was going to happen."

An hour later, police arrived with a child protective services worker. Again they gathered the children in the bedroom and the social worker quietly explained to the children that they were going away where no one would hurt them. It would all be OK, he said.

Mr. Brown tried to explain to the police how absurd the situation was.

"Children will say anything depending on your tone," he says now. "So I said, 'Squeak, does Daddy take glass and grind it up real good every morning and put it in your cornflakes every morning?' And Squeak said, 'Yep!' Just like that."

But the workers ignored Mr. Brown's attempts to show it was meaningless to question a two-year-old and continued to collect the children's clothing and some toys. Mr. Brown tried to remain calm, knowing that would be best for the children. He didn't realize that his effort to show absurdity about ground glass in cornflakes would appear in the children's files.

When a policewoman picked up three-month-old Roger, Angel showed more attitude. In response, the policewoman was brusque. Angel, too, would be going down to the Department of Children and Family Services, the woman told her.

"The policewoman was being all evil," Angel says. "I was being nasty to her because I didn't like the way she was acting." She abruptly turns away from the memory, still bristling.

Angel has never been able to play the system. She fights openly and sometimes viciously. She makes little attempt to charm or explain. Instead, her energy falls to harsh anger, retaliating at every slight or offense. Mr. Brown, for years a foster father, attempts to appease and accept. While not admitting fault, he recognizes that acquiescing can be the easiest way out of a bad situation. He calls it "playing their game."

Angel still bristles at the thought of child protective services workers taking her as well as her children into foster care.

"They was going to put me in a foster home too because I was under eighteen," Angel says, hands on her hips. "Yeah, they took me downtown, too. I was like, Oh God! They's taking me. I was packing my stuff up. But see, they knew, they knew they couldn't do nothing."

But they could have. Angel very well could have been put back into foster care. Only the note that Angel's mother had signed, giving her permission to marry, could be used to keep her from being returned to the system.

With Angel's fury rising and the children bursting into confused tears, Mr. Brown began to get frightened for the first time he could remember since World War II.

"When they took all of them, I felt that my whole life was chopped. I said, Jesus Christ, what am I going to do? This is my life. They're taking my life away from me," he remembers.

Angel's anger kept her from falling apart. She knew how to keep herself together by believing she could cope with the system if not beat it altogether. She knew, also, how to keep cool until she saw a chance to run. And run she would, she knew, if necessary to escape. Because Angel was also a minor, the child protective services worker called to the case required her to go downtown. They would give Angel the option of being placed in a foster home with her children. But Angel refused vehemently.

The children were bewildered when they were put in a car downtown and separated from their mother. Angel stood on the pavement trying to smile bravely to her children as she waved to them good-bye. "Angelica turned in her seat and looked at me. She suddenly looked so much older right then," Angel says. "I swear sometimes I look at Angelica now and she looks old, really old. She said 'Mommy?'—like that, a question—then 'Mommy!' And I saw her starting to cry when I waved.

"I was mad," Angel continues. "I was real mad. I was like that evil person who I was when I was growing up, and I was about to turn back into that person. That bad Najuwa. I thought I did all of this for nothing. Being good don't get me nowhere.

"I was so mad I thought I was going to go crazy," Angel continues. "I cried and I called my Mom at Latachee's and I told her what happened. And all she said was, 'Oh, un-huh.' I look at that now and I think she knew. She knew before it happened. Like if she caused it."

Linda Dillard, Angel's mother, did know in advance. Several days before, Mr. Brown and Angel had collected her from the streets to give her a few days' respite in their home. Angel slept over at a friend's apartment for a few nights, she says; in fact, she was out on a tear, "doing her thing." At home, her mother watched Mr. Brown apply a salve to his eldest daughter.

The salve was prescribed by doctors two weeks before, after a routine preschool examination. The doctor discovered that Angelica's vagina was closed. He told Mr. Brown and Angel that he could perform surgery, or they could apply a salve every night, to gradually open the vagina. He recommended the latter, and the parents agreed. Usually Angel applied the medicine, but now Mr. Brown rubbed it on, with Dillard watching.

Dillard told one of her older daughters, and the daughter convinced her mother that the medicine was an excuse Mr. Brown used to fondle Angelica. They had never been persuaded that he had not abused Angel years earlier. Dillard believes her daughter called the authorities. Angel and Mr. Brown believe that Latachee made the call. But Latachee denies it.

"I didn't think they were doing anything bad," Dillard says. "But my daughter said I'd be a bad grandmother if I didn't report what I saw. So I told them about it, medicine and all. I didn't expect they'd just focus on the touching part and not even ask about the medicine. Now that I think back on it, I realize that my daughter had her reasons too. She wanted to be on *The Jerry Springer Show* and she knew that when the authorities would take them kids away, there'd be room for her on TV."

Angel and Mr. Brown are quiet for several minutes at the end of that Mother's Day story.

Had the protective service workers explained the basis of their visit, Mr. Brown says he could have shown them the salve right there on the spot. The doctor would have confirmed it and the nightmare would have ended before it began. But once the children entered the system, it was too late. They were all caught now in a huge web.

"I've been through hell in my lifetime," Angel says after a long silence. "I've been in both sides. Child in the system, now with children in the system. I refuse to let my children go through what I went through. When you go through foster care system, you don't want to trust no one. You don't want to get close to no one. They mess with your head.

"Angelica was already afraid of cops because of the program *Cops* on TV." She laughs like a child. "I let them watch because my kids are not the type of kids that sit and watch *Sesame Street* and things like that. They wouldn't watch it. I tried it. They liked *Married with Children, Cops,* and Angelica loves *Days of Our Lives,* too, and *Beverly Hills 90210.* I thought, Oh well, they got to learn it sooner or later. They like to watch those shows and they the most goodest kids when you set them in front of *Beverly Hills 90210.* Angelica just loves Dylan."

What effect the removal will have on the children is impossible to know now. Children as young as four and a half who are taken from their parents into foster care remember the trauma. Many believe that they were kidnapped and that they were in part responsible for their kidnapping. Most recall believing it was a form of punishment for something they had done. Others, even those who say they were abused by their parents, fault themselves for not protecting their parents from the authorities, even if that meant hiding the truth. None of the children that I interviewed felt relieved when they were taken from their homes, despite the abuse they suffered.

One fourteen-year-old in Washington, D.C., who had been beaten regularly by her drug-addicted mother and father until the age of nine, as well as sexually abused by her uncle, who was living with her family, told me that more than anything she still wanted to be reunited with her family and to go home.

"Whatever anyone says, they're still your parents," she said one cold day over hot chocolate. "They're still all you got. With them at least you can pretend in your head that someone cares. But out alone in some strangers' home or group home, you know no one loves you and that you did something to be taken away. You know you're no good. You're a throwaway."

26
Charges

▓

ONE week after the children are taken, Angel and Mr. Brown are informed of the charges against them.

COUNT I: ON OR ABOUT MAY 4, 1994 AND ON PRIOR OCCASIONS, MINOR ANGELICA'S FATHER MARRION BROWN INAPPROPRIATELY SEXUALLY TOUCHED MINOR ANGELICA. FURTHER, MINOR'S MOTHER WAS UNABLE TO TAKE ACTION TO PROTECT MINOR . . . THE INAPPROPRIATE SEXUAL TOUCHING OF ANGELICA PUTS MINORS MARRION, FRANCIENA AND ROGER AT RISK OF THE SAME.

The charges are stated in clear bold capital letters on the first of a nine-page social worker's judicial review report. The first count was as shocking to Mr. Brown as the second.

COUNT II: ON OR ABOUT MAY 4, 1994 AND ON NUMEROUS PRIOR OCCASIONS ANGELICA'S MOTHER AND FATHER INAPPROPRIATELY PHYSICALLY DISCIPLINED MINOR. SAID PUNISHMENT WAS EXCESSIVE AND CAUSED MINOR UNREASONABLE PAIN AND SUFFERING. FURTHER, THE PHYSICAL ABUSE OF MINOR ANGELICA ENDANGER THE PHYSICAL AND/OR EMOTIONAL HEALTH OF MINORS FRANCIENA, ROGER AND MARRION AND PLACES MINORS AT RISK OF SEVER [sic] HARM.

Mr. Brown is confused, embarrassed, and frightened when he reads the charges. He has taken care of abused and neglected children, and now he is accused of being an abuser. More than most people, he knows that it will require years of effort to retrieve his children from the clogged court system, even if he can prove the charges are false.

The charges go on to contend that the children are at risk of SERIOUS PHYSICAL HARM INFLICTED NON-ACCIDENTALLY . . . BY THE MINORS' PARENTS, and further, that the children are inadequately supervised by their parents. The final accusation claimed that THE MINOR ANGELICA HAS BEEN SEXUALLY ABUSED, AND/OR THERE IS A SUBSTANTIAL RISK THAT THE MINORS MARRION, FRANCIENA AND ROGER WILL BE SEXUALLY ABUSED.

After looking at the files, Mr. Brown's lawyer first recommends that he plead guilty. Mr. Brown refuses. He insists he is innocent. It was the medicine, he tells his lawyer.

Mr. Brown's lawyer shakes her head.

"Look," she says, "the best you could do right now is plead guilty and then do what the court tells you to do to get your kids back. If you don't, they'll probably find you guilty anyway, and then if we appeal it, your whole past with marrying your foster daughter will come out and you'll almost definitely lose custody of your children."

Mr. Brown thinks for a moment.

"No," he says. "I didn't do anything wrong and I don't want my kids ever thinking I did any wrong to them. I'll do whatever the court wants me to do, but I won't say I did what they say I did."

In a compromise, Mr. Brown agrees to plead no contest. With this plea, he doesn't have to admit guilt and, he believes, they can move onto the critical issue of getting his kids back home. Several times in the files, his disclaimer is recorded:

> FATHER, MARRION BROWN, DISAGREES WITH DCS CASE PLAN. HE STATES THAT HE DIDN'T
> ABUSE HIS CHILDREN. FURTHER, HE STATES THAT HE PARTICIPATES IN COUNSELING BECAUSE
> OF COURT ORDERS.

Angel's lawyer has different advice for her client: leave Mr. Brown. If she does, she will immediately get her children back.

"No," Angel replies. "He didn't do nothing. He's a good father."

The wheels of the system grind on.

L.A. County Family Court, Room 416-26

When the bailiff calls the Browns, Angel is first to jump up. She tosses a plait of her long, woven black hair over her shoulder and marches ahead of her husband in angry, exaggerated dignity. She hardly falters in the high white heels that Mr. Brown polished for her that morning. Her attitude attracts attention, and her sexy walk particularly attracts men's eyes, including the bailiff's. She wears a loose white shirt above stretch pants that flatter her flat stomach, tight thighs, and slim calves.

"Is that the kid or the mother?" a woman whispers to her husband.

Mr. Brown quickly dabs sweat and hair grease from his forehead with a white handkerchief and pushes it, still folded, back into his suit pocket. He follows Angel through the door, head down, as if expecting the worst.

Room 416 is filled with the same faces that will gather four more times over the next year for this case. Judge Garcia sits on a raised bench, hunched over but still imposing with his stern demeanor. Facing him to his far right is a lawyer representing the children and another from the Department of Children and Family Services, as well as the children's social worker. Directly in front are Mr. Brown's lawyer, Mr. Brown, Angel, and Angel's lawyer. To the rear are a half dozen attorneys, whose clients are to appear later; they are busy writing out their coming presentations on long legal pads and flit in and out of the room between cases. Each proceeding takes only five to ten minutes.

On a scrap of paper, Angel has prepared all she wants to tell the judge. Mr. Brown has rehearsed his statement a thousand times in his head. Neither gets a chance to say a word except "Yes, Your Honor, I understand." The lawyers speak for them.

The judge has largely agreed on the outcome with the lawyers and social workers before Angel and Mr. Brown appear before him. After listening to the lawyers' presentations, the judge cuts in.

"So the perpetrator accepts guilt," he asks, looking at Mr. Brown.

Mr. Brown sits unmoving, realizing that in the eyes of the court, no contest looks like a guilty plea.

"You understand the charges?" the judge asks Mr. Brown directly.

Mr. Brown nods.

"This is a heinous act you've committed," the judge says severely. "I have to tell you that it's one of the ugliest acts that comes to this court."

Mr. Brown shows none of the fury and anguish inside him. His posture hardly twitches at the judge's condemnation. Instead he tries not to let the words enter his ears. But they do and they haunt him long afterward.

"I have to say, Mr. Brown," the judge concludes, "that there is little chance that you will regain custody of your children. You must complete all the programs that are ordered and you must pass several evaluations."

Then he turns to Angel.

"You too will have to take some classes and counseling," he orders. "Then we can think about placing your children back in your care."

Mr. Brown is distressed but determined to complete the programs as assigned. Angel is happy. Her impression is that if she completes the programs, her children will come home. All she has to do is attend some parenting classes and sexual abuse counseling and get some psychotherapy. Under supervision, she and Mr. Brown will be allowed to visit the children once a week.

The judge also imposes some basic conditions: that the parents keep DCFS advised of their address and telephone number at all times; that they sign forms necessary to release information to DCFS on court-ordered counseling and the minors' medical and educational needs; that no visits from the parents be allowed if they are under the influence of drugs or alcohol; and that the parents cooperate with DCFS in determining their ability to reimburse L.A. County for expenses incurred in supervising their children in out-of-home care.

A new court date is set for a year minus a day later to review the case. During that year, the Browns are to prove themselves worthy parents by completing parenting classes, domestic violence counseling, and sexual abuse counseling and by visiting their children regularly in monitored circumstances, as well as passing a number of evaluation tests.

In the meantime, authorities take the children from the Los Angeles Children's Center ("baby jail," Angel calls it), where they have spent the five days since they were removed from the Browns', and place them at the Masada Home in Los Angeles. Angel and Mr. Brown initially visit them one hour each week. But the staff at Masada soon allow the parents as many as three visits a week. All visits are supervised.

The staff notes, however, that Angel "wanders away frequently" from her children during the visits. "She spends time only with the oldest usually," one staffer reports. Mr. Brown, furious with his wife for her inattention, works hard to spend equal time with each child, knowing they are being watched.

After thorough examinations, the doctors discover Angelica's vagina is closed and prescribe the same medication Angel and Mr. Brown were using on her. The home supervisor, however, says staff members are not comfortable applying the medicine to the child. They fear being accused of sexual abuse.

Soon a foster mother is found for the children: Ms. Montario, a divorcee in her forties who has always wanted children.

Mr. Brown is relieved to have the children in a private home and initially likes the new foster parent. Angel has her suspicions, however, based on her own experiences.

"She's a religious woman," she says. "And when someone is that religious, you know something wrong with them."

Angel and Mr. Brown are allowed to visit three times a week for an hour. But after the first month, Ms. Montario asks them to visit only once a week. It was too difficult to get all the children dressed and ready for the visit, she says.

Mr. Brown and Angel agree without a fuss or mention to their lawyers. But Angel begins to feel uncomfortable.

"She is trying to take my place," Angel says jealously. "She has them call her Mommy. The social worker says she dress them so nicely, but I'm the one that got them those clothes, not her." She wants the children to remember they are a family, and the family does not include Ms. Montario.

The caseworker admonishes Ms. Montario. She is not to have the children call her Mommy.

Still, Angel is unhappy about the situation. Her children are growing rapidly and she claims their behavior is changing. She does not like the changes.

"I found something out," Angel tells me four months later after visiting her children. "Angelica laughs to keep from crying now."

Later that month Angel furiously relays stories her older children tell her.

"Squeak ran out into the street and Momm—I mean Ms. Montario spanked him," Angelica blurts out during one visit.

Angel is irate. She marches up to Ms. Montario.

"You don't spank my kids," she yells. "I don't spank them so you certainly don't. You got me? I'll whip your butt if you touch my kids like that again."

The social worker increasingly sides with the foster mother in the conflict. Angel becomes depressed. She visits her children less frequently but cries when Mr. Brown returns with recordings of their voices. For each visit she misses, she sends a tape of her own for Mr. Brown to play for the children.

"Mommy loves you and misses you very much," she says on the last recording. "You'll come home soon." And then she stops for a moment and clears her voice. "I know I keep saying that, but it's true, you'll be home soon."

"When's soon, Daddy?" Angelica asks after listening to it.

"Where's Mommy?" Squeak chimes in.

"Yeah, Daddy, where's Mommy?" asks Francina, copying her big brother as she does all the time now.

"She's sick with sadness," Mr. Brown tells them. "Because she misses you."

Angelica begins to cry.

"I miss Mommy," she says. "I don't want her to be sad."

Mr. Brown holds his daughter close.

"You smell like Vicks. Are you sick?" he asks her.

"Fish?" Squeak asks. "Fish, Daddy? Where the fish?"

Squeak is excited now.

"No, Vicks," Mr. Brown says.

"Fish, Daddy? Where the fish, Daddy? Are they big?" Francina follows her big brother's cue and they search the room looking for fish.

Mr. Brown wipes the tears out of his eyes as he and Angelica laugh.

"Daddy," Angelica says. "I want to come home. I'm tired of taking care of Squeak and Francina all the time."

27

The Jerry Springer Show

※

WITH the children in DCFS custody, Mr. Brown is having doubts that he and his wife should appear on *The Jerry Springer Show*. But a producer and Angel convince him that it will be a good way to clear his name. He has only a few days to decide. Maybe, he thinks, DCFS will recognize the misunderstanding over the vaginal salve and ground-up glass. Maybe they will acknowledge that he is a good father after all and return his children immediately, without the six-month evaluation. After the producer promises him every opportunity to explain himself, he decides it's worth a chance.

Angel refuses to fly, so the Springer show sends her and Mr. Brown two train tickets to Chicago, where the show is produced. Though the trip will take one full day and two nights, Angel is elated. It is her first train ride, and she is going to be on national TV. The first two hours on the train thrill Angel, but after forty hours, she decides to fly next time.

The show puts them up in a nice hotel. Angel is thrilled again. She loves such a life, calling room service and having producers ask if everything is all right. Everything is just fine, she says.

On the eve of the show, Mr. Brown learns that Latachee and Linda Dillard will be appearing at the same time. The producer explains that she invited Latachee to fill in because the children are in custody and the show needs to fill the chairs. Mr. Brown's estranged granddaughter, Gayle, is also to be present. The producer tells Mr. Brown that Gayle wants to repair her relationship with him with a surprise apology on national television.

"They set up a lynching," Mr. Brown says later.

First the audience attacks Mr. Brown for marrying a girl so much younger. Then Gayle accuses Angel of seducing and exploiting Mr. Brown.

From the moment she walks onstage, it is clear that she has no intention of making peace with her grandfather. "I can't stand to be around either one of them," she says. "She just a whore. She always using him. Those kids aren't even his kids. She go out all the time with different boyfriends and he stay home with the children and they aren't even his."

"Yes they are," Mr. Brown interrupts.

"No, no they are not," she insists.

"Yes they are," Angel breaks in. "And I'm a good mother too."

"No you ain't either," her sister Latachee interjects.

"You're just jealous because you ain't got no kids!" Angel shouts.

"No, I'm not. You don't deserve to keep your kids the way you are with them," Latachee retorts, nose in the air.

"You!" Angel screams furiously, her face pale and drawn. "You the one who called the authorities on us. You did, didn't you?"

Springer belatedly restores calm. Mr. Brown looks away. Angel is still stunned that her sister turned her in. But Latachee is not at all embarrassed. She is preparing for the next round.

Mr. Brown, she announces, has always been a pervert. When she and her sister lived with him and his wife, he propositioned her several times, she claims.

"I said no, so he went to her." Latachee points at Angel.

"You just jealous," Angel spits back. "She is, cuz she always liked him and he didn't like her."

Mr. Brown has decided to ignore the whole affair, leaving Angel to fight alone.

The audience is virtually rioting by the end, caught up in the excitement of such a real-life drama. Springer closes the show speculating on why seventy-year-old men marry fourteen-year-old girls.

Nobody has won. Certainly not Mr. Brown or Angel.

But Angel is proud and excited afterwards. She cherishes the video of her appearances and watches the Springer show faithfully afterward. Mr. Brown wants to hear nothing more of the show.

"They lied," he says of the Springer producers. "They just lie to get people to go on there. Then they tear people up inside and then they throw them away. They don't care about truths. And they don't care how they mess up lives.

"It's a using game," Mr. Brown explains. "Latachee used DCFS to make space for her on *The Jerry Springer Show*. The show used us, and she used them. It has nothing to do with the truth; only we're left to clean up the mess they all make of our life."

SOON after Angel and Mr. Brown return to Los Angeles, the anonymous child abuse complaints against them are dropped. The person who had called originally simply rescinded the complaint. But by then it is too late. The children are in DCFS custody.

28

Six-Month Review

▩

In the six months following their court appearance, Mr. Brown and Angel attend the required parenting classes, therapy sessions, and group counseling. Much of the day Mr. Brown spends in the car, going to or from these sessions himself or ferrying Angel to and from them. Scheduling is almost impossible at times, with some classes in Long Beach and others in Los Angeles. Angel cannot drive their stick-shift car, and she has totaled their automatic on the freeway on her way to her boyfriend's one night. Besides, her license has been suspended for a series of moving and standing violations.

Despite the scheduling difficulties, both Angel and Mr. Brown complete the parenting classes and group counseling sessions. Angel then demands that the caseworker give her children back. The caseworker refuses.

"I'm taking all these therapy things that aren't for me," Angel complains. "I took the parenting class and now I have to take a domestic violence class. Why? He didn't hit me and I didn't hit the kids. Neither of us did. So why do I have to take it?"

She also sees no reason to attend classes for victims of sexual abuse. "All the women in there were beaten or raped by their boyfriends or husbands. I wasn't, so why I got to be there?" she asks.

Her attendance begins to slip, and in her frustration she fights with her children's caseworker. When the caseworker visits for the last time before the six-month court review, Angel barely acknowledges her in the living room with Mr. Brown. Instead, she walks past into her bedroom, shuts the door, and turns on her TV loud enough "to drown out the problem." She refuses to come out when the caseworker asks to speak with her.

By now, Angel hates her children's social worker, Mrs. Zhang. The social worker tells Angel nice things about the children's foster mother, which makes Angel seethe with jealousy. "She don't even speak English; she don't understand what I say," Angel says. "She's Asian, you know, and they hate black people."

"Mother states that . . . she just does not feel good enough or not in a good mood to see her children or attend counseling on several occasions," the caseworker reports. "Father is still in denial stage," she adds, because he refuses to admit guilt.

The caseworker concludes that the parents are not yet ready to be reunited with their children. Furthermore, "there should be no change in minors' status and it is not appropriate to liberalize monitored visit for both parents at this time," she writes for the judge in her six-month court review of the case.

"All minors have been observed to be bonded well with each other and with their caretaker," the caseworker writes. "They have also been observed to be well taken care of by their caretaker."

Angelica is four years old now and enrolled in preschool. Teachers report her doing "very well." She is participating in a prelatency group for sexual abuse counseling once a week and "doing fine" in the group. So fine that the doctor wonders at times why she is in the group at all. Her health is good, but a psychological assessment report finds her "in the significantly intellectually delayed range."

Squeak, who is three, has mastered toilet training. He has also developed a nervous stutter since he left his parents, and recently he has begun speech therapy. A psychological evaluation confirms his delay in speech and language skills. He is shy among other children and keeps closely to his sisters. Staff at Masada Home initiated play therapy for him, which he continues at the foster home.

Play therapy, intended to help children participate and socialize with their peers, was also begun for Francina, who is two. "She is quite shy," the social worker reports. "But when prompted she shows a very happy sweet affect and personality."

Roger, the baby, ten months old at the time of the evaluation, appears happy, relaxed, and "well bonded with his caretaker."

The caseworker's plan for the children now is to reunite them with their parents one year later, in November 1995, a full year and a half after they were removed from their home.

29

Court

░

A̲s their December court date approaches for the six-month review, Angel and Mr. Brown—unaware of the social worker's recommendations—are excited at the prospect of recovering their children. Not only have the abuse charges been dropped, but Mr. Brown has received an outstanding psychological assessment, which goes so far as to doubt that he was ever guilty of sexual abuse in the first place.

"I believe Mr. Brown is capable of rearing his children in a responsible manner, and is deserving of the opportunity to demonstrate this to the court," the psychologist concludes in his final report to the social worker.

In court, however, Mrs. Zhang, the children's social worker, claims never to have received the psychologist's report, although it was postmarked November 4, 1994, more than a month before the court date. When she is made aware of his recommendation, she says she disagrees with it, particularly the portion that suggests Mr. Brown's age is enough to ensure that he cannot sexually abuse his children.

For his part, the psychologist is disturbed by the social worker's assessment of the case. In an unusual move, he appeals directly to Mr. Brown's lawyer, offering to appear in court if necessary.

"Mrs. Ling-Ling Zhang, C.S.W., prepared a document for the court regarding Mr. Brown in which she disagreed with my recommendation that the children be placed back in custody with Mr. Brown and his wife," the psychologist writes to Brown's lawyer.

Ms. Zhang indicated that the reason why I think Mr. Brown is not a physical or sexual danger to his children is due to his age. While it is true that Mr. Brown is currently 72 years old, this is not my only reason for believing that he is not a danger to his children.

Mr. Brown has been in individual counseling with me, as well as having taken classes in parenting. Both in my clinical experience with him, as well as supported by a battery of psychological tests, I have found that Mr. Brown does not constitute a threat to his children. Mr. Brown shows a balanced outlook with regard to the custody of his children. He is dedicated to their well-being, and has committed himself to their growth and development. Mr. Brown has demonstrated time and again that he has fine impulse control and is not subject to outbursts of temper, nor is he given to inappropriate expressions of anger."

To send such a letter as well as his evaluation report to Mr. Brown's lawyer is very unusual. Rarely does a psychologist go around the social worker.

Mr. Brown intends to argue his case in court. But the social worker does not appear in court. She is in the field on another case. With such a large caseload, this is not unusual.

"DCFS is recommending that the children stay in their foster home at this time, at least until the next evaluation," Mr. Brown's lawyer tells him hurriedly just before entering the court.

"Yes, but the social worker says she didn't see this," Mr. Brown says, handing her a copy of his psychologist's letter and evaluation.

"You're right," the lawyer agrees with him when she reappears. "We should appeal her recommendation."

Angel's lawyer is also shown the report, but chooses not to join in the appeal, because Angel has not complied with the court order by attending all of the prescribed sessions.

Judge Garcia is sympathetic when he learns of the psychologist's evaluation and agrees to an appeal of the social worker's recommendation. Meanwhile, he allows the children to visit with their parents as long as the visit is monitored by a court-approved outsider. If all goes well, he says, he will no longer require Mr. Brown's visits to be monitored.

Angel is a different story, the judge says, turning to her as she squirms restlessly. To him and most people, her movements and attitude are defiant. She is demonstrating an irresponsible lack of concern for her children by refusing to attend court-ordered therapy and classes, he warns sharply. She will continue to be monitored on visits to her children.

Ironically, Angel is practically right in the end. While it was accusations against Mr. Brown that brought the children into custody, the court has found another reason for keeping them there.

But Angel misunderstands the court's action. She believes the system, backed by the court, looks for excuses to punish her. "Since I was little they decided I was bad and that they were going to keep punishing me. But, see, they're punishing my babies too," she says, breaking into tears. "And they didn't do anything bad."

The court sees Angel's behavior not as rebellion against the judgment she thinks they have made of her, but as lack of responsibility and care for her children. To Angel, participating in the court-ordered programs to get her children back would be admitting to fault. But to the court, her lack of participation is a sign of noncommitment to her children, and even disinterest.

30

The Night Before

✖

ANGEL storms out of the courthouse well ahead of Mr. Brown. "Let her go," he whispers to me. And he allows her space all the way to their dented brown Honda. He has tried gently to explain that the proceedings have turned out in their favor. But Angel is furious that he has emerged in a more positive light than she.

"Why are they going to take *you* off monitoring status and not me?" she pouts. Then she storms: "It was because of you that we're here in the first place, not me."

The larger picture is lost on her, that their children may actually be able to come home for the holidays and that they could eventually enjoy them without an outsider looking over their shoulders. The system is starting to trust them, slowly.

But Angel is fully into her tantrum and beginning to enjoy it. She marches ahead, pausing only once, briefly, to say hi to a guard by the metal detector at the front door, who looks her up and down with one raised eyebrow, flirtatiously.

THE sting of that court experience is still with her at the next date.

The night before the second custody hearing, months later, Angel rages in her apartment. Her anger is targeted on her own court-appointed lawyer.

"I don't like that woman at all," she rants. "I swear I almost popped her in court last time. She was being real evil. I said, 'Whose side are you on? You're not working for me. Why do you just sit in court like an idiot?' She was just agreeing with what everybody was saying. She agreed with everybody, the Department of Children and Family Services, his attorney," she says, pointing at Mr. Brown. "Everybody. I said, 'What's your problem?' I was sitting next to her and kept pushing her. 'Say something!'"

If Angel and Mr. Brown complete several classes and participate in both group and individual therapy, the judge said last time, "then I might consider awarding you custody of your children. But frankly, it doesn't look good.

"I know a lot about you," he told Angel directly. "I've looked through your files and I know everything about you. Don't run, because I'll find you."

So on the evening before the third hearing, she proposes to Mr. Brown exactly what the judge warned her against.

"Let's run," she says. "We could just take the kids out of that home for a walk and leave."

Mr. Brown shakes his head. "No," he says. "We'd be on *America's Most Wanted.*"

"But see, I figure then people would listen," she urges him. "We never had an opportunity to stand up and say our side in court. Never. We never got to talk to the judge."

Mr. Brown shakes his head again. "But we aren't going to say it by running. Not that way," he says.

Angel pauses.

"Well, next time I'm talking," she says of tomorrow's court date, lifting her chin indignantly. "I'm talking no matter what. Even if I have to raise my hand and say, Look, Your Honor, may I speak to you a moment? You listening to what everybody else say, but let me say something.

"I'm talking no matter what, if I have to tell Valerie [her lawyer] to shut up, it's my turn. I wish I could fire her. Can I? I can't. Can I?"

She looks at Mr. Brown.

He knocks one shoe against the other.

"There'd just be another one," he says.

31

Third Hearing

❖

ON the morning of the third hearing, a full year after the children were taken, Angel and Mr. Brown are to pick me up at my motel between 7 A.M. and seven-fifteen. Roll call at Family Court begins eight-thirty, but Mr. Brown worries about every possible delay, from traffic on the freeway to Angel's inability to get ready in less than two hours. They have already missed one parenting class because Angel could not get her hair right and refused to go.

The day breaks gently at the horizon as I wait outside the motel, about a mile west of their apartment, past the oil refinery, tire stores, and several drive-through Chinese and Mexican restaurants.

A small boy walks by, his brown hair smoothed down neatly and an oversized knapsack sneaking off his shoulders and riding almost down to his knees. A scar-faced man with mean, glazed eyes slows his red Bronco to ask me for directions. Where? To a liquor store maybe, wherever I want to go. Get in, he tells me, his mouth moving slowly and numb. He'll pay, he says, for my company. The little boy quickly looks down and picks up his pace. A van shrieks around the corner all too close to the boy as he crosses the street; a gin bottle tossed from it smashes and splinters on the black pavement a few inches from him. The red Bronco finally crawls away, slowly, to the back of the motel. Three police cars swoop around the corner on their way to an alarm. The boy continues his walk; his eyes again focus on his feet. I wonder how he will make it three more blocks to school all alone. Today and every day.

"In a place like this you have to be on your toes every moment of every day," Mr. Brown says when they arrive, at 7:45. "If you have kids you have to be with them every second. That's what scares me so with my kids. Look what happens if there isn't anyone. Look at Angel."

32

Room 416

Mr. Brown is anxious. His hair is slicked back and he reeks of aftershave as he drives wordlessly. Angel chatters away, pulling silver curler clips from her black hair. We arrive in the courthouse parking lot with thirty minutes to spare.

"Smile," a police officer tells us as we walk through metal detectors.

An elevator rises to the fourth floor and arrives opposite a long waiting area for Room 416. The chairs and cushioned benches are almost full. Angel sits for a moment but then runs off to stand in line at the door. She is second.

"Who's here?" the bailiff asks after she gives him her name for the docket list.

"My husband and a close family friend," she replies.

Angel rejoins us on the bench, which faces a large open window looking out to a golf course. She jabbers on about last night's TV shows and a radio station party that she spent the morning trying to get invited to through numerous phone calls. Mr. Brown sits quietly, sad and serious. He smiles only once, when Angel mentions an episode of *Married with Children* that they watched the night before. Mr. Brown's lawyer stops by briefly and tells him her expectations are not high because of Angel's continued poor attendance record at court-ordered classes. Mr. Brown says he understands, that all he wants from this hearing is to have the judge allow his children home for Christmas Day. Then Angel's lawyer comes to speak quietly to Angel, careful not to let anyone overhear. She has urged Angel not to talk to me. But then she has also told Angel not to return to *The Jerry Springer Show,* and Angel will do so once more.

The bailiff calls for Brown. We walk, as other fragmented families did before us, through a narrow door into the courtroom. As before, the judge faces us and presides from his seat on an elevated platform, facing one long bench with the DCFS's lawyer, Mr. Brown's lawyer, Mr. Brown, Angel, and Angel's lawyer.

The judge looks closely at Angel and Mr. Brown as they take their places. To everything the judge says, Mr. Brown will nod. But Angel's attitude hardened the moment she entered the room. As before, she is not the image of the young mother eager to get her children back. She is an angry, defiant juvenile again, with little trust or respect for the justice system.

The judge commends Mr. Brown for his good attendance at court-ordered classes and for the recommendations he received. Then he looks at Angel and asks why she has not attended hers. She shrugs. He tells her, in a stern judicial voice, that he will not allow her to take her children back unless she abides by the court's order. How could he trust her, he asks, when she can't follow these directions? He adds that he might be willing to allow the children to visit on Christmas, but he needs to consider it further.

After merely six minutes in the courtroom, Mr. Brown and Angel are told to return to the waiting room to be called again later.

Mr. Brown is elated. Angel is quiet. Suddenly she erupts, furious that the judge has criticized her again.

"It's cuz of you we're here in the first place," she spits out once again at Mr. Brown. "Why was he so mean to me? It's not fair."

"I know." Mr. Brown tries to appease her. "But we might get the kids for Christmas."

"I don't care," she says. "I don't like it."

She stomps off. As she has before, she will flirt and collect men's phone numbers. "Putting herself on display" is how Mr. Brown puts it.

He learned how to play in the white man's world in the 1940s and 1950s, especially while serving in the Army in World War II and Korea, by appeasing and accepting and working twice as hard, he says. The court and foster care system is a white man's structure, he says. It may not be as obvious, but it's in the cultural differences and even the language. Angel, he says, never learned. "She fights every step of the way, right down to the way she talks," Mr. Brown says.

Some might consider this rationalization for her actions. If she truly cared for the children, she would have complied with the court's directives as Mr. Brown did. If she so badly wanted to keep her children from the foster care system that maltreated her—and that she despises as a result—she would have attended the required classes. It is sometimes difficult to avoid seeing her as a petulant, self-centered girl who would hardly be able to survive if not for an overly indulgent old man.

But Angel is the product of her upbringing, or lack of it. She is no better or worse than most who have had the same experiences. She is expected to play by rules that she was never taught and that, as she sees it, were not made for her. They have never helped her. The system that imposes the rules she does not trust, even though she fears it. Just as she has not been able to look past the immediate to build her future, she has never learned how to act responsibly to earn what she wants.

33

Back to Court

As we wait outside the courthouse to be called the second time, Angel's irritation grows palpably. She stubs out her cigarette, then looks up.

"They're playing God up there." She flares, thrusting her chin toward the courtroom high above us. "What right do they have to play God?" she demands.

"I know people who blow marijuana smoke into their babies' mouths, people who beat their children. Why are we here? For nothing. It's not fair. I hate it. I wish I didn't have no kids," she says, looking away sadly. "Then I wouldn't hurt, I wouldn't cry."

Mr. Brown starts to talk about getting the children back for Christmas, but she refuses to be placated.

"It's not going to happen. You know it just ain't gonna happen," she insists.

"I was thinking we could stop on the way back for a quick drink. Just one," Mr. Brown says, looking deeply into his foam cup of bitter coffee.

"You're not supposed to," she snaps. But then she pauses as her own temptation takes hold.

"Ooooh," she says excitedly. "We could stop at that place and I could get a kiwi-strawberry soda." She almost claps her hands in her childlike enthusiasm.

"No, you're right," says Mr. Brown. He is a reformed alcoholic who has forsworn drinking.

Angel looks at her watch again and again.

"Where are they? We should have heard by now. I just want to go home. I need to be home for *Days of Our Lives*. I don't care. You know I'm addicted to that show." She laughs and playfully pushes Mr. Brown.

"I just want to go; it doesn't matter anymore. Let's just go," she whines.

Mr. Brown begins to speak placatingly again; but Angel tells him to shut up.

"You're the reason I'm here in the first place. It's all your fault."

Mr. Brown's body seems fluid with fury. He leans forward to glare into her face, but she will not meet his eyes. He seems on the verge of speaking terrible words that will crush her and change their relationship forever. His thoughts seem powerful enough to strike her. But after a visible effort, he walks away.

"See," she says, arms folded before her. "We don't have a perfect marriage. That's why I went on *The Jerry Springer Show* the second time. They had another couple; she was seventeen and he was sixty-five. Not as much an age difference between him and me, but enough. I told her, Don't do it. You have your whole life to live; his is almost over. Don't do it. See, it's not perfect. We fight."

But she is quiet now, satisfied to have provoked her husband so deeply. Mr. Brown's lawyer finally reappears. The judge will not allow the children to visit Angel and Mr. Brown without a monitor, she says. A third party, with no criminal record, must agree to be with the family on Christmas to make sure the children are not mistreated. Angel and Mr. Brown must suggest someone to the judge when they return to court in a few minutes, so that police can run a check on the monitor.

Just as the lawyer leaves, Mr. Brown appears down the hall.

"Oh no, he's back," Angel says. "Why can't he go away?"

He sits in silence. Angel is so intent on punishing him that she has either forgotten to pass on the lawyer's message or willfully refuses to. Finally I break the silence with the news.

Mr. Brown's eyes light up. Angel looks away, still angry.

Angel's lawyer rushes out and asks for the name of a monitor.

"We don't have no one," Angel says.

"Your mother," Mr. Brown suggests.

"No!" Angel flares.

The lawyer studies the two. "OK, but you need someone fast," she warns. "They're not going to wait."

Angel and Mr. Brown offer names to each other. All are rejected because they have criminal or drug records.

In desperation, Angel decides to phone her neighbor. She doesn't know her entire name, but she has her phone number. But before she can phone, they are called back into the courtroom. They have no monitor to propose.

Angel again adopts her attitude. Her face hardens into an insolent stare. She fidgets as the judge criticizes her again for missing classes. Her lawyer glares at her. She raises her hand to her shoulder and waves it faintly, unsure, as if trying to signal that she wants to be called upon to speak. If the judge understands, he ignores her.

Mr. Brown's lawyer tells the judge they were unable to contact a possible monitor. The judge gives them a week to find one.

When dismissed, Angel stomps out of the courtroom, her arms crossed, marching into the elevator and then out the glass doors. It has become her standard behavior. Mr. Brown only shakes his head. But his step is lighter. He doesn't know how he will deal with his wife, but he does know that his children are coming home for Christmas.

34

Knock

▓

LATE that night, there is a firm knock at my motel room door. Thinking of the incident in the parking lot the morning before, I ignore it. But early in the morning, the front desk calls to say Mr. Brown is waiting to see me.

He is not in the lobby but outside on the street, wearing a navy blue Adidas jogging jacket and brown slacks. He motions me into the passenger seat of his Honda, which is heavy with cigarette smoke. The ashtray is overflowing, the butts smeared with Angel's purple-red lipstick.

"When we got home, she went berserk," Mr. Brown says immediately. "She just went off."

She was admitted to St. Francis Medical Center in downtown Los Angeles last night. A checked box on the admissions form told the reason bluntly: "Depression/suicide."

"She said she had nothing to live for anymore and was going to end her life," Mr. Brown says. "She agreed to go to the hospital. At first she agreed to talk to you at your motel, and we got to the driveway here before she said no, she wanted to go to the hospital, she needed help.

"We filled out the forms and they put one of those bracelet tags on her. But then she said she'd get bored there in the hospital. So she just got up and walked out with her bracelet still on.

"It's not the first time she's threatened suicide," he continues, searching his hands in his lap as if for an explanation. He carefully unfolds a white paper. The handwriting is round and, like that of a child learning to write, seems uncomfortable, almost unnatural, on paper. Dated May 26, 1994, a few weeks after the state took custody of the Browns' four children, it read simply:

> To whom it may concern. I, Najuwa Holts AKA Angel Jackson, am taking my own life. I have no kids, no heart. I want everyone to know that daddy had nothing to do with this. Please let my kids know mommy loves them. I'm sorry for all those I hurt, but I hurt too
> Najuwa Holts

And then, almost as an afterthought, the more confident signature, "Angel Jackson," is added.

Mr. Brown found the note among a scattering of pills. He knew how many pills had been in the bottle, however, and realized she had taken only a few.

"She's always looking for attention," he says, and offers me three more scraps of paper. Each had a man's first name and address. One address was a prison. "That one," Mr. Brown points, "that I know about. He's in jail for about a hundred years for taking pornographic pictures of his children having sex with him, and probably with Angel, too.

"Sometimes I don't know why I took her back," he says. "She wrecked the car on the freeway two miles from where we live, but kept driving all the way downtown to see a boyfriend, with no water in the radiator. That was the end of the car."

Do you regret taking her back?

"No," he says. "Either she'd be dead or on the street if I hadn't. I have an obligation to her, but sometimes, I just don't know why I put up with it."

Why do you stay?

"My children," he says. Then after a long pause he adds, "And I guess it comes down to that ugly four-letter word: love."

35

Mr. Brown

✸

I ARRIVE at the Browns' around six in the evening to take Angel to dinner. The sky is almost dark. Orange cones of light hang from arching street lamps. Compton's East Artesia Boulevard takes on a more sinister face at night. Already the police have a man sprawled across a fence while they search him, his car angled on the sidewalk. Their blue lights stab out at the encroaching night. A few blocks away young men gather at a corner; their cursing seeps through the car window. I park on the street behind a dented Honda and in front of a smashed Chevrolet.

Mr. Brown looks through gray curtains before opening the door. He is apologetic; Angel has gone. She left for the store to buy perfume three hours ago. He was hoping she had swung by my motel on the way back. We wait for Angel, and as we wait, Mr. Brown tells me his history.

His life has not been easy, but he came from a loving home. Born in Crystal Springs, Mississippi, on February 22, 1922, he believed he was Cora and Melvin Brown's son until he was fifteen years old. Melvin worked in a steel factory. Cora and her daughters doted on young Marrion.

"Oh, they were good to me, real good. My dad used to take me fishing. He'd make this dough bait out of cornmeal and sugar and roll it into balls. I used to sneak a pinch here and there and then roll it up again good so he wouldn't notice. One time I saw him scratching his head and he said, 'Boy, you come over here. Have you been eating the dough bait?' he asked me. 'Yes sir,' I said. 'But just a little bit.' He said: 'Now by the looks of it you've eaten about half. You should have told me. Next time I'll make a special one for you.'" Mr. Brown laughs, a warm laugh, rich in memory.

"Oh, yes, they were good to me. They taught me love and caring. No matter how tight things got during the Depression when work was slow and my mom had to go clean houses, white people's houses, they made sure there was plenty of food on the table and clothes too. They weren't my real parents but I didn't know that and you'd think they didn't know it either, the way they cared for me like I was their own. It was the South, you know, and back then people took care of their own," he says.

"My mom always told me to be good to women, and I have," he says.

Around town there were rumors that Melvin Brown was not his real father, but not a hint that Cora Brown was not his mother. "I was sure she was my mother until that visit," he says.

"This lady came with a boy. I was fifteen then. I was talking with the boy and she came out the porch and into the road and gave me $5. I said, 'No, I don't need that, thank you.'

"It made me feel funny, you know, why's this woman giving me money? She said take it, and I wouldn't. Then she said, 'Don't tell Cora I told you this, but I'm your real mother.' I felt like someone struck me, I remember so well."

He never told his aunt that he knew she was not his mother and that he kept in touch with the boy who had visited, his brother (as he did until his brother's death, a few years ago). He never met his older sister, who was born to his mother when she was thirteen years old. By way of his brother and mother, he found out his biological father was a porter on a train that went from New Orleans to Chicago. It stopped right there in Gary, Indiana, where his family moved during the Depression.

"I tracked him down later, you know. I said, 'Why didn't you come find me?' He said he didn't know where I was; he said he didn't have an address.

"So I know how important it is for my children to know their father and that he's fighting for them," he says finally.

"My parents raised me right. The love and care they showed me . . . well, I have responsibility for my children. They're mine, they're my responsibility, no one else's."

Mr. Brown seems to be applying the principle of adoptive love that he learned so well from his aunt and uncle to Angel's children. He accepts them as his own, though at times it seems he also recognizes that they may not be his biological children.

"I know what happens to them in the places the system puts them. Look at Angel," he continues.

"I'm fixing to buy a house for the kids, so that they have a home. Even when they go away they'll have a home. I put in for a loan with my GI bill. I'm going to fix it so that the property can't be disposed of by her, only by the kids. I have to have something to leave them. She might get in with someone who abuses her and wants money from the house. Only the children all together will be able to dispose of the house," he says pointedly.

WHILE Mr. Brown has plenty to concern himself with his kids, Angel is also on his mind.

"I know what's going on," he says abruptly. "She told the lady at Larry's [restaurant] that she was going to divorce me and marry a woman. Yep, a woman. The lady told the manager, Mr. Martinez. He came up to me and said, 'Why is your wife saying things like that? It's not good. Not good for a mother to be talking that way.' I know she's angry about my getting off monitor status and blowing off steam, but it's hard to hold my head up sometimes."

Angel has been having a relationship with a woman for some time. She is confused about her sexuality, she says. Her first sexual experience with a girl occurred at MacLaren Hall. It was, she says, her first real sexual experience, her first consensual intimacy.

BY midnight Angel still hasn't returned.

"It's falling apart," Mr. Brown says as I leave. "It's all falling apart."

36

High School

"I'D be finishing high school now. I'd be in my last year," Angel says the next day, picking at her turkey club sandwich in a back booth at the neighborhood Denny's restaurant.

The waitresses fawn over her. They fed her through three pregnancies, when, she says, all she did was eat. "We felt responsible," one waitress jokes after an elated hug. "We thought maybe it was something in the food we served her. Every time we turned around, she was pregnant again."

Angel smiles politely, masking, as best a young person can, her feeling of boredom and betrayal. When we are alone, she speaks about her marriage.

"At the time it was what I wanted," she says. "It was a way out of the system. The only way. But I didn't know what I was getting into."

She licks her finger and looks off.

"I'd be getting ready for prom now," she says wistfully, back in her day-dream, "buying a dress. Getting in a limousine.

"Maybe with someone like Dylan," the rich rebel on *Beverly Hills 90210*.

But boys are not the main element of this dream. The focus and attraction is herself. The purpose is to escape from responsibility and criticism. She is as hungry for experiences now as she once was for security. She wanted a home, so she married. Now, like a child entering adulthood, she wants to spread her wings, to find adventure in new things.

"Oooh, I just love limousines," she says, squirming as she imagines herself in a posh car.

Which brings up *The Jerry Springer Show*. Its producers called recently, wanting to update Angel and Mr. Brown's story. Her husband reminds her of the mess it got them into the last time and tells her to refuse. But the producer tells Angel to think about it, and says they will call back in a week.

"I want to fly this time," she tells Springer's producer when she calls back a few days later, "and I want a limo."

She is unconcerned that a second flamboyant appearance on the program, with her again running off at the mouth, could end chances of getting her children back, as well as end her marriage and perhaps even herself. Now she's looking for an adventure to overtake her disappointment. She hangs out with friends Mr. Brown doesn't approve of. They fill her with trouble, he says.

They also give her the lead to a new adventure, in Dreamland.

37

Dreamland

ANGEL walks into the Dreamland with a defiant look she thinks will get her a job. A long-sleeve, short-waisted T-shirt hangs loosely from her shoulders to the middle of her rib cage, far above the waist of her black stretch pants. Her nails, as usual, are brilliant red. Her white heels click over the dance floor as she tries to grab at some attention and ooze sex like her idol, Madonna.

Her friends have promised adventure and sex here. "Lady," they said, using her nickname, "you got to see it to believe it. It's a mess."

Customers pay Dreamland $20 an hour for the company of young women. The girls receive $5 per hour plus tips and expensive drinks just to sit, dance, or let men buy drinks for them. This job she could do, Angel thinks. She could make money. Then maybe she'd have more freedom, maybe a wild life, the one she missed out on while she was at home, pregnant.

She saunters up to the bar, feeling eyes following her as she moves. The manager takes one look at her and barely a glance at her fake ID. Start tonight, he says.

Daylight can't fly fast enough. But when it turns dark and butterflies dart around in her stomach, she wishes it would have paused. Almost all the customers are Japanese businessmen. The way they look at her, the way they move, the way they talk, she senses it is very unlikely that her version of Mr. Right will find her here. But she stays.

The girls keep to the house rules on the dance floor and in the booths while they tease and flirt with the men.

"What's you doing that for, man?" A bar girl's voice flares harshly across the smoky room. "They couldn't pay me enough to let you touch me. No way. Uh-uh. You want a prostitute, you go find your way to the boulevard. I ain't no prostitute, uh-uh. I'm leaving. I don't care how much money you got."

The young woman rises from the booth, the man scurrying to his feet, pushing a $50 bill at her. She swoops it up like a gull skimming a minnow from the sea and is gone. All night he follows her around, but she has other customers.

Although apprehensive at first, Angel quickly adjusts and even enjoys her new job.

"It was flattering," Angel says. "Men paying just to be with me. I had complete control over what they could touch and what we could do. If he wasn't too bad, I'd let him touch. If he was ugly, I took money and gave him the finger."

A week later, however, Angel is disgusted by most of the clientele.

"They are sick," she says. "I mean, who pays money just to talk to a woman or dance with her?"

She begins to spend less time with rich customers and more time with the better-looking ones. Three really good-looking white men sit together watching her. They don't look like money, but they are buff. One reaches out past his drink for her.

"You can look but not touch," she sasses, throwing her hair over her shoulder. She leans forward toward him, shoulders back, breasts forward. She likes the muscles in his arms and his broad shoulders.

"Oh, I can touch," the man says, a dangerous flirtation burning his eyes.

"Not here you can't," Angel says.

"I can touch anywhere at the right time."

Angel feels chilled and straightens up.

"I don't think so," she says and walks toward the dance floor splashing in pink and silver lights.

"We'll see," he calls after her.

Another client meets her on the way and asks for a dance. He bows and hands her some bills. She takes the wad and moves with the man, swaying and undulating, lost in the lights spinning around. The white men, she knows, are watching. All the men are watching. And she feels powerful.

That night, as she walks to her car, the three men jump her.

"I told you, bitch, I could have you anywhere," the first one says as he rapes her.

Angel never returns to Dreamland.

Months later she tells her husband of the rape.

"What did you expect?" Mr. Brown demands when she tells him. "Dress in those outfits, running around those shaky-shaky places. What did you expect?"

38

Return to Springer

❖

In late August the Springer show calls. Mr. Brown initially won't hear of returning to the show. But Angel sweetly convinces him.

"We know how to do it this time," Angel says. "The last time was a mess and we can clean it up this time. Please," she pleads. "For me?"

And he agrees. When she is like that, he can refuse her nothing.

Then, through a friend of his first wife, he learns that Gayle, his granddaughter, is also preparing for the show. And Latachee. Again, the producer has not warned them of this. It has the earmarks of another debacle.

He tells Angel they are not going on the show. "I told my wife she's not going and I think I'm in a position to make that decision," he says.

Angel doesn't think so. She is angry.

"He won't do it," she complains to one of the segment producers. "He never cares about what I want."

"Is it that bad?" the producer asks.

"It's worser," Angel replies. "It's terrible."

"So terrible you might divorce him?" the producer asks.

"N . . . Yeah, it's that bad, I might," Angel says, picking up the cue. "I just might."

"You could come on the show without him and say that," the producer says. "We'll fly you up. And you could ride in the limo."

The idea of a divorce takes hold on Angel. "I'm tired of playing house. He's old now, and I'm young," she says. "I'm tired of this. He shouldn't have married me. I was too young. He took advantage of me. I was forced into it."

Has she spoken to Mr. Brown about this? I ask.

"No," she says. "I'm going to tell him on TV about the divorce because he might get violent."

"Has he gotten violent before?"

"No," she mumbles. "But [the producer] says he might."

So it was all set without Mr. Brown's knowledge. Angel would be flying to Chicago in two days.

"I've never been on an airplane," she says, her voice brimming with excitement. "Have any of your planes crashed?"

"No," I reply. "Get a window seat."

"Oh my God!" she squeals. "Well, maybe I'll peep out and look. I don't think so, though. I think I'll close my eyes the whole time, like this."

Over the phone, she squeezes her eyes tight. It is impossible not to smile.

BEFORE Angel leaves, her mother phones. Gayle and one of Angel's sisters are going to railroad her on the show, Dillard warns. They got on the show the first time by calling DCFS to have the children taken away. "Now they plan to tell stuff from your past," Dillard tells Angel.

Angel is confused. For the first time she can't turn to Mr. Brown for help. She realizes how much she depends on him.

She phones the producer, to cancel.

"She says she would get fired if I didn't show up," Angel tells me. "And I told [the producer], 'If I go on and say that I'm divorcing him, I'm going to be homeless.' "

"No, you won't," the producer replies. "You'll have a place Thursday night. The show will keep you in a hotel Thursday night."

Angel sighs. "Mm-hmm, I thought. She don't care about me. She just care about herself."

So Angel tells it all to Mr. Brown. And they drive to Las Vegas for the weekend to celebrate her decision not to appear on the show.

39

Tired of Waiting

❊

BUT their new togetherness is short lived. Soon after they return from Las Vegas, Angel and Mr. Brown's relationship is quivering between anger and disgust. Angel blames him for the loss of their children. He feels his wife is unmanageable. Angel is back doing her thing with boyfriends and girlfriends. She is increasingly confused about her sexual preference.

"She's been so deceived by black people, by black men especially, she's shoving off them," Mr. Brown says. "Now it's the opposite race and sex, whites and Hispanics and women again."

When the Springer show calls again, Angel is with Raul. She agrees to go on the show with her boyfriend and calls him "the love of my life."

And this time, she does.

Mr. Brown knows nothing of these plans until the limo driver arrives and asks for Raul. Mr. Brown tells the driver that he has the wrong address. But Angel runs after him.

"The driver made a mistake." She giggles when she tells me the story. "He got our two addresses confused. I told him he was looking for me."

Mr. Brown stands at the window, confused, as Angel steps into the limo like a princess, waves, and rides off.

He watches her appearance on television alone, astounded, as she announces she is divorcing Mr. Brown for this new "love of her life."

Mr. Brown immediately phones the producer. His wife lied, he says; they aren't having such serious problems. They have never talked about divorce. It wasn't fair to find out like this. It wasn't even true.

"You're right," she replies. "I thought something was fishy."

But the show airs as a repeat at least once again.

Angel does not return to Mr. Brown after Chicago. She stays with Raul in an apartment he shares with a roommate.

Before long, she becomes restless. Raul likes to go to bed early, with Angel. Angel wants to stay up late and watch television. One night, as Angel is sneaking out of bed to watch TV with Raul's roommate, Raul wakes up suddenly and becomes enraged.

"You want to go with him, you whore? You go then," Angel recalls his saying before slapping her and standing up to throw her against the wall.

She runs into the front room, where Raul's roommate sits before the TV. "He just watched while Raul hit me," Angel says. "And then he went back to his room."

Angel runs out the front door with Raul throwing her clothes after her. Half dressed, she calls Mr. Brown from a phone booth.

Police arrive just before him. They see blood and bruises on Angel but have no evidence that Raul beat her. The roommate says he saw nothing.

Mr. Brown takes Angel home. She cries most of the way.

"You're my husband," she strikes out at Mr. Brown. "You should have beat him. Any man would have."

"She's just so bumfuckled," Mr. Brown explains, resigned. "But we're back together. I keep telling her we have to stay together. She needs me to take care of her and I need her to get the kids back."

"Do you really think it's best for the kids to come back?" I ask.

"Oh, yes," he replies immediately. "Before this whole mess, we were fine together. Sometimes she'd get her thing and go off for a night or two, but I'd always be here with the kids."

"But what if you weren't here any longer? If something happens to you?" I ask the seventy-two-year-old father.

He hesitates just a moment. "I wouldn't trust her alone with those kids for one week," he says flatly. "I don't doubt that she loves the kids. But she would go off and leave the kids without thinking. Sometimes she doesn't think beyond what she wants at the moment. Her urges are strong, I suppose you could say."

"Is Angel a good mother?"

"When I'm there, yes."

"When you're not?"

He shrugs. "It will never come to that. I'm going to see those kids graduate from college," he says.

He will have to live past ninety to realize that dream.

40
Letting Go

▨

Angel calls collect from a phone booth in Compton early in August. She is seven months pregnant with her fifth child. It will be a girl, and she will name her Samantha Marie Brown. She will call her daughter Sammy, after a character on her favorite soap opera, *Days of Our Lives*.

It is not Mr. Brown's child, despite the intended surname, but Mr. Brown says he will raise Sammy as his own if Angel does not broadcast the fact. Raul is the father. Despite the beating he gave her, she returned to him long enough to become pregnant. Now she is no longer seeing him.

"Yeah," she admits hesitantly. "I did love him. But I got over it cuz I know he been cheating on me."

She had also left Mr. Brown, as her lawyer had counseled, in an effort to retrieve her four children. But Angel lasted in a women's shelter just one week. Feeling caged in by the curfew, required group meetings, and other restrictions, she went back to Mr. Brown.

Angel learned she was pregnant the same week she returned. It was a surprise. Angel says Raul had claimed he was sterile. Having broken up with Raul and unsure whether to stay with Mr. Brown, she had serious decisions to make about the baby. She did not consider abortion, but thought seriously about offering the child for adoption.

"At first I thought the only reason I want the baby is cuz I'm lonely for the other children," she says. "And then I thought that DCFS is going to take the baby from me at the hospital anyway, which will cause me to go absolute berserk. I'd rather give her away to someone who would take better care of her than them or me. I know what they [DCFS] do to girls.

"The counselor at family services told me that if I keep doing what the court tells me to do, they can't take my baby. And I started thinking how pretty the baby is going to be. Her father is Mexican and Samoan. She's going to have pretty blue eyes and beautiful long hair. She's going to be much lighter than the rest of my kids."

So she decides to keep her baby.

• • •

HER sister is trying to get Angel on another talk show. Subject: "My Teen-age Sister Is a Baby Maker." Angel laughs. She refuses to go. She has learned from the Springer appearances.

Her battle with authorities over her four children continues, with confusion over court dates causing another—perhaps the final—setback.

A custody hearing for her children in foster care was scheduled for July 26, but a mix-up occurred, resulting in Mr. Brown and Angel's failing to appear. So the court rescheduled the hearing for the next available date on the court docket, November 6—one year, six months, and five days after the children were taken into state custody.

"I can only see my kids for an hour on Mondays. They're all doing fine, though. They're getting so big! Angelica is in school and doing good. She can write and read a bit now. I try to get along better with their foster mother. She is taking care of my kids. I have to be grateful for that at least," she admits. "I try to talk to her some now. It's better for the kids. I can see it in them. They're happier and more relaxed when Mama and their foster mama get along."

She wonders for a moment whether she was a better mother to the children than their foster mother.

"Sure I was," she says, but she seems unconvinced.

"Do you realize that I do not have one good story to tell my kids about my childhood?" she adds softly. "They're starting to ask now for stories about when I was a kid, and I don't have anything to say. I can't tell them that I was molested and that I beat people up. Kids don't need to hear those things.

"There's nothing good I've had, besides babies. Kids don't need to hear that either. I don't want to tell them that. The girls have to go to college before they marry and *then* they can have children, *maybe.*"

She worries about being a mother again.

"Good grief, five children!" she exclaims. "Some people ask me if I'm having babies to get back at DCFS and I just look at them like they're crazy. No way. I don't know why I do it. But I think sometimes that if I didn't have children, I would have ended it a long time ago. After what I've been through even strong people would have. All that molesting and beating and all the people coming through my life like a freight train."

Then she talks about what she's learned from the weekly sessions with her court-appointed therapist, Ms. Gray. She no longer calls Mr. Brown Daddy.

"I call him Marrion now. Well, sometimes I still call him Daddy. He doesn't always understand that. But I said to him," she continues, with an edge of frustration in her voice, " 'Sometime you want to be my daddy, sometime you want me to be a wife. I don't think you know what you want.' I'm not here for his fantasies."

"Well, you sound like you're doing well," I say, thinking of the new maturity in her voice. She was looking beyond herself now, looking to build a future on her own foundation.

"Yeah." She laughs. "But I'm still going through this bad old thing they call life."

I didn't want to let her get off the line then. She sensed it and stayed with me a moment. Then her voice came forward, quietly, without the childish intonation she had used frequently in the past. Now her voice was so pure it shook me.

"I'm too young for this," she says wearily, sounding small and scared, tunneling through the darkness at age seventeen.

"It gets easier as you get older."

"How?" she asks. It is the first time she has ever asked me a question.

"You start understanding things better, clearer. And you know your mistakes, so you don't make them again." Cliché, I think, but true.

"I hope so," she responds. Then after a long silence: "I still think of ending it sometimes."

"Don't."

"I know," Angel says. "I just have to remember sometimes how strong I am." Then she pauses. "I am strong, aren't I?"

The doubt is as new as her maturity, and it stings my eyes.

"Yes," I tell her truthfully. "You're the strongest person I've ever known."

"You think I'll get my kids back?" she asks.

"I don't know," I reply.

"I do know," she says, perhaps sensing my pessimism. "But I have to keep thinking I will or I'll go crazy. You know? I will go crazy."

She pauses again.

"But you know, I think they're happy," she says.

And I can feel her letting go.

41

Starting Over

▓

As Angel's due date approaches, she becomes more sick with worry. She complains that her hair is falling out, her ankles hurt, she is breathless every time she moves, and she has never gained so much weight. She cries all the time now. And she has lost her appetite for life.

It isn't the pregnancy that weighs on her. It is the fear of giving up her newborn.

"Before I just couldn't wait to get the baby out," she cries on the phone. "Now I don't want to let her out, because they'll take her, and I'll never see her. She'll never know that I loved her. That's what hurts the most: she won't know I fought so hard to keep her and that I wanted her so bad. She'll think she just like all the rest of the kids [in foster care], like I thought I was, that no one wanted me bad enough, and that isn't true. I love my baby."

Her voice breaks, and then takes an angry turn.

"I know she gonna be mean because I felt mean during this whole last part [of the pregnancy] because I'm mad," she says. "They told me in the beginning I could keep her and now they're turning around."

A meeting in late September decides who will take the baby. Angel, her therapist from the Department of Children and Family Services, Mr. Brown, his therapist, Angel's sister Maria, Maria's boyfriend, and the Brown children's caseworker all attend. The caseworker wants to take the newborn directly into DCFS custody. Angel's therapist suggests alternatives. The first is agreed upon. Angel can keep the baby if she goes to live with Maria and Maria's boyfriend. Although Maria and her boyfriend are not married, the caseworker concedes they have a stable home. Maria has been drug free since her rehabilitation five years ago. Maria and her teenage daughter, Maria's boy-friend, and his eleven-year-old son have lived together seemingly peacefully for two years. The other possibilities are that the baby would be adopted by Maria or put directly into DCFS custody.

Mr. Brown will not be allowed near the child. Ever.

How does he feel about the arrangement? Mr. Brown's therapist asks him before the group.

"Does it matter what I think or how I feel?" Mr. Brown answers evenly. "You're going to make the decision without me, right?"

"Yes," one of the counselors says.

So he shrugs.

After the meeting he speaks his mind quietly.

"Angel wants our children back even if it's without me, and I'm not going to stand in her way," he tells me. "That's why we've stayed in California. We considered taking off to a new state with Angel pregnant so they couldn't take the newborn away, but then I said, 'What about the other children?' So we stayed so we could keep fighting for them."

But Mr. Brown now knows they have lost the fight.

Maria is excited about having a baby in the house. After her teenage daughter was born, she wasn't able to conceive again. Angel is a bit con-cerned her older sister will take over parenting. But she knows if things get messy between her and her sister, and if Maria complains, DCFS will give the baby to her. That is part of the deal. Like a vulture, her children's caseworker is hovering, waiting for that moment, Angel believes. She sees evil in the caseworker's eyes, she says.

And how about Maria's boyfriend, who will be at least half supporting Angel and the baby?

"Basically, by me being in love with Maria right now, anything she says, goes," he says with whipped humor. "But once we get past that honeymoon stage, its gonna be, What we doing with that baby that's not even ours?!"

42

Mom Again

▓

Samantha Marie is born two weeks early, on September 25, at 8:55 A.M. She weighs in at seven pounds and is nineteen inches long. "Oooh," Angel says with a giggle, "she's so fat! She's adorable, she really is. Pink mouth, pink cheeks, pink everything. She's almost white," she whispers. "She has hazel eyes. She's wiggling now. The angels is playing with her. I'm so happy."

There is a warm smile in her voice.

"In a little bit," Angel tells me, "seven minutes exactly, she'll be twenty-four hours old. A whole day old."

Mr. Brown is not as high as Angel. In fact, Angel says, he was bringing her down. He had taken Angel to the hospital at 6:15 A.M. for the delivery. The night before, he stayed up reading the Bible and watching her sleep for the last time. He knew that after the birth, Angel would leave him.

Maria will be picking Angel up from the Bellflower Medical Center tomorrow to take her and Sammy home.

"I don't really want to leave Marrion," Angel says with a light sigh. "But I have to try this. Our way didn't work. Our way was to stick together and get our four children back. It didn't work. So now I've got to try this alone."

43

Looking for an End

▓

ON November 8, 1995, the day of her nineteenth birthday and a month after giving birth to Sammy, Angel awakes in a hospital room. The nurses have told her she attempted suicide. Angel doesn't remember it all. Toward evening, the memories begin to return from the dark corners of her mind. It's like waking to a fragmented nightmare, she says. She puts the fragments into words that tumble out.

She remembers being depressed. She had been in court two days earlier. Raul had called DCFS claiming Angel was abusing Sammy because Angel refused to let him visit his daughter as often as he wanted.

Then in court that day, she had given up custody of her baby, Sammy, to Raul and his fiancée. Raul had been engaged for two years, Angel learned that morning. During the year of their relationship, she heard rumors that he had another woman.

Sammy had been in state custody for almost a week, ever since Raul's call. The judge would never take Raul's word, she believed. Her therapist and her lawyer were both surprised that the caseworker had even acted on Raul's complaints to take Sammy away in the first place. Angel was confident and cheerful when Mr. Brown picked her up that day for court. She couldn't wait to have her baby back. Sammy was all Angel had left now. Her four other children had been taken.

But the court directed Angel to give Sammy to Raul and his fiancée, or else put the baby in foster care.

"He looks like the kind of man who would take care of the baby," her lawyer said, encouraging her to take the deal.

"No way," Angel said, flying into a rage.

But then, in the mediation room with those two lawyers, things became confusing to Angel. Each lawyer seemed to argue more for the other's client, having little confidence in the parenting ability of his own client. None of it made much sense.

So Angel agreed to give Sammy to Raul and his fiancée. It was the only way to keep her child out of the foster care system. At Raul's, she could visit her daughter every day if she liked. And she would have weekend custody.

Mr. Brown took Angel home with him. She was quiet most of the ride. It was unusual for Angel to be so quiet. Usually, in the face of defeat, she would rattle on, talking almost nonstop about inconsequential things to take her mind off the situation. But now, nothing was left. A dark sadness seeped in. At Mr. Brown's residential hotel room, they watched soap operas.

That night, she asked Mr. Brown to rent a video, but before he left, she asked for a glass of milk. When he was gone, she swallowed a bottle of Tylenol PM pills and cough medicine. She wasn't trying to hurt herself, she claims now. She just wanted to numb her pain.

"Say 'Happy Birthday' to me," she told Mr. Brown dimly when he returned.

"It ain't your birthday yet," he told her. "It's not midnight yet."

"I know, but say it anyway."

He did.

"Kiss my babies for me tomorrow, and tell them Mommy loves them," she said, her voice groggy with the numbing.

"Aren't you going to be there?" he asked. They had been planning to visit together.

"I don't think so," she said. And she closed her heavy eyelids.

Mr. Brown rushed to the medicine cabinet to find the empty bottles. He and his neighbors slapped Angel and stuck ammonia under her nose. But her pulse was low, her heartbeat too slow.

Mr. Brown knew that another suicide attempt would prevent Angel from ever regaining custody of her children. But a neighbor who is a nurse insisted on calling the paramedics.

SEVERAL hours later, Angel woke in the hospital. Her nose hurt, her mouth felt dry and sore, and her stomach ached from being pumped.

"Maria yelled at me. Marrion yelled at me. Even Maria's boyfriend yelled. Maria hasn't talked to me all day. She lost her best friend, Tanya, to suicide two weeks ago, the night Sammy was born. But I don't think I was trying to hurt myself." She tries a weak defense. "I really don't. It won't happen again. That's for sure.

"I'm nineteen today," she continues wearily, "but I think someone's made a mistake. I'm way older than nineteen, I think. I'm just so confused," she says in the end, her voice trembling.

"You're so beautiful and smart, Angel," I say honestly, trying to encourage her.

"I know," she cries. "That's what they keep telling me in the hospital: 'You're so pretty, why would you want to kill yourself?' I'm so confused.

"What does pain have to do with being pretty or smart anyway?" she says, her voice quivering. "The smarter you are, the more it hurts."

IV

BRYAN
Chicago, Illinois

1

Orphans of America

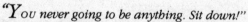

"*Y*OU *never going to be anything. Sit down!*"

That's what Bryan Friday learned and remembers from Cuneo, his third foster placement in Chicago. The words still echo through his mind at times, usually during bad spells or when he's under stress—as he often is in his young life.

"The staff was terrible there," he says, shaking his head through a difficult memory. "I was calling my caseworker every day to get me out of there. She'd pick up the phone and I'd say—before hello or anything—'Have you found a place for me yet?' She'd know right away it was me."

Finally, just after his fifteenth birthday, she did find him a new placement.

"I fell in love with Mercy Home the first time I saw it. People acted like they cared there. It was startling. They knew my name and said, 'Good to have you here,' and stuff," he says. Anxiety, worry, and sadness have made deep inroads across his brow, creasing his forehead and the corners of his mouth.

"It took me a while to get in," he continues. "Five or six interviews and an evaluation. But they decided to take a risk and accept me."

His usual seriousness breaks into a bright smile. His teeth are straight and white, a handsome contrast with his dark brown skin. When he laughs, his cubic zirconia stud earring pales to the sparkle washing over his brown eyes. He's average in size, but his solid and confident posture makes him seem larger, with a lean, muscular build that testifies to his track-and-field ability. He earned an athletic scholarship as well as an academic one to Lewis University in Chicago.

Bryan survived foster care. His experiences and their lessons say a good deal about what works and what does not in the system. His story shows that even children with the most troubled pasts can succeed, although often with serious bumps along the way. And it offers some clues for predicting which child will make it and which one will not.

"Is it genes?" asks Eileen McCaffrey, who runs the small, well-respected Orphans Foundation of America in Washington, D.C. The foundation has given Bryan a modest scholarship (large according to their financial ability) and arranged for him to spend Christmas and part of his school vacation with a local family in exchange for some office work. On this frigid December day, the foundation's only staff member besides McCaffrey is out sick, leaving McCaffrey and Bryan alone to race around the office answering phone calls and shooting out faxes. They finally find a moment to sit and talk.

"It's not intelligence. Well, not entirely. Some real smart kids don't make it. It's not looks. It's not a program that I know of. If we could just find what it is that makes kids do well and take advantage of every little thing they're offered, if we could bottle that up"—McCaffrey's hands fly up, accenting her pixie haircut as she leans sharply forward—"we'd be out of this mess. But what is it?"

She sighs and sinks back into her chair, frustrated.

Bryan pulls a red knit ski cap off his shaven head and looks down at his white sneakers.

"It's a mystery," McCaffrey says rhetorically now, looking again at Bryan but not expecting him to come up with an answer.

He sits forward on the office couch, hands folded together, legs bent outward. After a moment, he looks up.

"It's inside," Bryan answers finally.

ONLY months later, when I know his entire story, do I understand. Bryan would turn out to be less than perfect, but it's not perfect behavior that sets him apart; it's his ability to analyze his actions and take responsibility for them.

2

Home

BRYAN watches his mother pick up the bright yellow mug with a black smiley face. The yellow dims in her hands. He knows something is wrong then. Very wrong. He remembers everything after that in slow motion—from the moment she reached for that mug to the end of the day his world collapsed. He shakes his head, freeing himself of the shivering memory temporarily. But it always comes back.

Bryan is not quite seven years old that day in Del Monte, California. He loves Del Monte, particularly after Chicago. It is big, fresh, and beautiful. The sun always shines. Everything is open, so different from the gray, wind-whipped streets of Chicago, where he couldn't get away from the cement. Here there are trees and sky. People are warm and smiling. His family goes to church regularly—his mother, father, and two older sisters. His oldest brother, Bill, was left in Chicago, placed in a group foster home before Bryan was born. But that's one of the many family stories he does not know then. The family never talks about it. He doesn't know, either, that the reason his family moved to California two years earlier was that his dad and mom had been using drugs in Chicago. Lots of drugs. And his uncle, attempting to help, had relocated the family far from Chicago to California, where they could make a fresh start. Bryan does not know his parents worked hard to stay clean. And he doesn't notice the few times they slipped, though he senses something is not right at times.

What Bryan knows best is that he likes to play outside with his friends. He has a bike. He loves his family and he counts on them. He enjoys school and he likes church. His father has a construction job and his mother works for a rich lady, as a health worker or something. They have a lot of friends. It is a good childhood.

His family goes to a park once a week, a huge beautiful park where the sky meets the trees and even the ground. It's like church, they go so regularly; it's almost sacred to them.

This day, the family is going to the park.

His father is in the shower and his mother is rushing him.

"Come on, William!" she calls to her husband over the sound of hard-flowing water. She reaches for the bright yellow mug and it dims in her shaking hands.

Bryan looks around with new eyes then. In his memory, it is a premonition, and things start slowing down.

She goes to the patio, first calling to her husband, then screaming at him. Her hands are jittery. Black coffee splashes over the sides of the yellow mug she holds. She is talking to herself, mumbling, jumping, jerking, her eyes darting anxiously. She puts the mug down.

"C'mon William! Let's go," she screams again.

She goes back inside, mumbling louder, pacing, nervously shifting kitchen dishes, picking them up and putting them down, harder each time, less aware of their fragility each time. She picks up the yellow mug for the last time, walks with it into the closet, and closes the door.

Bryan looks at the door, confused. Something is wrong. Something isn't right. A trill of panic runs through him. He stares at the door.

Suddenly there is a thud, a big, solid thud from inside.

He runs, never swiftly enough in his memory, to the door. He opens it and sees his mother in a way he has never seen her before. She lies awkwardly, mouth open as if surprised. Her eyes are glassy and staring, scared, as if she has just seen a monster.

His sister dashes in and begins howling in her grief. His dad runs dripping from the shower and cries as he lifts his wife onto a bed. In between his sobs, he attempts mouth-to-mouth resuscitation. But her limbs fall to her sides, lifeless.

Bryan stands aside, ghostlike and removed, like part of the wall or the ceiling, invisible as the ambulance pulls up and takes his mother and father away. His sisters, Felicia, fourteen, and Crystal, twelve, sit together on the couch, waiting, though he doesn't know for what.

The phone rings. Felicia jumps up to answer. Crystal is holding him too tight. His sisters begin to cry again.

"Bryan, Mom is dead," Felicia says finally.

He starts crying, too. He doesn't know why exactly, except that he is scared. His sisters are crying and they never cry. He doesn't know that their lives have changed forever.

IT would have been helpful, Bryan thinks now, if he had known to cry for the loss of his mother and the loss of his life as he knew it. But he didn't understand then that his mother was gone for good and that her death would also claim the family. The Friday children never retrieved the family life they lost that day. None of the four children found any semblance of that love and unity in the decades they were to spend in foster care. Their mother had been the family anchor and strength. Without her, their father would be unable to keep them together.

"When my dad lost my mom, he lost everything," Bryan says now. "Without her, there was no him. When she died, he lost it."

3

Bryan's Dad

WILLIAM Friday Sr. would like you to believe that he moved the family back to Chicago immediately after his wife's death from a drug overdose. He wanted to bury her back in her hometown. She'd always missed her family and he didn't want her alone now in an exiled graveyard. The children would need their extended family's support while he struggled through the crisis.

His life passed with her, or he wished it had, he told them. Fighting drugs and alcohol had been almost impossible before, but at least it was a fight. Now it took too much effort even to breathe. Without his wife, the goals they had built for each other and their family were empty, like shells from another lifetime. He knew he had little strength or heart to fight his drug and alcohol addiction anymore.*

The truth is more sordid. After Mrs. Friday's funeral, in Chicago, the family returned to California, where they lived until Crystal called the department of children's services to report her father was inappropriately touching her. She was placed in foster care on her birthday, and returned to her father two days later after no charges were filed. Soon after, William Friday moved to Chicago with the children.

There they stayed with relatives, mostly with their stepaunt, Cookie. She and her husband owned a big house on the West Side, around Huron and Laramie Streets. Big trees lined the roads. A solid stone high school stood from the days when high school was a big deal. It is still in use, but the kids milling around aren't the rich white kids who attended it before World War II. The neighborhood never revived from the war years, when owners began letting out rooms and taking in boarders to help the war effort. By day, it is still a real neighborhood. Most neighbors mow their tight lawns. And on that block many families, like Cookie and her husband, an auto mechanic with his own small shop, own an entire two- or three-story house. Several, like Cookie, take in less fortunate relatives, which, one neighbor says, "adds, let's say, spice to the neighborhood."

The Fridays were to stay with Cookie until Mr. Friday could find work and save enough money for an apartment. But as Cookie struggled through her first pregnancy, she began to believe her husband had eyes for Bryan's sister Crystal. She told William that he and his family had to leave.

William found work and a town house apartment virtually around the corner, but in a less well-kept neighborhood. The front and back yards were smaller than the porches, and few people bothered to cut the strips of green, where more weeds than grass grew. By day, the neighborhood still belonged to families, with old Mr. Richardson's Fourth of July fireworks for children and Mrs. Shepard sharing produce from her backyard vegetable garden. But at night, trash was discarded from slow, cruising cars with booming hip-hop and tinted windows. And youths began to gather on the street corners and toss about trouble.

William Friday was soon back into alcohol and drugs, his children say. His using got progressively worse. One job after another released him, until he finally was refused employment altogether.

---

* William Friday Sr. refused to be interviewed further for this book.

Crystal looked after Bryan as much as she could. But her school was farther away than his and its day was longer. Before Crystal got home, William started his son Bryan on drinking.

First it was beer. "Here, have this," his father would say, and Bryan would fight hard to swallow the nasty yellow stuff bubbling sharply on his young tongue. Then the stuff got harder and the colors changed, to the deeper amber of moonshine and then the clear thick transparency of gin.

"I don't know why he did it. I guess he liked it and wanted to share, or he wanted to keep me quiet or something. I don't know," Bryan says.

And yet Bryan remembers his father warmly from that time, despite an overall stormy relationship.

"He took care of me. He loved me," Bryan says with a child's eye. "He did his best, I guess. He was my father. He was all I had, and I loved him.

"He would take things from stores for Crystal and me, you know, like clothes and underwear and stuff, because he couldn't afford it, or food. To this day, I don't think that was so wrong." Bryan shrugs with embarrassment. "I mean, I know it's wrong. He was the adult and he taught me how to do it. How to rob and steal. But, well, he did what he had to do."

Love and loyalty are values Bryan never forgets. Even his sharpest, meanest memories of family are laced with a childlike trust and forgiveness because he believes his parents loved him in their own way.

Crystal sees it differently. She associates love only with her mother, never with her father. Her mother was the family's protector as well as unifier. Every Mother's Day, Crystal feels the loss of her mother as strongly as she does on other special occasions, like her high school graduation, her marriage, the birth of her first child. She reruns the treasured memories of her mother over and over in her mind. With time, they grow richer rather than fading. She remembers sitting with Bryan on her lap and watching her mother cook dinner. During those times they were a family, and her mother would tell her things, personal things. Now when she cooks dinner, she is sometimes overwhelmed with grief. If her mother were alive today, she often thinks, she wouldn't be married or have a child. She and her mother would be living somewhere together, alone. And Crystal would be happy.

The father Crystal remembers is not the same man Bryan remembers. Her father was a bullying and controlling drudge who used his strength and meanness to terrorize his children, particularly her older brother, Bill Jr. She remembers the whuppings he gave her almost as well as she remembers the way he beat Bill.

"He didn't do nobody like he did Bill," she says.

He used extension cords, leather belts, ropes; anything that he could find that he could bind with electrical tape he would use to whip Bill. Afterward, he'd throw Bill in a tub of boiling water, or freezing water; usually boiling, though, Crystal recalls.

One day of that pre-California life in Chicago stands out in particular horror.

Bill came home with a ring, which he intended to give his mother. She worked in the post office from three in the afternoon to eleven at night, so she was not home yet.

"Where'd you get that ring, boy?" his father demanded. "You stole it. You stole it, didn't you? You bastard. Good for nothing . . ."

The cursing flew out with his belt. Crystal and Felicia screamed. Felicia swore she had seen Bill pick the ring up out of the street, but her father ignored her words. After thrashing Bill with his belt, Mr. Friday threw his son into a tub of boiling water. When it was over, Bill and Crystal ran to their one safe place, their beds, and drew the sheets over their heads. In their beds, they would lie still so their father would forget about them. Only then, it seemed, were they safe.

When their mother got home, she felt something was wrong. Maybe it was the look on Felicia's face.

"Why Bill and Crystal always asleep?" she asked her husband.

"Don't know." He shrugged.

In the next room, Crystal shook under her sheets.

"Bill," she whispered, wanting to know if he was still alive. He had stopped whimpering because he didn't want his mother to know about the beating.

"We never said anything to our mother because we were afraid of him," Crystal says now of her father.

Mrs. Friday went into their room, threw the sheets back from her son, and gasped air that expelled into a scream. She flew into a rage. Her son's body was red and swollen. In a rage, she carried him to the hospital. Crystal ran to keep up with her mother's brisk, angry pace.

"What kind of animal would do this to a child?" Crystal remembers the doctor asking.

The hospital called the police. A child protective services worker arrived shortly afterward.

This was an extreme case of abuse, the social worker said. Under these conditions, Mrs. Friday could legally divorce her husband immediately for $1 —bypassing the state's required separation period for a divorce, the court fees, and the legal fees—or alternatively, Bill would be taken that night and put in foster care. The social worker encouraged Mrs. Friday to divorce. It was only $1, she said. Lawyers fees and court fees would be substantially more expensive later. It would be immediate. And a restraining order could be issued on her husband that night. If Bill were taken away, it would be very difficult, maybe impossible, the social worker said, to ever get him back again.

Mrs. Friday cried as she said good-bye to her oldest son.

"Bill never got over it," Crystal says now. "He knew what happened and he always thought he was worth less than a dollar. He knew she picked our father over him."

Chicago's Department of Children and Family Services placed Bill in a foster home seven blocks from his home. Though the court forbade visitation, he wandered home whenever his foster mother wasn't around, which was often. Several times he told his mother that his foster mother had pulled guns on him. Mrs. Friday fought to get her son back. But when the caseworker told her that reunion would be impossible as long as she lived with Mr. Friday, she fought to have Bill moved to a better home. The better place turned out to be Maryvale.

WHEN the Fridays returned from California, Crystal managed to get in touch with Bill again. She called every relative to find him and finally, her great-grandmother knew. Always thereafter, Bill kept in touch with Crystal.

"I used to say, 'Bill, Bryan and Felicia say hi,' " Crystal remembers. "He'd say, 'I'm just a stranger to them,' like he felt guilty. 'They don't love me because I didn't send them cards or anything.' I would say, 'Bill, why you say that? You the victim.' But he always felt guilty. He was always looking for Bryan. He wanted to take care of his little brother. But Bryan was always on the streets and we could never find him when Bill came. Bill would go looking for him. He was scared for Bryan and wanted to do things for him. He used to say, 'My little brother needs me and I'm not doing nothing for him.' "

Bill regained his strength at Maryvale and went on to the University of Illinois at Champaign-Urbana with a full track-and-field scholarship. Years later, as a muscular college student still bearing his childhood scars, he hunted down his father to ask why he had been beaten and tortured. Bill cornered his father in a neighborhood bar.

"I'm sorry, Bill," his father said simply.

"That's all he said. 'I'm sorry, Bill,' " Crystal remembers. The fire of anger and hatred that burned in Bill's eyes during the hunt for his father suffused into a white hot scorn and then pity. "Bill just looked at him, but he didn't hit him or nothing; he just walked away. Even with all his trophies and things, I was never more proud of Bill than I was then."

In contrast, Felicia and her father were close—too close, according to some relatives. Even before he was accused of molesting his daughter, many of his relatives suspected that Mr. Friday sexually abused his older daughter, Felicia. But none spoke up at the time, nor were charges ever brought.

"My sister was on the streets from early on," Crystal remembers. "Felicia told me that she used to shoot t's and blues [heroin] with my father, so they bonded over that, I guess. I don't know."

Crystal prefers not to think about it. When she does, she remembers that her father never whupped Felicia as he did Crystal and certainly never as he did Bill. But the abuse, she thinks now, could have been much worse.

"One night, it was Thanksgiving," Crystal remembers specifically. The family had not yet moved to California. "At three o'clock in the morning, Felicia started screaming. Screaming and screaming. I ran into the room . . ."

There she found her eleven-year-old sister grabbing at her abdomen, her sheets soaked with blood. Crystal stood, staring at her older sister while her mother called the ambulance. By the time the ambulance had arrived, Felicia had delivered a stillborn child, the umbilical cord wrapped around its neck.

No one had known Felicia was pregnant, perhaps not even Felicia herself. She refused to talk about it.

Felicia left home first, at age eleven. She just vanished one day soon after that night. The authorities tracked her down several times and placed her in one institution after another, but she never stayed for long. She'd run away. She was afraid of them, she later confided, because of "some weird experiences." She instilled the fear in Bryan, warning him that in such a place there is no escape. Fear of the unknown for Felicia was worse than the danger of the known. She told her little brother of a ghost she still maintains she saw in one of the group homes. After that apparition, she refused to stay in any placement even during the day. The fear overwhelmed her. The streets with their violence were less frightening to her. By the time she was eleven, she had been so violently raped and beaten that even Crystal had a hard time identifying her.

Felicia gave birth to four more children after the first. Her youngest, born after her older three were placed in foster care, died recently. Felicia's drunk boyfriend took the four-month-old baby from its crib to the couch with him. The infant suffocated between the cushions. No charges were brought.

INEVITABLY, the time came when William Friday, three months behind in his rent, having already borrowed from every available relative and their friends, was evicted along with his two remaining children.

Crystal had expected it. Every morning for weeks she had packed a suitcase full of clothes for herself and Bryan.

"I didn't want our stuff on the street all messed up," she says.

"My aunt would say, 'Crystal, why you take a suitcase to school when other kids take a knapsack?' But I knew it was going to happen and I wanted Bryan and me to be ready to go when it did."

Several days later, Crystal and Bryan came home from school about the same time that the sheriff arrived. Their father had gone off to buy drugs. Crystal carried their suitcase to her stepgrandmother's home, a few blocks away. Together, she and Bryan dragged what they could of their parents' remaining possessions through the alley to their stepgrandmother's.

Their stepgrandmother, Mrs. Beecham, lived in a three-bedroom house, where she was raising thirteen children—five of her own, four grandchildren, and now four foster children, including Crystal and Bryan. It was a big house, but not big enough for the number of children flying in and out at all hours. Always one of the kids was messing with Bryan or Crystal. And Crystal, who had kept a tidy house since her mother died, didn't like the stains on the wall, the peeling paint, the roaches that lumbered along the walls, or the rat droppings in her shoes. Initially Mrs. Beecham had called children's services to take the Friday children away. But instead, the caseworker struck a deal with her. The state of Illinois paid for the Friday children to stay with her as foster children. They were now wards of the state.

Life had been unstable and tough with their father. But at their stepgrandmother's, they encountered a whole new set of difficulties. Mr. Friday had usually fed his children, even if he had to steal to do it, and even if he himself went hungry. The children had to conform to a new way of living at their stepgrandmother's. At Mrs. Beecham's, Crystal and Bryan had to compete with the other children for food and space, and fight to protect their clothes and few other items of property. The meal line formed at the front door some days. Most nights Bryan was left hungry. Sometimes no food remained by the time he reached the table, particularly if he napped through the beginning of dinner.

Crystal looked out for him. She would save food for him. She also tried to keep him out of trouble. "Bryan, come straight home from school," she'd say. Or, "Bryan, take a shower." Or, "Do your homework."

Thanks to Crystal, he was in all accelerated classes at school. He loved school, too. It was the one place he felt appreciated by adults, and the one place he escaped home life safely. On Parent's Day, when students could show off their work and grades, Bryan was without a parent. Not even Mrs. Beecham came. But Crystal was always there.

"She was my mother, really," he says. "She was great. Without Crystal, well, Crystal took care of me, she really did."

Bryan shared a room with two of Mrs. Beecham's sons, who were technically his stepuncles. The boys got along well. When Bryan's money from the state arrived each month, Mrs. Beecham took the two boys shopping for clothes, dividing Bryan's foster care check between them.

If money was scarce in that household, love was scarcer. Crystal remained Bryan's only advocate and source of consistent care. When she left, Bryan felt more lost and alone than he has ever felt. He searched for the love and protection he missed. And he found affection existed only in the streets—when Crystal disappeared.

"I don't know what happened, why she left. She just vanished," Bryan says, exasperated. His expression clouds in a muddled and confused memory of the event.

"If Crystal told me she was going, I don't remember," he says, trying to clear his memory from the hurt. "But she didn't. I would have remembered that. I *know* I would have remembered that. She was just gone one day, vanished. I guess she got smart."

4

Crystal's Reason

CRYSTAL'S situation turned out to be more complicated than Bryan ever suspected.

She did not plan to vanish from her brother's life. She wanted to take him with her. She had asked her caseworker to find them both another home. Their caseworker delayed acting, expecting that Crystal would change her mind or forget her request altogether. He considered Mrs. Beecham's home a good placement. He suspected Crystal just needed to get used to it and then her complaints would quiet down.

Some of her complaints, he had to admit, were valid. Rats did creep into the house from the alley, and the bathroom floor upstairs had a hole through which the ground floor was visible. But other foster homes were far worse off. At least the children were not being abused.

But Crystal kept pushing for a new placement. She was tired of fighting for food for Bryan and herself. She tried hard to stay clean and neat, as her mother had taught her. But when she hung up her clothes and Bryan's at night, one of the thirteen kids in the house often stole them by morning, or stuffed them into the toilet. The nights were as much a struggle as the days. While Bryan slept, his stepuncles, who were Bryan's age and slightly older, would fill his ears with toothpaste and sometimes toothpicks, and he'd wake up crying.

"I was tired of it," says Crystal. "Even after I left I would get calls saying Bryan was in the hospital for different little things. Like once his stepuncles were watching *Little Rascals* or something and put firecrackers in Bryan's back pocket and burned up his whole backside."

Crystal's caseworker finally found a home for her, but she had to move quickly. Could Bryan come with her? she asked. The caseworker said he would speak to Bryan, alone.

Did he want to leave his stepgrandmother's home?

"No," Bryan replied. He thought that would mean he would have to leave his sister Crystal.

The next day, while Bryan was at school, Crystal was taken to her new foster home.

"I never got a chance to say good-bye," Bryan says, pain lining his face.

"I never got to talk to him face-to-face," Crystal says, shaking her head. "It was too hard. I thought he had chosen to stay even though I had decided to go."

Bryan felt lost without his sister. He knew Crystal still lived on the West Side, but he didn't know where. He walked for blocks each day, hoping to find her.

They were out of touch until Crystal visited Bryan in the hospital after the firecracker incident. When she realized how much he had missed her, she wanted to stay close to him, but living in another foster home made that difficult. So Crystal arranged for Bryan to call collect at least once a week at a payphone around the corner from her foster home. Her foster mother did not permit her to use the home phone; it was reserved for her and her biological children. The phone booth plan worked for a while, but then drug dealers threatened them for hogging the phones. Bryan and Crystal lost contact again.

Meanwhile, Crystal called their caseworker often, complaining about conditions at Bryan's home and begging him to move Bryan out. She had urged Bryan to do the same. She saw the effect of his troublesome uncles on his attitude and behavior, and always in her mind she saw Bryan as she had last seen him, sad and uncared for. She'd lie awake at night wondering if Bryan had found a bed for himself that night in the overcrowded house, or if he was sleeping on the floor because someone else took his bed. It often happened.

"Look," she'd tell the caseworker, "even if you don't put us together, you got to get him out. It's terrible there."

She told Bryan to tell him the same thing.

"But Bryan was so small, the caseworker didn't take him seriously. He just figured Bryan wasn't getting beaten, and the uncle stuff was just kids' pranks. But I told the caseworker about how Bryan had to sleep on the floor some nights because there were so many kids in the house. My stepgrandmother's kids started having kids and moving back into the house. And I told him there was no food left for Bryan. But it didn't make any difference until Bryan was bigger and could speak for himself."

Crystal worked for the state Department of Children and Family Services that summer.

"I tried to tell them [department officials] about the problems too, but they were tight with my stepgrandmother and didn't believe me," she says. "They think kids complain just so they get attention."

While working in the office, she discovered that she had a right to ask for a specific placement. She knew that she could push to be moved, but there was the uncertainty that the next placement would be worse than the present one. She asked to go to Maryvale, because her older brother, Bill, lived there. Maryvale is one of Illinois's best-run and best-known group homes. Directed by Father Smith, Maryvale has been particularly successful in managing children with troubled pasts, providing them with security and love and outlining discipline so they can develop normally and plan for a future.

Bryan was too young to be aware of his right to ask for a new home. Like all kids in the system, he had a caseworker that made his decisions for him. His old caseworker left the Department of Children and Family Services. His new one inherited not only his case, but the problems of his old caseworker. The problems kept her too busy to give much attention to any one child's needs. Crystal had told him to keep pushing, but Bryan had never known his words to sway anyone in the foster care system. His caseworkers seemed to work independently of him. He didn't know he had any choices. If he had known about the programs available to him, if someone had sat down and explained it to him, even at eight or nine years old, he thinks he could have understood and acted to change his situation. Instead, he felt like a puppet, worthless, with no control, adapting to where he was set.

He did not know that both private and public homes for children like him existed, and that the private ones were usually better. He did not even know that there were homes that cared whether he was home at night, that fed him regularly, that never left him hungry for anything. He could have avoided the trouble too—the drugs and the gangs—most of it anyway, if he could have left his so-called friends and their neighborhood on Chicago's West Side. He even wanted to get away from it, because inside he knew it was bad and that it could destroy him as it had destroyed his father, mother, and oldest sister. But he never knew he could leave for any reason, least of all because he felt in jeopardy and sometimes felt an impending sense of doom. Even when Crystal left, he did not know why. He did not know he had only to ask his caseworker to move, and then push hard.

Crystal wanted to be with Bill, not because she loved him more than Bryan, as Bryan had thought, but because Bill was her older brother. He would look out for her. Bill awed Crystal. She saw her brother as a star at Maryvale. Caring for Bryan drained her with too much responsibility. She had tried to save both of them, but when her caseworker told her Bryan had chosen to stay, she knew she needed at least to save herself. After a series of interviews and evaluation tests, the private children's home accepted Crystal.

But at Maryvale, she cried at night and sometimes during the day. Crystal shakes her head when she thinks of that time. She felt generally happy at that home. Maryvale seemed to her the best placement yet. She cannot understand why she cried so much there. Her counselors believe it was because Maryvale was her first safe home, the first place where she could stop reeling from the trauma of her early life and start feeling all the emotional pain she could not let herself feel while still in danger. She had buckled down the hatches, emotionally, and now she began to let her emotions free. She rocked back and forth, sometimes crying and sometimes just rocking. Counselors told her that she rocked because she had not received enough comfort from her mother at a young age. But Crystal refuses to accept that explanation. Her mother, she says, always comforted her. She remembers crying while fearing for Bryan and feeling guilty for leaving him. She rocked back and forth in an effort to comfort herself, she says. Maryvale staff almost immediately placed her in therapy.

"I was scared for Bryan the whole time," she says. "I didn't know if he had what it takes to make it. He had to fight the streets even at home because of his uncles. I didn't think anyone could do it."

AT first, Bryan had help from his older brother. When Bill was on home visit from Maryvale, staying with his great-grandmother, Bill would ride his bike all the way from the South Side to the West Side to visit Bryan. He would put Bryan on his handlebars and they'd ride away. Bryan never wanted to come back.

Bill was goodhearted and smart, fun and strong. Bryan wanted to be just like him. He loved to look through the newspaper clippings of Bill's track-and-field feats, which Crystal carefully cut out and pasted in a thick scrapbook.

Bill did well in school. His grades were high. Staff as well as other children in the home liked him a great deal. His track-and-field work and talent earned him an athletic scholarship to the University of Illinois at Champaign-Urbana. Bryan looked up to his big brother.

"Crystal always says he was a lot like me," Bryan says, his smooth voice clouding. "I didn't know him, really. But she says he was motivated, determined. All of us are. He was smart, too. And he was a great track star. We both liked to run. And I'm, like, Man, I didn't even know he liked to run."

But while Bill ran in high school so he could go to college, Bryan learned to run for other reasons.

"When I was eight years old, there was a girl down the street who used to beat me." Bryan smiles. "She was my inspiration to run."

Bill's visits stopped abruptly after one summer. In the fall, he went away to college. Bryan did not understand. He had assumed that going away to college meant Bill was just going somewhere across town and would still be around to visit him. He didn't realize that the move downstate would prohibit his brother's regular visits.

Bryan saw his father sporadically after Bill left.

"It was wild then," Bryan says. "Crystal was gone, I was alone. She didn't call me. Wouldn't even come and see me. My brother was just gone too. And

Dad, it was like, Damned if I see him and damned if I don't. Dad would ask me for money. I was hustling and stuff. He would ask for change. It was kind of rough. I was always trying to have money because there wasn't any around. I knew he was into drugs. But I'd give him whatever I had, $5 or $10. I knew he was using drugs, but I'd give it to him anyway and then I'd hate myself for doing it."

Bill did well at the university his first semester. But after a year, he dropped out.

"I just keep thinking, why did he do that?" Bryan says even now, as if it just happened. "He had it all. He had it made."

Bill went to Florida with his new girlfriend and her sister. He did really well there at first. None of the family knew exactly what he did, but he had a nice house, a bike, things they only dreamed about.

Then he went to prison. Bryan and Crystal never knew why. When he was released, they resumed limited contact. He was working construction down in Florida. Then he went back to prison.

After that, Crystal and Bryan lost contact with Bill. He called and wrote to Crystal and Bryan when he was doing well. During difficult times, he stopped. But he had always kept in touch with their great-grandmother. She hasn't heard from Bill in several years. Bryan and Crystal never say it directly, but they would be relieved to find him in prison now, or in a rehabilitation or detox center. If Bill were alive, he would have dropped some sort of Mother's Day card to their great-grandmother one of those missing years. He never forgot Mother's Day. He had always remembered their birthdays, too.

From the day Crystal turned twenty-six, she started hating her birthday because each one is a reminder that Bill is missing. If he is alive, he'd have sent a card.

5

Catching Up

▓

THIRTEEN years later, Bryan still hasn't asked Crystal why she left without telling him, and why she never visited afterward except that once when he was in the hospital. It hurts too much to remember. Besides, she's going through difficulties in her own life now. At twenty-nine, she's been married three years, has a one-year-old baby daughter, and has successfully fought a heroin addiction for three years. Bryan spends most holidays, including Mother's Day, with Crystal, her daughter, Amber, and her husband, Eric, who recently graduated from the police academy. Crystal tries to keep the family together as much as she can.

Felicia lives with her boyfriend and his mother. Her three children are wards of the state, living in the same foster care system she fought so hard to evade herself. She never cared for her oldest child, Shawanna. Her younger ones, Jamie and James, were taken by the state after two consecutive fires in the apartment. The children were so badly burned in the second incident that they were out of school for a year. Crystal has kept track of them through foster care. She has them over for the weekends and holidays whenever she can. Jamie is living with a foster family that specializes in mental illness. She was placed there after her first foster mother reported seeing her and James kissing, though Crystal can't imagine that that would happen. James was placed in a group home in Wisconsin because there was no space available in Illinois for foster care boys with his special needs. He has little immediate memory, whether because of the drugs he is given to control his behavior, or from Felicia's drug use during pregnancy, or from the trauma he experienced as a child.

Felicia's eldest child is fifteen now, the same age as Felicia when Shawanna was born. Shawanna has just given birth to her first baby, two months prematurely. His fragile body weighs under three pounds. When he is released from the hospital, he will live with his mother in foster care.

Crystal and Bryan stay closer to their nieces and nephew than they do to their sister. Though Felicia is now in outpatient treatment for her heroin addiction, she often struggles in her fight against drugs. Bryan also has difficulty, sometimes, around Crystal, but during good and bad times, Bryan talks to her often, about once a week. Whatever their personal problems at the time, they keep the conversation light and upbeat. They support each other that way.

One day, Bryan hopes, they'll talk out the unresolved issues in their past. There's a time for everything, Bryan says, but this just isn't the time.

6

Juvenile Detention

▓

Bryan was twelve and in sixth grade when Crystal left. He was scared and lonely until he found a family of friends, mostly high school students, who hung out on a street corner he passed on his way to school. They called him Smiley because of his wide, trusting smile and his eagerness to please.

"Hey, what's up Smiley? Come hang with us," they'd say. "Smiley, try this. Here's some reefer," or, "Hey, Smiley, do this. That's cool."

"I was doing things that wasn't good," Bryan says now. "Using and selling marijuana. I was in a crowd that was totally, totally bad. And I was back and forth to the Audy Home so many times I couldn't see straight."

The Audy Home, as it is known familiarly to street kids because that's what it was called when many of their parents and relatives went there, before 1973, is now officially named the Cook County Juvenile Temporary Detention Center, or JTDC. The average stay for children is about twenty to twenty-five days. Like Bryan, about 60 percent of the children sent there are sent there again for later offenses.

The facility is divided into about thirty units. When Bryan attended, the children were set apart by sex in units of sixteen to eighteen children. But boys and girls attended the facility's school on the second floor together. There was a little privacy, Bryan says, but not a lot. At night before bed, all the children would be taken to the showers. A few children got to be on the cleanup crew, which meant they could stay up a little later and gorge themselves on peanut-butter-and-jelly sandwiches and milk as their wage. That was the best food in the place, so you had to eat as much as you could to fill up. It was far better than the morning's powdered eggs.

"The staff watched you for eight hours at a time," Bryan explains. They were guards, not residential counselors. "They were OK, but not nice. They didn't care about you. Each were different. Some were less snotty than others. You just had to figure them out and deal with the situation."

Any time you got to leave the dorms was good. "You'd even look forward to going to the [medical] clinic because you'd be leaving the dorms. Leaving the dorms was like leaving hell." The best part was school, which was in the same compound.

Bryan always liked school anyway. Classes were interesting, not difficult. What he missed most at Audy was his regular grade school with Miss Placek. "Miss Placek was really good," Bryan says. "She knew certain people had problems at home, and she'd keep you focused on the education."

Audy stifled his education, but with Miss Placek's help, he would catch up quickly. It became so common, catching up became almost a ritual. While he fell behind at school, he came out ahead on the streets.

"They would keep me for a month or three weeks at Audy and then I'd go right back to my old so-called friends on the street and get into more trouble," Bryan says. But that was OK by Bryan because it gave him standing where it really counted, on the streets with his friends.

"The more time you spend in a place like Audy, the cooler you are, the more status you have with the other guys. So when I'd come back, I'd think, OK, I'm not going to get into it with them again, but then they'd be all cool about things and happier to see me than my stepgrandmother or anything. I'd fall back into trusting them and wanting them to like me even more."

Bryan looks back on the year after Crystal left as a blur. He moved swiftly between court, the Audy Home, and his stepgrandmother's house. Drugs were getting the best of him, he now says, though he didn't notice it at the time. First came reefer, then the harder stuff like cocaine, heroin, and PCP. Sometimes he was sent to Audy not for anything he did specifically, but because he was with a gang that the police knew was running drugs. Even when the crowd didn't do something wrong, their behavior and records made them prime suspects for the police. The questioning, arrests, court, and punishments all became so common that Bryan never considered whether the police were right or wrong, or even why he was stuck in the cycle.

"I didn't even know it had anything to do with the crowd I ran with. I was in and out of court so much it was pathetic," he says now. "They'd say, 'There's Mrs. Beecham [his stepgrandmother] and that bad little boy.' I just thought that was the way it was and there was nothing I could do about it."

Should the court have done more, either in punishment or in educating him on what he was doing wrong?

He looks puzzled by the question.

"It wasn't the court's problem," he says. "The problem was in the home. No one, not my stepgrandmother, my caseworker, or anyone took me aside and told me what I was doing wrong. No one told me that the people I was hanging out with were doing me trouble just being around them."

And Bryan caught himself up in real trouble. His crowd used him to run errands, like dropping off drugs, that would get them, as adults, into far more trouble than Bryan, a juvenile. Beyond that, they were instilling dangerous standards and values in him.

"I was living with a distorted image of what a man is," Bryan says now, after several educating programs. "I thought being a man was working like this, hanging like this, doing this. No one told me otherwise. My stepgrandmother, I don't remember her saying a word to me. She just showed up in court."

Eventually, the court gave him more than just another term at Audy Home —and he is thankful for it. He came before a judge whose name he can't remember, on a charge he can't remember. But the sentence, he says, saved his life.

"I think it was a battery charge," he says, "but I'm not sure. There were so many times."

His gang got into a fight on school turf with another gang. Bryan had not been there, but he was on the corner later when the police scooped his crowd up. It wasn't cool to try to excuse himself out of punishment when his crowd took a fall, so Bryan, as usual, said almost nothing in court. The judge, also taking into account previous drug possession counts, sent him to Cook County's Department of Correction (DOC) prison in St. Charles, Illinois, for however long it took Bryan to get straightened out. The time he served would be decided by the DOC administration at periodic reviews.

The time Bryan served at St. Charles turned his life around, he says. Someone was finally talking to him, and what they said about his world started to make sense. He learned a new way of looking at his life.

"I did a lot of thinking there," he says. "That's where I got old. I was fourteen then."

7

St. Charles, DOC

BRYAN'S time at the Illinois Youth Center at St. Charles turned out to be the most positive experience of his first fourteen years, he says. It was far, far better than the foster home or group homes he lived in, he says eagerly. The detention center proved a better environment. There were more authority figures, there was structure, and there was discipline. He learned more, was taught more, and he was given more direction than ever before. For the first time, respect, attention, and discipline were demanded of him. And he responded.

He didn't find it easy at first. In fact, it was wrenchingly difficult. It forced him to reevaluate what he'd learned of life so far, reject those values, and adopt new standards.

"That's when I started having feelings again, like love and things," Bryan says. "Before, I was just a bad person. I didn't think of anything or care about anything, myself or anyone."

ST. Charles is a medium-security juvenile detention facility. It was built in 1905 as the first prison for youths in the country. Illinois had adopted the first juvenile penal code in 1899.

Today St. Charles is one of the state's six juvenile detention facilities, which range from low to maximum security (the last of which is mostly for murderers). Like most correction facilities nationwide, it is filled beyond capacity. Designed to hold 318 youths, it currently holds 460 boys, aged thirteen to sixteen, among them felons, sex offenders, and attempted murderers, as well as so-called normal delinquents. Because of the overcrowding, most of the rooms designed for single occupancy have a bunk bed. Rarely, if ever, is any of the boys alone. And never do they leave the self-contained facility.

Children admitted to St. Charles have committed an average of sixteen crimes or misdemeanors by age thirteen, according to Nick Howell, its public relations official.

"Generally," Howell says, "delinquents are sentenced to DOC as a last resort. They have to use up all the community resources before they're sent here."

St. Charles looks like a prison. The 126-acre facility is totally self-sufficient, with a school and a medical facility, so that no inmate ever needs to leave for any excuse. A double row of twelve-foot chain-link fence rings the facility. Razor ribbons crest the tops of both fences.

The youths are grouped more by physical stature than age or crime. Boys who are truant are placed among those found guilty of sexual assault and attempted murder. Some claim that combining so many youths of different crimes only exposes them to more sociopathological behavior. But Bryan claims that spending so much time with such a crowd straightened him out.

"I didn't want to be anything like them," he says.

The high staff-to-resident ratio is greater than one staffer per two boys—659 to 1,000—far higher than at any foster home or group home Bryan stayed at during his tenure in foster care. DOC claims that with so much supervision, the boys have little time to get into trouble, no matter how varied their criminal experience. Unlike in prison, they wear their own clothes.

Time for detainees is strictly regimented, but many respond very well to this form of discipline. The boys are counted each morning and herded to breakfast at seven. School starts at eight and, with a break for lunch, goes to three. With extra attention, and free of the distractions of the street, many boys have astonished St. Charles officials with their learning ability. More than one has entered at a fourth-grade reading level and left a year later at the seventh- or eighth-grade level.

After school and a light break, most boys are required to do odd jobs on the facility, like cleaning the latrines. Some are allowed recreation instead. At night, there are almost always specialized programs. For many, it's drug rehabilitation. The rest join visiting community groups, often religious groups. Then, before lockup, is private time, when the boys can go to a dayroom and watch TV or read.

St. Charles has a large mental health component, not meant for deeply disturbed boys (defined as those that hurt themselves or others) but for treating delinquent behavior. Most of the kids have had some mental health treatment before they arrived at St. Charles. It's almost universal among delinquents.

Unlike adults, juveniles are given open-ended sentences to the Illinois DOC. All juvenile detainees must pass through St. Charles, regardless of their crime. At St. Charles, their needs are assessed when they first arrive. Some are moved to a low-security facility, others to a maximum-security facility. In all cases, a contract is drawn up that describes goals they must work on. Each inmate is required to sign the agreement. When he has achieved those goals, and on the recommendation of the staff, a review board releases him. The average stay is twelve to fourteen months, though some kids are sentenced to life there. Bryan served eight months.

It was not the tough experience that turned Bryan around, he says, but the kindness and sensitivity of the visiting groups. At St. Charles, college students often visited the boys. A few exposed Bryan to a kind of spirituality, not a formalized religion, but a sense of himself and his power to be loved, he explains. When asked to define himself in religious terms, Bryan says he is Muslim. And if he had to choose between the two main branches of Islam in America today, he'd choose the Nation of Islam, whose membership is all black and which demands the discipline he feels many boys like himself needed. But his new attitude is less about religion than spirituality, he says. It was the visiting students, with their lives together and their generous caring, that made him see the world differently.

"They had meetings with us and they'd just hang out with us," he says. "I started thinking, Man, what am I doing here? I could be like them."

He started to realize that his friends and family back home did not care for him the way he had believed.

"In the whole eight-month period, I heard from one uncle, and I got one call from Felicia," Bryan remembers. "It was hard. I didn't hear from no one else. I thought, Man, this isn't right. What have I been doing?"

The students and staff made more and more sense, the more time he spent alone, away from his old friends and family. He had thought selling drugs to survive was normal, even a job. Shoplifting was OK too, if you needed to eat. Your standing on the street among friends and associates was everything.

"At St. Charles I started really thinking, Man, this isn't right. This isn't the kind of life I want," he says.

While in St. Charles, Bryan was assigned a new caseworker. Bryan and Crystal's first and second caseworkers, who never listened to their complaints or prepared them for or even explained the changes in their lives, were replaced by Vera DuBoise. Bryan was never told why. All he knows is that DuBoise came along just at the right time.

Bryan describes Vera DuBoise, an older black woman, as "like a mother to me. She would just show up when I needed her. When I got out of St. Charles, she came and got me. She was the only one there for me. I don't know if she knew how much she helped me. She had so many kids [in her caseload] to take care of."

DuBoise took Bryan back to his stepgrandmother's, a place he knew would be a struggle. He still did not know he could ask for another placement. He did talk to DuBoise about changing his life, however, finding a different crowd to hang out with. She suggested that he enroll in a different high school, keep busy, and stay off the streets.

After elementary school, Bryan had had a choice between two high schools, a magnet school some distance from home and a neighborhood school, which his crowd attended. If he had been encouraged to go to the magnet school, things might have been different. It's the only subject on which Bryan still harbors some anger. He needed some guidance and encouragement to set him on the right track at that time. If someone had talked to him then, things might have turned out OK. Instead, he wandered onto the wrong track. Now, with his record, it was unlikely he could gain admission into the magnet school. So with DuBoise's help, he enrolled in a third high school, away from the neighborhood. Though underage, he also got a job in the Hanes factory to earn spending money and take up any extra time he might have spent on the street.

But soon he began skipping school and working all day in the factory. Each day he would pass the old crowd of friends on the street. He began hanging with them again. It had been only three weeks since he left St. Charles.

He called Crystal at Maryvale. She urged him to talk to his stepgrandmother and his caseworker about moving to Maryvale. That night he spoke to his stepgrandmother. He didn't think this was a good place for him, he said. She didn't seem to be bothered, or even to care.

The next day, DuBoise took Bryan to a Maryvale campus. But it was not the same Maryvale where Crystal stayed. Bryan arrived on the Columbus campus. Neither he nor Crystal had realized that Maryvale had more than one campus. Still separated from his sister and brother, Bryan felt scared, disappointed, and angry. He lasted only three weeks there.

"MARYVALE was OK," Bryan says of Maryvale, Columbus. "It was clean. They fed you."

But it was another placement that lacked security and respect. Bryan learned early on at his stepgrandmother's to protect his things. When he arrived at Maryvale, he asked to store a few of his expensive clothes, for safety. His clothes were put in a staff closet. The next day, when he asked for them, they were missing.

"They didn't care about it either," Bryan remembers. "They just said, 'They're gone,' and walked away. They wouldn't pay for them or anything."

The staff, he concluded, stole his clothes. He was furious. He had to protect himself. He had to be listened to and respected. He yelled and kicked things, but they still ignored him. So he picked up a bat and stalked around the narrow gray halls, shouting.

"Where's my clothes!" he shouted over and over. Staff and kids fled the hallways before him. He didn't swing or hurt anyone, but he terrorized the staff. Even after he calmed down, he was not punished. He wondered why until he was transferred the next day to the gray halls of Cuneo.

8

Cuneo

CUNEO was terrible, the absolute worst. On the North Side of Chicago, across the street from the Michael Reese crazy home, is how Bryan begins to describe it. Its rooms seemed like army barracks—wide, cold, colorless cinder block. Cabinets for clothes lined the wall, and each boy was given his own lock. Early each morning, the boys were wakened to take a communal shower. There were no curtains for privacy. Bryan could find no security or protection in the other boys or the staff.

"I was around all these guys and I really don't know what's going on, that's how I felt," Bryan says.

He did not know what was expected of him at Cuneo or whom he could trust. Almost all of the other boys were into gangs. The staff wasn't much better.

"You're up against people living there all the time," Bryan remembers. "And the staff would swear at you, man. They treat you like dogs. 'You nothing. You ain't ever going to be anything.' It was terrible."

Bryan was thankful that he was still on a court-ordered work release program. He went to school half a day and did piecework half a day, stacking boxes of hair care products at a nearby factory.

"The job gave me a little bit of sanity," he says. "It was a blessing to get out of Cuneo. Going back was hell. I stayed in my own world, not getting involved with the other youths there. They were in groups like gangs and you had to join one or another, but because I went out to work and I guess because they knew about me from the street before Maryvale, I was OK. I didn't have to get involved. I'm glad about that. Otherwise, I wouldn't have gotten into Mercy. One fight here and a couple of bad incidents there and that's it, you're done. No one will take you."

Bryan shut himself off at Cuneo. He had no friends because he didn't trust friends now. They always got him into trouble. He began to believe he was different and better than the boys around him. He wanted to build on those differences.

"Most of the kids there don't know their family," he says. "They don't know nothing. Fortunately, I knew my family. I knew where I came from and that they were out there somewhere. It was just a matter of keeping track of them. I started to think of how important they are. Family don't do you like friends do when you turn your back. Family don't do you like that. I would go out [to work] and come back to this place that was supposed to be home but it was a hellhole really. Vera DuBoise, she already knew it wasn't good. But I tried to deal with it and keep to myself."

In his free time away from Cuneo, however, Bryan went to the West Side and used drugs he thought helped him cope. They were only to get him through, for now, he told himself, while he tried to find a better home for himself. He did not notice he was slipping into dependency.

Bryan phoned DuBoise everyday, asking her for another placement. He didn't even have to say his name.

"You got me a place yet?" he'd ask his caseworker.

"No, Bryan," she'd say. "Hang in there, OK?"

She knew how difficult it was for kids to hold their own in a place like Cuneo. If the streets are a bad influence, places like Cuneo are simply bad. Just as in prison, the boys are surrounded by others who are trouble and have committed just as serious or more serious crimes than they have. There is no trust. There are few friendships. Staff keeps the kids out of trouble by force and intimidation. But unlike St. Charles DOC, there was not enough good staff to monitor the boys. The inmate to staff ratio was about sixteen to one. According to Bryan, the staff often took payoffs in drugs or money from the kids.

Soon after Bryan's stay there, Cuneo was shut down quietly and disappeared from the system, but not from the memories of the boys who were held there.

"If a boy said the wrong thing or did something wrong, staff restrained him," Bryan remembers vividly—at least one of the reasons he believes it was shut down so quickly and quietly. "There was no talk about it. They just restrained him by kneeling on his arms, pushing his face against the wall with arms behind his back. Sometimes kneeing him in the groin. There was a lot of blood sometimes. No one cared. I saw a lot of staff beat up on kids."

There was little good about living at Cuneo, and for other kids today there are places just like it. If you are too clean or keep your distance too much, the other boys try to bring you down. If you play their game to become acceptable enough so that you don't have to constantly watch your back, the attitude and incidents recorded on the rap sheet could forever prevent a better placement. DuBoise warned Bryan of this, and he took her words to heart. She was the first person in the system he trusted, and in good faith, she lived up to his trust.

9

Mercy

"Bryan, I found a very good place," DuBoise told him on the phone one evening. "But it's going to be extremely hard to get in. You're going to have to work for it."

Bryan was frantic with excitement. That night he could not sleep. He hardly wondered what the new place was like. Instead he thought about how hard he would try to get in. The next morning, on the way to the new home, DuBoise coached him for his entrance interviews, about posture and sitting up straight, making eye contact, shaking hands eagerly, and most important, answering questions directly. When he toured Mercy's campus in downtown Chicago for the first time, his excitement turned into even more solid determination.

"I fell in love with Mercy the first time I saw it," he says. "The people were nice. They acted like they cared. They even knew my name. It was really thorough, their procedures to get in, though. It was rough."

First he met Brother Dan King, and they talked about Bryan's background. Bryan never saw his child welfare service files, but he knew that they recorded everything. He made no attempt to hide incidents. In fact, he went out of his way to accept blame, not intentionally but because it was the way he felt. The method worked well.

King set up another appointment, for an evaluation test, which included a personality test and an IQ test. These entrance exams and psychological evaluations cost Mercy $350 for each applicant; neither the state nor the children are asked to contribute to this cost.

"I must have passed, because they set me up with a psychiatrist for an interview," Bryan says. His IQ score was above the 80 that Mercy considers the minimum for children capable of benefiting from the therapy they will receive. Bryan tested in the low average range, but after an interview, the psychologist noted that he was clearly intelligent and believed Bryan would have scored higher under less stress and with a better education.

Unlike many homes, Mercy explained to Bryan exactly where he was in the admission process and what tests he had to pass. Bryan did not feel he had to needle around to figure out what was happening to him now, or the alternative, to ignore everything and go with whatever happened. For the first time, he felt that he was given a way to work toward what he wanted— not just avoid trouble, but try for something good.

"Ultimately I was accepted," Bryan says, his voice still proud. "And, man, I was happy. I was grateful to the caseworker and everyone. Mercy was the best thing that happened to me. I did a lot of growing there."

There was only one thing Bryan didn't tell Mercy when he interviewed.

"I didn't tell them about the drugs," he says. "During the whole cycle, through everything when I had no family or friends, drugs were my friend. I didn't tell them I was still using."

Bryan pauses.

"Probably a good thing you didn't?" I ask.

"What?" he replies as though waking from a memory.

"It's probably a good thing you didn't tell them," I say. "You probably wouldn't have gotten in."

"Oh, yeah," he says, polite but still confused. "But it was a good thing I told them in the end."

Rather than feeling that he had to lie to save himself, Bryan is still ashamed of the lie.

"I should have told them right up front," he says. "Not for any reason, but it was the truth."

10
Mercy's History

▨

"IF it hadn't been for Mercy, I don't know where I'd be," Bryan says, shaking his head. "On the street or in a gang, or dead probably. Mercy was there for me when I needed them, and they stuck with me. Man, they stuck with me. I still can't believe they did. I'd be dead without Mercy."

Bryan tosses his head back with a laugh free of pain.

Brother Dan King, who admitted Bryan to Mercy and then fought to keep him there after serious setbacks, takes Bryan's life more seriously but comes to the same conclusion.

"That boy would not be alive today," he says flatly, his blue eyes steady. "I know that for a fact."

Looking through Bryan's files, anyone experienced with troubled youths would make the same prediction, probably accurately.

While Brother King is proud of Mercy, he is modest about the home's role in Bryan's success. "He wanted help and we were there at the right time for him. We didn't do everything we should have," he adds honestly. "No program does."

But Mercy comes closer than almost any other home in providing its boys and girls with what they need to overcome their troubled pasts and become productive and stable members of society.

"It's very unique," explains Mike Liberto, who became Bryan's caseworker when DuBoise retired. "Mercy is the elite of these programs."

The home's success rate alone proves that. Father James Close, Mercy's director, estimates that half the youths who enter its 109-year-old boys' home or its four-year-old girls' home respond positively. When they graduate its programs, they are able to hold down jobs, pay taxes, and establish a healthy family—one that will break the cycle of pathological behavior among foster care children that often passes from one generation to the next.*

---

* Social worker William Marrow counts Central Children's Home fortunate to have one or two such successes every few years. "The truth is, few kids out of the foster care system are successful," he says. "Most grow up with social workers making decisions for them, and when they turn eighteen, the ties are cut. No matter how good the kids are, you find that five

About 15 percent of Mercy's graduates do even better—going on to compete with the best and brightest of their generation for undergraduate as well as graduate degrees from such prestigious universities as Harvard, Stanford, Notre Dame, and the University of Illinois. But about one third fall to Mercy's shadow. They either run away or are kicked out because they respond negatively to the program.

Most of the kids, like Bryan, are not drawn to Mercy because of its success rate, though that's why area counselors, teachers, and social workers refer their favorite troubled kids to it for admission. The youth are attracted by its comfortable accomodations—even lavish by most standards—including chandeliers, leather couches, computers, televisions, and loft beds. Its clean and well cared for rooms widen the eyes of most kids and give them a greater sense of their self-worth, child care workers say.

But what first struck Bryan was that the staff knew his name and genuinely welcomed him during the interviewing process. And what strikes him still is that the individual attention never waned over the years. Through good times and bad, staff watched him, looked out for him, and counseled him. That, Bryan says, is unbelievable in foster care. And it has proven irreplaceable in resurrecting the best in a troubled youth.

Because of its reputation and because it is a private institution, Mercy can be selective. Only three out of eight applicants are accepted. And those accepted have to want to be at Mercy.

"No one is placed at Mercy," King says. "We won't have it." The 140 kids at Mercy must sign admittance papers declaring that they want to be at Mercy and that they will take their education seriously. Choosing the most motivated children for admission helps explain why Mercy has a high success rate.

Mercy's kids come from all socioeconomic backgrounds. They come from wealthy suburban families, from public housing projects, or like Bryan, from the streets. Together they form a therapeutic "small society"—a far cry from the way Mercy started out in 1887, as an Irish Catholic orphanage in downtown Chicago.

Mercy's original building, on Jackson Boulevard, was only a block or so away from the boys' campus of today. Its purpose was to house and feed street boys set adrift during the country's great wave of immigration in the latter half of the nineteenth century. Community churches throughout Chicago and in other large cities took on the duty of finding shelter for these

---

years later, if they haven't had good follow-up or are not in an independent living program somewhere, they're not going to make it." Follow-up programs, in which caseworkers check on their "graduates" periodically, are not part of most public foster care programs. In the follow-up, the caseworker looks at whether the youth needs anything from emotional support or more therapy to more food stamps. In independent living programs, social workers are more heavily involved in the kids' lives, regularly.

waifs crowding the streets as newsboys, bootblacks, and out-of-town run-aways. In Chicago, Jewish, Catholic, and Protestant denominations had their own orphanages, as did German, Irish, Italian, and Polish parish communities. At that time, most of the orphans were children from unwanted pregnancies and from impoverished immigrant families, left to cope with the death or disappearance of one or both parents.

Until the Depression, Mercy was well funded by Catholic women's groups, which staged benefit drives throughout Chicago. When the stock market crashed, Mercy struggled more successfully than most homes in staying open. The staff still tell stories of how its then director, Father Edward J. "Jake" Kelly, got the home through the hard times by dodging bill collectors and scrounging slightly damaged food from sympathetic wholesalers.

He also came up with one of the many innovative plans that helped Mercy survive at first, and then excel. He had the boys spend an hour each night scouring out-of-town phone books for names of likely Catholic families to send handwritten appeals to for funds. Whether or not Mercy was the first to use direct mail fund-raising as it claims, the method was indisputably successful. It continues to be the mainstay of Mercy's support. Last year, $3.5 million of the home's $5.5 million of revenue was generated by direct mail. Mercy is better know nationally than locally. Approximately 90 percent of its donors are located beyond Illinois.*

The number of the nation's orphanages declined during the Depression. Most closed under extreme financial strain. But after the Depression, few were revived, due to weakening church and community support. In the 1940s and 1950s, the number of children in need of care dropped with improved economic conditions and government-funded family aid programs. But over the next two decades, the numbers rose swiftly, until by 1980, they had doubled and tripled in many states. Child services workers blamed this population explosion on the wave of drug addiction, particularly crack cocaine. But even though the crack epidemic has since waned, the number of children placed in state custody is still on the rise. In the 1990s, the numbers escalated even beyond the scare-formulated predictions.

The types of children filling the institutions have also changed. Increasing alcohol and drug addiction brought serious problems into the lives of chil-

---

* Sixty-two percent of Mercy's budget depends on donations. Only one percent of the budget is covered by parent contributions. Mercy does ask parents to pay tuition based on a sliding scale. Of some parents, they ask as little as $50 or $25 a month, an insignificant amount in terms of the estimated $25,000 a year spent per child on schooling, treatment, and housing. But Mercy believes tuition, even if nominal, reminds parents of their responsibility to their child and is a way of keeping parent-child contact. Mercy's primary goal in most cases is to reunite the child with his family, if not so they can live together, then so they can at least maintain some form of familial ties. Bryan's father did not pay any tuition because Charles Murray, Chicago's appointed guardian of the children, was listed on his application as his guardian. Bryan was officially a ward of the state.

dren, including violence, crime, and sexual abuse. Like most such institutions, Mercy was slow to recognize the needs of this more troubled population. In 1973, when Father James Close was appointed to head its boys' home, Mercy was still run like many children's homes today, as an old-fashioned orphanage. Caring for ninety boys were eighteen child care workers, who could do little more than make sure the kids got up in the morning, went to school, and studied. The home had only four social workers. The few kids troubled seriously enough to be designated as "disturbed" got to see a social worker once a week.

"We didn't really try to get into fixing the dysfunctional kid," says Close now.

At the time, social work of this kind was totally new to him. Today Close makes no attempt to conceal his initial reluctance in taking over Mercy. He had been a content and successful parish priest when John Cardinal Cody asked him to consider taking over Mercy boys' home.

Father Close did not think the idea a good one. Explaining he had no experience with children, he declined the offer. Cardinal Cody suggested he think about it more and pray on the decision. Father Close did as the cardinal suggested and came back some time later even more convinced that this was not the job for him. The cardinal then told the priest: "I've prayed over it too. And you are going to the boys' home. Tomorrow."

Close found Mercy overrun by tough street kids, not down-on-their-luck orphans looking for the kindly Spencer Tracy figure in *Boys Town*. If they weren't in trouble, they were halfway there.

"What the hell's the program here?" Close asked the outgoing director, Father Kelly, who was suffering from cancer. Kelly answered his question by suggesting that Close get a black belt in karate, adding that he was pleased that Close was big and looked mean.

After Close took over, he became convinced that Mercy needed reform. With his fresh eyes, he decided that boys sent to the home needed more than a bed and food. They needed counselors and therapy to repair the damage in their shattered lives.

Deinstitutionalization was in full swing across the country, reaching beyond mental institutions to orphanages. Social workers were placing their wards in foster homes rather than the traditional orphanages, now called children's homes (mostly for politically correct reasons). For about 15 percent of the children placed with a surrogate family, foster homes do not work out, and they are shifted from home to home, left rudderless in what has come to be known as "foster care drift," until they age out of the system. Only the troubled children who "fail out" of foster care homes are placed in group and children's homes like Mercy. Most of them, Close decided, needed therapy.

But Close found Mercy caught in the depressing cycle most children's homes still are slave to—of surviving by taking children they are not equipped to help. He did not believe that Mercy was up to caring for the seriously troubled kids the state was sending them. They hadn't the staff or funds. And the children Mercy felt more prepared to help, those with firm values already instilled and intact, were placed not with Mercy but in foster homes. Still, Mercy could not refuse the children the city sent to it. It was bound by a contract with Chicago's Department of Children and Family Services. Moreover, Mercy, like Central Children's Home, was paid according to a per diem schedule for each kid. This per diem accounted for almost all of Mercy's budget. If it did not accept all the DCFS kids, or if the city became critical of Mercy, the home was vulnerable. Fewer children would be sent to it, which would reduce its income. Without DCFS business, Mercy would go bankrupt.

Father Close responded with a daring approach. Despite the danger of going bankrupt, he terminated Mercy's contract with Chicago's Children and Family Services and asked the city to remove their wards from the home. Close took another revolutionary step. He enrolled in business school at Notre Dame.

Armed with a master's degree in business administration, he returned to modernize and then computerize the home's fund-raising methods. Within only a few years, he successfully set Mercy on solid financial footing. And with the healthy finances, he gradually built a staff of professional child care workers to help the children. Unlike most homes struggling under DCFS's minimalistic contract, Mercy has been able to attract and hire staff with at least college degrees. The turnover rate is high, not because of burnout from unreasonable schedules and demands, but because many of the energetic staffers go on to graduate work. Salaries are also significantly higher at Mercy. Most impressive, Mercy is able to maintain a student-staff ratio impossible in most foster homes. In its Kelly Home, one of the three within Mercy boys' home complex, four staff members care for seven kids. In another, ten staff care for sixteen kids. In some of Mercy's programs, as many as six staff care for seven kids.

"You can't say Mercy is your average program any more than you can consider Bryan your average ward," Bryan's caseworker, Mike Liberto, concludes. "They're both exceptional."

11
Campbell

▓

Mᴇʀᴄʏ has six programs for boys. The Young Boys' Home, for boys eleven to fourteen years old, provides individual and family therapy and a very structured schedule, and focuses on teaching its ten boys "appropriate behaviors and communication skills." The boys are expected either to be reunited with their family within eighteen months or to graduate to the Mahony Home.

The Mahony Home, for teenage boys between fourteen and sixteen, has twelve beds. The boys are required to attend high school (most enroll in nearby private schools) and take individual and group therapy.* The boys follow a very structured schedule with a little free time. Within twelve to twenty-four months, they are expected "to develop mature interpersonal skills and coping mechanisms."

For the more troubled, streetwise boys, like Bryan, there is the sixteen-bed Campbell Home, a transitional living program for older adolescents fifteen to eighteen years old, who are expected to leave after one or two years. In the morning, Bryan attended school. In the afternoon, he worked a part-time job, like all the Campbell residents. He was exempted from family therapy because there was no family to return to, but he regularly and even eagerly attended his individual therapy and group meetings. He was on a busy, disciplined schedule, but one that allowed him some freedom. He progressed well toward the Campbell Home's goals of "developing self-reliance, initiative and personal responsibility."

Bryan was eager to please and impress the staff. It was his best placement to date, and he did not want to mess it up. He did not feel that he fit in entirely. But he knew good accommodations when he saw them—a small room to himself with a desk, a bed, and a dresser. It offered more privacy and space than Bryan had ever known. There was a communal kitchen, where Bryan learned to cook. He liked the staff, and though he was still wary of friendships, he got along well enough with the boys.

---

* Mercy pays the tuition if they choose to attend private school. Most of the children choose the local private schools.

"I began to grow there," Bryan says.

The only problem was that Campbell was too close to his old neighborhood and his old friends, most of whom were now full-fledged drug users. While he tried to fit into the program at Mercy, he was still more at ease with his old street friends. It was like living two lives, one that he pretended to be a part of because it was better, and one that he sank back into when he feared he was not good enough for the better life. He hid his double life and his drug use from the staff in the mistaken belief that he had his addiction under control. Bryan would attend school, work part-time, and complete his chores. But as soon as he had free time, he was back to his old neighborhood and his oldest friend—drugs.

No one seemed to notice. At least, that's what he thought for weeks. Until, one Saturday afternoon, he had a bad trip. He returned ill and went directly to his room. The weekend counselor on duty was herself recovering from an addiction and had been watching Bryan for weeks. Her suspicions were confirmed several times by his bloodshot eyes, his mood swings, his weight loss. But she waited for the right time to talk to him. At eight o'clock that night, when most of the boys were out, she went to Bryan's room. She sat on his bed, and without saying a word, she hugged him.

"I was so surprised," Bryan remembers. "It was warm. I hadn't been hugged in a long time, I guess. She said, 'It's going to be OK,' and I felt totally better even though I hadn't told her yet."

"What's wrong?" she asked Bryan. "Are you using?"

Bryan answered truthfully. It might have been the understanding and acceptance in her deep brown eyes. Or it might have been the hug. It could have been that he didn't have time to think about lying. He doesn't know.

"Yeah," he said. "I am."

"It's going to be OK," she assured him again. "We're going to get you some help."

Mercy sent Bryan to detox at Saint Cabrini Hospital a couple of days later. It was a ninety-day program primarily designed for teenage boys. Every week, the boys' parents would join in a session with their sons.

"They all had parents," Bryan says. "The first time I was scared and sad because I knew I had no one. I knew no one would come for me and I'd be all alone. But there was Joe. Joe came and sat right next to me every time, just like a parent."

Joe Winn was Mercy's drug counselor. He kept close contact with Bryan during the ninety-day treatment at the Chicago Addiction Center.

"I was really helped then," Bryan says. "He was always there. Mercy didn't turn their back on me when they had every reason to. I broke the rules but they stayed with me anyway. I never thought they would take me back and give me another chance, but they did. I come to find out later that they knew about my using."

Bryan recognized what he had in Mercy and in Joe. He swore he would do everything possible not to be unworthy of their attention and trust, and never to take it for granted. He saw drug use in a new light.

"At the addiction center they told me all about my disease. Because drugs are a disease. Mine ran throughout my family. But I was still in denial, I think, because I still thought I didn't really have as big a problem as everyone else there."

But Bryan learned something almost more valuable.

"I'll never forget that first day. All these guys had their mom or dad or both there, and here was Joe, for me, sitting next to me. It was like, wow. He used to talk to me and things. He made me feel OK, that I was worth something and that I could do it. I wanted to do it for Joe and for me. But I never had someone who cared like that."

While in treatment, Bryan became friends with two boys. He told them about Mercy and when it was time to leave the program, they joined him at Mercy. Like many of the kids at Mercy, they had parents, but the relationships were poor. Bryan began, then, to be a model to the new boys. He also talked openly about his problem with the boys already at Mercy. The staff encouraged him to do so. As he did, other boys began coming forward to talk about their alcohol as well as drug problems. With Bryan as an example, they lost their fear of being thrown out of Mercy. They were more confident that Mercy would stand behind them as it had Bryan, so they were willing to seek professional help.

"I started being a leader of the whole floor," Bryan says, amazed that he could be looked to as a role model. He began to grow in self-respect and pride because he could help others. But a setback began to develop soon after, when Joe left to take a job elsewhere. Bryan could always tell Joe his fears and cravings. Joe understood him like no one else, Bryan thought. Without Joe, Bryan feared he would stumble back to his addiction. He did not believe that he was strong enough to stay away from drugs, and the responsibility of being looked up to weighed on him.

"Bryan doesn't like being a leader," Mike Liberto, Bryan's caseworker, says. "He feels he has to be perfect, and he won't come forward with his own problems. He thinks having problems fails others. It's something he'll always have to watch out for."

A few months after Joe left, Mercy told Bryan he was ready to graduate to the Kelly Home, the next phase of the Mercy program. Bryan was hesitant. Each day since Joe left was a struggle. He thought of drugs often. He worried about the extra freedom he would have in the Kelly program, a six-to-nine-month program for boys eighteen to twenty-one years old. The six boys in the program are enrolled in secondary or higher education, work part-time, and attend individual therapy as needed. The program is less structured than those for younger boys since its purpose is to prepare them for independent living, advanced education, and careers. They have much more freedom and spare time. He told the staff that he wasn't ready.

They allowed him to stay a month longer, then decided that he needed a push. They had seen such hesitation before in kids who became too reliant on Mercy's tight schedule and readily available staff. They find comfort in Mercy's cocoon, safe and free, cut off from their past with its temptations and failings. But Mercy's goal is to guide the children toward self-reliance and to build in them strength to resist whatever temptation lies outside its coveted walls. So Bryan was told he would move to the last-phase housing at Mercy after the home's camping and canoeing summer trip to Colorado.

12
Crisis

"I HAD a crisis," Bryan says about the Denver trip. "I had to come back."

Since he was nine years old, Bryan had known he had sickle cell anemia, a genetic disease that tears almost exclusively at African-Americans. But he never really knew what it meant. He did not know the effects of the disease or the limitations it placed on him, and he didn't know it often proved fatal. Just as many children are tossed in the system, so too their medical histories are transferred from placement to placement but often not examined or thoroughly explained to the child. At age seventeen, all Bryan knew of the disease was that, as he put it, "If I have a girlfriend who has sickle cell anemia too, and we have a baby, the baby will also have it." Nothing had been told him about the disease's effects on his own body.

So when Bryan began to feel queasy as the Mercy group drove higher and higher in the Colorado mountains, he believed it was only the elevation sickness the counselors told him it was.

"That's one bad thing about group homes," Bryan says. "If you're not literally dying, they don't really want to hear about it."

As they climbed higher, Bryan felt as though someone were stealing his breath.

"Staff told me, 'Don't worry about it,' " Bryan remembers. "I tried that, but then it was getting worse. I was like, No, I'm losing breath. I was having a crisis."

Bryan passed out and he was rushed to a clinic, then airlifted to a Denver hospital, then to a Chicago hospital. He spent the next three weeks there, first in critical, then in stable condition. His spleen and liver were dangerously enlarged.

"Stuff was happening and I couldn't stop it," Bryan says. "They wanted to give me drugs [at the hospital] and I didn't want that. I told them I was recovering and didn't want it. I told them that I had a problem with drugs. But they had to put me on synthetic drugs. It brought back that feeling. I relapsed mentally."

By the time he was released from the hospital, Bryan had a thirst for his old drugs. He looked forward to being back in Mercy's Campbell Home, where he had made a safe, drug-free life for himself. Instead, while in the hospital, staff had graduated him to the Kelly Home. They were proud of Bryan's accomplishments and eager to have him move on. They thought he needed to be nudged, as many fledglings do. Bryan thought otherwise.

"I explained that I wasn't ready to move on," he says. "But they moved me anyway."

Liberto sees it a little differently. While Bryan's promotion may have been slightly premature, Bryan needs to be able to face his successes no matter what their timing.

"Unfortunately," Liberto explains with his usual, keen awareness, "Bryan's setbacks are often due to his successes."

"What did I do in my free time?" Bryan asks, shaking his head. "I went back to the West Side." There he hung with his stepuncles and eventually relapsed.

"Man, I felt really, really bad," he says. "I was the role model. I thought, Should I tell them? No, they'll kick me out. But my using got worse."

Bryan's actions told them anyway. First his punctuality slipped. He was late to meetings, then slept in meetings, and finally missed meetings altogether. Some of the staff suspected he was relapsing, but they failed to get to him before other trouble did.

Cook County Jail

Bryan barely mentions his stint in Cook County Jail. It turned his life around for good, he says. But other than the outcome, he does not want to talk about it.

"When they took him from Mercy and locked him up, Bryan was really hurt bad," says Crystal. "Bryan, he was really hurt by it, really hurt. He still don't like to talk about it."

He doesn't talk about it, and he doesn't think about it. Crystal told him just before he was locked up not to dwell on it because he'd just get bitter, and not to get angry either because that would hurt him, too. Just look ahead and pray for the Lord to give you strength to get through, she told him. Bryan did as his sister said. And he finds that her advice is as effective looking back as it was in getting him through that time.

He is clearly embarrassed by the incident that landed him in jail. He would like to brush it aside, as he has done in his own mind, claiming he can't recall much about it. He even invents a story he thinks is plausible, accepting the blame, just to get it behind him.

"I was doing drugs and stuff, and selling it sometimes," Bryan first told me. "They caught me or something. I think that's what happened. Possession and not going to school, I think. I don't really remember."

It was an improbable story, particularly since he was taken to a high-security detention facility. The true story came from Crystal.

"Armed robbery was the charge," she says, "only everyone knows Bryan didn't do it. Bryan's done plenty of things, but not that. It was Bryan's [relative] who pulled a gun, which turned out to be a BB gun, on a neighborhood girl, and robbed her of her coat. While the girl's father called the police, Bryan's [relatives] climbed up a fire escape to the girl's window and bribed her to point the accusing finger at Bryan. Bryan wasn't even there; he was buying drugs on the corner. It was all a mess, they admitted later, but never to the police."

"It just don't sound right," Bryan's father said when Crystal called him just before the police arrived. "Bryan got three coats of his own now. Why would he steal one? He don't even have a girlfriend to give it to."

Besides, Bryan's father and sister agreed, Bryan never took from anyone. His problem was that he was too giving and wanted to be liked too much. He accepted blame to protect others and because he learned early on that what he said didn't count much, but handling well what was dealt to him did.

"My father went to the girl and her father and raised sin," Crystal remembers. "She admitted that our [relatives] had paid her to accuse Bryan of the incident. But then my father left and the police went to her, and she told them Bryan had done it. It was too late. Nothing we could do. The girl and her father weren't as afraid of Bryan and our father as they were our [relatives]. Then it was too late. Nothing we could do."

His head bowed, Bryan later tells the story. Crystal was only partially right. He had been there when the coat was stolen. He was right alongside his relatives when one of them pulled the gun. Only Bryan did not know it was going to happen. They did not tell him what they were up to. It was a cool spring evening, with a hint of summer's restless air. They were going, Bryan thought, to buy drugs. But they hesitated on a block. Bryan didn't know why. It was for a girl, the relative told him. Bryan assumed his relative liked the girl and wanted to mess with her in a flirtatious way. They never flirt alone. He'd need the other guys with him. Then the girl came and his relative asked her for her coat. A red coat. Demanded it, really. And Bryan felt things spiraling out of control. She said no. When his relative pulled the gun, Bryan ran. He ran all the way back to Mercy and swore to himself not to go back to the West Side, ever, for drugs or anything. That was too close. It was wrong. He did not question whether he should have stayed during the incident to make sure no one got hurt. He knew his relatives weren't capable of hurting the girl. To them it was a game.

It would have been easier if he had been completely guilty, he says. It would have been right. He did not fight in court to clear his name because when he tells the truth like that—he was there but he didn't pull the gun, in fact he didn't even know that they were going to rob the girl—people think he's making excuses. But even more than that, he believed he was guilty, maybe not of armed robbery, but other things. He was a part of the mess. Again he was hanging out with the wrong people. But he had trusted his relatives. He even loved them. They were like his brothers; they were his protectors on the street when Crystal was gone. He had failed to see the signs that they weren't for him—the tricks they played on him, the drugs and stuff they got him into, the things they got him to do. It all adds up now. But then, then, he was young and foolish.

"I'll never forget that," Bryan says, still upset about the moment his "bad old world" collided with and almost destroyed the "new good" one he was building.

It was a hot day for Chicago's spring. And this was the day Bryan had to wear a long-sleeved shirt and tie. He walked from school, Truman Middle College, to a job interview. He tried, unsuccessfully, not to sweat. He didn't want wet spots on his white shirt during the job interview. Fresh dress and cleanliness were firmly imprinted on him from the days of Crystal's influence. Bryan had even had his jeans dry cleaned so they'd have the starched crease in them. He had pressed his only dress shirt three times the night before. He wanted to be perfect. He wanted this job for the summer. He'd be working in a lawyer's office. A lawyer! He'd have made it.

"You have quite a history, Bryan," the interviewer said, scanning the résumé Mercy helped him put together.

"Yes," he said seriously, without a smile.

"You've moved around quite a bit," she said.

"Yes," he said.

"We need someone reliable, not someone who is going to show up just when they feel like it or just when they *can,*" she said.

Bryan said nothing but sat up straight, eagerly. She looked up over her glasses at Bryan, impressed by his looks and that he had held his tongue.

"But I understand from Mercy you have a good attendance record," she said. "We're not in the business of taking risks, Bryan, so I hope you have it together."

She was looking at him for a response now.

"Yes, Mrs. Smith," Bryan said firmly. "I believe I do. I've made mistakes before. And I really do believe I won't make them again. I want this job because I'm building a real life for myself with Mercy's help. I know I can do it."

It was the first time Mrs. Smith's scowl softened, almost into a smile. Bryan felt pretty good. He hoped he had it (and he thought he did). He would keep hoping all the way home. He wouldn't even say he thought he got it if anyone asked. That would presume too much. He would be *lucky* to get it, he kept telling himself. He went through every one of Mrs. Smith's questions in his mind on the way home. He hoped one of the counselors would remember about the interview and ask him how it went. He wanted to talk about it. He knew someone would remember. They were good about that, and he had been talking about this interview for two weeks, since he was graduated to the Kelly program and a counselor suggested he might apply for this job. Once the counselor mentioned it, Bryan knew he wanted it. Now, especially after that incident on the West Side had shaken him up, Bryan wanted it and that new life. Kelly was the last-phase, independent living program, and he was going to prove to Mercy that they did right by accepting him. He was going to be a success. He smiled.

Once he reached Mercy, Bryan jumped the stairs two and three at a time. He was looking forward to talking to the counselors about his day. He came in, as usual, looking for all the counselors so he could say hi to them. Kelly was starting to feel like home, and it felt nice.

They seemed funny, the way they looked at him. Something didn't seem right, but he didn't know what. No one asked about his interview or even his day, but that wasn't it. It was the way they looked at him that stirred a funny feeling in him. He went to his room to put away his stuff and change.

Before he even came out, the detectives came in. Bryan was frantic, shocked, as he describes it, beyond scared. As the detectives spoke he felt jittery; all his nerves were on end. He could feel everything, sense everything. It was one of those moments of utter fear and terror he's felt a handful of times in his life. But this was worse, because this was real. It wasn't as it had been when he was a child. This he understood. He had failed.

Their words blurred together. But he picked out some of the ones they repeated over and over. He knew what they were talking about, even though he hardly heard their words. All he understood was that it was something about a jacket and someone had pressed charges. He knew inside that he had been with the wrong people in the wrong place at the wrong time. It had all happened before. But this was different. This was worse. There were people here he cared about; he didn't want to let them down, not like this, not after all this. A counselor and a therapist had come into the room with the detectives. He didn't notice them at the time. He was too focused on the detectives. Slowly he recognized their faces as if they were coming into focus. First he registered their fear, then their surprise, and then he recognized who they were. Later he realized that they had probably asked the detectives to stay in a closed office and make the arrest in the privacy of his room rather than in front of the other students.

Jean, the therapist, asked if she could talk to Bryan alone. The detectives looked skeptical. They looked out the window and found that, through it, there was no escape. They handcuffed Bryan to the foot of his bed and guarded the outside of his door.

"It's OK, Bryan," Jean said smoothly. She saw the terror leaping in his eyes.

"I was trying, Jean, I really was. I'm sorry. I thought I was going to do well. I really did. I don't know, Jean. I don't know," he said shaking his head, frantic still.

"It's going to be OK. It's going to be all right," she said knowingly. "Don't give up."

Those simple words stuck with Bryan. They meant more to him than anything at that moment, and they gave him the strength to walk, hand-cuffed, out of Mercy, and look into the scared and disappointed faces of the counselors he passed. Thankfully, most of the other kids were at their after-school jobs. But walking those grand halls of Mercy, past the support staff, the counselors, everyone, was one of the most horrible moments of Bryan's life.

"The police came into Mercy and handcuffed me there with everyone watching. And I was supposed to be the role model," he says, shaking his head, still more disappointed in himself than anything else.

After the shame came fear.

"I thought, Man, I'm through now, my life is over with. But Mercy was still with me. Laura, the director of the Kelly home, sent me cards and letters. She came to court with me. I think it was because of her they put me in drug rehab rather than prison," he says. "Mercy realized that I relapsed."

Bryan smiles. Mercy stood by him.

Bryan had just turned eighteen and was prosecuted as an adult. He was found guilty and sentenced to serve eight months in Cook County Jail, but then with Mercy's recommendations and character reports, the judge agreed to the rehab program and a long probation, rather than the high-security detention center at Cook County Jail Bryan was placed in awaiting his trial.

The treatment was intense, Bryan says. The first time he had undergone treatment was when he was still denying he was an addict. This time he accepted that he had a problem, however humiliating.

He remembers one exercise in particular from the treatment course that still tears at him. Each man took turns standing on a red line, called the life line, with all the others looking at him. Then the questions would start bombarding him from all sides where counselors and guards stood.

"Do you love yourself?" a counselor booms.

"Yes."

"What?!" the captors yell.

"Yes!" Bryan's voice breaks.

"You love yourself and you're here?!! You stupid or something?"

"No."

"What? Yes you are." They pause. "Aren't you?"

Bryan doesn't answer.

"Aren't you stupid?"

"Yes," he mumbles.

"What?!"

"Yes."

"Yes what? Yes, you're stupid and a drug addict?"

"Yes."

"Say it."

"Yes, I'm stupid and a drug addict."

"Louder."

"Yes, I'm a stupid drug addict!"

"Good."

"What's your occupation?!"

"I don't have one yet."

"You a loser or something?"

"Yes."

"Do you love your family?!"

"Yes."

"What?"

"Yes!"

They said something about Bryan's mother and he broke down. He doesn't know if they knew she was dead, but it wouldn't have mattered anyway.

"I was just like, Man, I am an addict. My name is Bryan and I'm eighteen years old and I am in jail."

When Bryan was freed, Mercy didn't want to take him back. A new program manager reviewed his files and was convinced this youth would not work out. He had failed too often, and then severely.

Bryan's caseworker, Mike Liberto, went to bat for him. Liberto is a typically overworked social worker in the West Area Chicago office. The Association of American Social Workers' guidelines require that social workers should carry no more than seven children on their caseload. But DCFS says there are simply too many kids in the system, so the caseworkers are stretched to work in the best interest of far more children. Liberto's load fluctuated between fifty to seventy cases, once reaching 180 cases.

"It was horrible," Liberto says. "Unbelievable, but that's because there are just too many kids and not enough workers."

"With Bryan, the problem was that he had turned eighteen," Liberto says. "You can't place someone who's eighteen. If Mercy didn't take him back, it would have been over for Bryan."

So Liberto appealed to Brother Dan King, who had been the one to accept

Bryan originally. Liberto had an advantage there. King knew Bryan and he shared Liberto's suspicion that Bryan was not guilty of the armed robbery charge.

"I just told him that Bryan is afraid and this is what he calls his home," Liberto says of his meeting with King.

King was swayed in part by Liberto's commitment to Bryan. It was unusual for a social worker to take such an interest in a case. King went over his program manager's head and readmitted Bryan.

Brother Larry, the director of the Quille Home program, to which Bryan was admitted, was still unconvinced. He told Bryan that he was giving him six months to prove himself.

"They came to see me," he remembers from Cook. "And then they accepted me again. Man, it was unbelievable. And when I came out, I was stronger than ever. It helped me a lot mentally. I realized I was up against myself. I thought, What do I want to do with me now? Who am I? What do I want to do to get there?"

That was in 1991, and five years later, Bryan is still clean.

Bryan got a job at the Hilton in downtown Chicago and worked for his graduate equivalency diploma while still in treatment. He graduated at the top of his program. His graduation ceremony was held in a church. Both Crystal and Felicia attended.

"Bryan was the only student to speak," Crystal remembers five years later. "I was so proud of him. He spoke so well. I knew he had it then."

Brother Larry now urged Bryan to enroll in the ACT prep course.

"What's that?" Bryan asked.

"The ACT is a college entrance examination," Brother Larry told him. "C'mon, we're going to get you in college."

Bryan was stunned. He hadn't considered college.

"Don't you want to go to college?" Larry asked.

"I don't know," Bryan replied. What he really meant, he now says, laughing, is that he didn't think he was smart enough to make it there.

"You want to make money, don't you?"

"Yeah," Bryan said.

After that, he went with the flow, working hard at whatever Brother Larry put in front of him.

On the ACT pre-test, Bryan scored 14. After the course, he scored 16. "I thought that was low," Bryan says. "But Larry said it was good."

Bryan applied to the schools Larry suggested. To Lewis University, a small school outside of Chicago, Larry wrote a long letter. A few weeks later Bryan received a letter from its president.

"I couldn't believe he wrote me directly! He said they would help me as much as they could and that he *hoped* I would go to Lewis," Bryan says. "They were behind me a hundred and ten percent!"

Not only had he been accepted, but they actually wanted him at that school, he thought. It was the first place he felt that he was not a burden— that he was actually invited. He was determined to succeed at Lewis.

He enrolled initially in a program for students with low ACT scores. He earned a 3.7 grade point average out of a possible 4.0. The next semester, in regular classes, while running track and cross-country as his brother had, Bryan earned a 3.4.

Bryan was part of Mercy's postresidential program for boys twenty-one and older, which provides access to social services and career and educational support. When Bryan turned twenty-one, Liberto asked the courts to allow him to stay in DCFS custody. Cases in Illinois are automatically closed when children reach twenty-one. Although Bryan had done very well, Liberto felt he should continue to have access to Mercy's support system until he was fully self-reliant.

"From experience I knew that if Bryan were emancipated, he'd fall through," Liberto says. "We [DCFS and Mercy] were his security. Based on his history and background, his ups and downs, I knew it would be difficult for him without us.

"My first impression of him had been that he was a friendly and likable kid, but to be honest, I compared him to my other cases and I didn't know if he would work out. I wouldn't have predicted Bryan would come so far. You just can't do that with any kid. But Bryan was working against the odds. He was raised on the streets. When you get those kids as teenagers, they say they want to go through high school but they don't make it. Bryan's the only one who has followed through in my cases. I wanted to make sure we didn't leave him before he was ready. He had come too far."

In a landmark case for Chicago, the judge allowed Bryan to remain in DCFS custody until he graduated from college. And on the basis of that case, Liberto was able to hold on to a twenty-one-year-old girl just like Bryan, enrolled at Northeastern Illinois University in Chicago. DCFS pays tuition for foster kids like Bryan if they attend the public university system, and provides them with a monthly stipend. Bryan chose a small private school initially because he needed more attention than large universities can offer. After his first year, he transferred to Northeastern, a public school, because of money. But the semester proved difficult. He missed the individualized attention and transferred back to Lewis, where the state chipped in for some of the tuition, and the school awarded him an academic scholarship. He also had small scholarships from the Orphans Foundation and the Urban League. Still, despite the financial aid and working part-time during the academic year and full-time in the summer, Lewis put him $14,000 in debt each year, he says.

The summer before his junior year, Bryan worked at the Daley Center in the Records Department, pulling files from the warehouse to fill lawyers' and public requests. He entered Lewis again in the fall. He's more comfortable there, he says. While the student body is predominately white, he feels at ease with the area it's in and the tutoring available to him. He's majoring in social work and minoring in English. He's chosen classes with subjects he knows a lot about—minority issues, research in social work, chemical dependency, Christian actions and values (which is required), an AIDS seminar, and sexuality in the nineties. Because he registered late, unable to pull enough money together for the regular registration period, he was left without a dorm. He stays over at Crystal's some nights. But then there's a forty-five-minute commute to school, when there isn't any traffic. Sometimes he stays with his father, who lives much closer to campus. Mostly he stays with a friend whom he plans to get an apartment with. His friend still lives with his family in Joliet, the suburb where Lewis University lies.

"The main thing now is maintaining in school," Bryan says, still shaken by his bad grades at Northeastern.

But there are other things too. On campus, Bryan had been accused of stealing a $72 jacket. He was with three "associates" at the time. One of the three stole the jacket, but all three were charged. Bryan missed his court date and a $5,000 warrant was put up on him. He missed the court date, Bryan says, because he had another court date in Chicago, for a stolen television. He showed up to that one, and the charges were dropped.

Even with all the hurdles Bryan has cleared, and all the barriers from the inside and out that Bryan has torn down and rebuilt, Liberto knows Bryan is not home free.

"Bryan can be swayed," he explained even before the two recent incidents. "He wants to be liked. He doesn't have anyone to say you really screwed up when he does. That's what I'm here for. To show him I'm on his case and let him know we care. If you leave him alone too long, he'll feel abandoned. And his addiction is very much a daily battle."

Liberto was recently promoted to assistant supervisor of the East Regional office. He asked to continue working on Bryan's case and nine others. It was an unusual request. He was in effect asking to work two jobs, mostly on his own time—a request the overburdened system could never afford to turn down.

"I have a lot of strong feelings for Bryan," Liberto explains. "He's rare."

13

Narcotics Anonymous

❖

Bryan was tired when he picked me up at about 7 P.M. on his way to a Narcotics Anonymous meeting on Chicago's South Side. He brought Tijuana with him, a friend who is also recovering. According to Bryan, the two are virtual relatives. Tijuana's grandmother was the original foster mother of Felicia's children, and she also raised Tijuana. Though Tijuana is two years older, Bryan watches over her like an older brother. It was on her request that Bryan was driving from his apartment on the North Side clear to the South Side to attend this particular meeting. Tijuana wanted to see her girl-friend, who would also be there.

In the car, Tijuana was serious and reserved, shying away from conversation. Bryan was quiet too. He had had a long day of work at the courthouse pulling files for lawyers. It was made longer because he had spent the previous day in line to renew his food stamps, then in a hospital waiting room for the doctor's final inspection.

Now Bryan parked on a full curb near the back entrance of Jackson Park Hospital. The Narcotics Anonymous meeting was already under way in a basement room. About thirty people were seated in child-sized chairs when we walked into the middle of a testimonial.

For two hours, recovering addicts told of drugs that had torn at their hopes, loves, and lives. Women told of selling their bodies for a hit. Men spoke of beatings they gave and jobs they lost. Many admitted violating the NA rule that they forgo relationships for a year in order to learn about themselves and become self-reliant. Some had become involved with people they met at NA meetings and discovered, during a relapse triggered by the stress of new relationships, that their partners had been attending meetings only to satisfy families or employers.

"If you're not here for yourself, you're not going to make it," one woman declared during her testimonial. "You are going to fail."

"Mm-hmm. That's right," the group chorused, as they did repeatedly through the meeting.

Each testimonial drew me deeper into despair. Each story glanced not one or two, but hit several tragedies straight on, along with some hopes and many fears. So many relapses. It was an emotional roller coaster ride to hear these stories and then see members of the group jump up to embrace and congratulate those who had been clean for thirty days, for sixty days, for ninety days, for a year, for a year and a half. No one claimed the two-year award, a key chain, or the five- or ten-year prize, but there seemed to be no disappointment. Someone called out, "Keep coming back!" and the phrase was picked up and called forward around the spartan room. Pain and struggle seemed to echo off the gray cinder-block walls.

Always it was a struggle, each person said. Staying away from drugs wasn't easier after ninety days or two years. Relapse always lurked just around the corner. Always, you had to be careful of the friends you choose, the chances you take, the life you lead.

Never, it seemed, would Bryan or anyone there be free. The thought became almost suffocating. At twenty-one, young, curious, and brave, Bryan should be expanding his life rather than concentrating on keeping some of its doors closed. Always now, he has to be careful not to get too hungry, too lonely, too tired, too sad. All those conditions are precursors for relapse.

As we left, I was concerned that Bryan had sat through the two hours for my benefit, so I could see what it was all about. I was depressed that he had undergone another painful reminder of his past. He had hardly spoken since we left. We waited in the car for Tijuana, who was talking with her girlfriend. Orange cones of light fell from high street lamps uniformly lining the wide, desolate street. I turned to look over at Bryan after a while of silence. That's when I noticed there was something different about him. He was not tense, as he had been when we arrived. And he was not upset. There was something very different about Bryan. There was a serenity about him. His eyes glistened. He glowed. Bryan stared ahead, his eyes wide and open as if gulping in some beauty I could hardly see. I looked out at the desolate street again, but now the streetlights looked bright against a peaceful dark. It was transformed into a different world in minutes.

As Tijuana slid into the car and melted back into the cushioned seat, she let out a relieved sigh that sounded as if she had breathed fresh air for the first time. Then a new smile lit up her face. She was beautiful then. Bryan was leaning back, both hands on the steering wheel, still gazing at the street.

"You all right, Tijuana?" he asked.

"Yeah," she said.

"Ready to go?"

"Yeah."

Bryan slowly moved forward as if reaching for a bar of soap in a soothing bath, and started up the car. He pulled out smoothly. They were quiet until I broke the silence.

"Did I miss something?" I asked. "I thought that was depressing."

They did not say anything, only smiled separately, together.

"Something went right over my head, didn't it?" I persisted, confused.

They laughed at me easily then. Bryan reminded me that weeks earlier, he had told me about the "ninety-day glow." NA recommends that recovering addicts attend ninety meetings, such as the one we went to. "There's a glow people get from them," he said. "People offer you jobs, scholarships. Things just fall into place." I had dismissed it as too magical until that night, when their glow lightened my heavy sadness.

Together Bryan and Tijuana eagerly explained each of the twelve steps of recovery as Bryan drove along Lake Shore Drive, past the darkness of Lake Michigan. On the way down, the gray waves crashed chaotically onto the shore, angry at the day's storm and warning of the night. Now they had a certain beauty to them. A contained unruliness.

The meeting was unnerving and depressing to me. I was sure of that. I left feeling weighed down, even imprisoned, burdened with learning what addiction is. But they left feeling free. It was as if they had stepped into a fresh new world and they were breathing it all in for the first time.

"I don't want to lose this," Bryan said, lights filling his eyes after a peaceful silence.

"What?" I asked.

"Life. I love life. Every moment. I love this."

14

The Stars

ONCE a year, Eileen McCaffrey's Orphans Foundation of America brings a handful of its scholarship recipients to Washington, D.C. There they meet with lawyers and legislators, attend receptions, dabble in some work, and if they're lucky, one of their dinners may make the local news.

Bryan was pleased to be invited for a second year in a row, this time as a sort of chaperone for the rest of the crew.

His experiences in Washington bubbled and flowed out of him even weeks after he returned to Chicago.

"You know what got me most?" he asked. "It was I got to be around all these young professional African-American males, and I thought, Hey, I can do this too."

Then, with hardly a breath in between, he launched into the most memorable day of his trip.

"I was at this law firm in the morning and then they took me to lunch, Michael Rasheed, this guy who kind of sponsored me at the law firm," Bryan said. "I loved it so much I was like, Man, I don't want to leave. They didn't want me to leave either, but they said things were planned for me.

"So then in the afternoon I went to Capitol Hill to meet with Representative Watts. He's into welfare reform. I thought I was just going to sit there awhile, but, man, they get you busy. They said, 'Do you type?' And I said, 'Yeah, I type.' I was busy interning for him the rest of the day. I wrote up a bio of myself for him to introduce me at the reception that night. He is a beautiful person. And in fact, that night they had a congressional reception for us. And I was picked to give him an award. They thought I did really well. I stumbled over a few words and I don't think I did so well, but they said, 'Bryan, it came from the heart, and that made it great.' "

But back in Chicago, things had taken yet another bad turn. Bryan is excited about starting school, but Tijuana is not doing well. While Bryan was gone, she relapsed. Bryan's voice dropped in sadness for her and the loss of their friendship. He had allowed her to stay in his apartment when he went to Washington. When he returned, he found the phone cut off because of an astronomical phone bill he could not pay, and his TV and VCR missing. Tijuana had sold them and his number for drugs.

"Is it possible she might just have a few hits and go back to NA?" I asked Bryan.

"That's not how it works," he said. "One hit is too much, and a thousand isn't enough."

He had to change his locks in case she came back. He could not afford to get caught up in her relapse. Seeing her would be too dangerous.

"As soon as I can I'm going to leave this place," he said. "This city has so many reminders of my past and people I have to stay away from, like my dad. And now even Tijuana. Crystal I'll always keep in touch with because I know she really cares about me, but she always wants to tell me about my dad and Felicia and stuff and their addictive behavior. It's not always good for me. If I could, I would leave Chicago and start a whole new life."

He plans to go to graduate school for degrees in social work and law after he finishes college in two years. He can't wait.

"So, are you going to be a congressman, Bryan?" I asked.

"Oh no," he said with a light, full laugh. "I'm going to be the president. First I'm going to reform the whole juvenile system, though. I know I'm reaching beyond the stars. But I'm going to try."

15
Holidays

❖

Two weeks before Thanksgiving, Bryan calls at 2:45 A.M. exactly. His voice is hushed into a whisper. He doesn't want to wake up his roommate. He is sorry to phone so late, but he wants to catch up. The semester is going fine. He has dropped one class, Christian Values and Ethics, because his load was too heavy. He is working at the Joliet Boys and Girls Club, which he loves. He plays basketball and talks to the boys, mostly, pointing things out to them that he wishes somebody had pointed out to him. The staff has become like a family to him.

"But we've got these holidays coming up," he says with a heavy sigh. Like Jamie and Angel, Bryan dreads the holidays. The feeling sweeps over him before he can distinguish whether it is because he has to make plans for himself, or because he doesn't belong somewhere exactly, or because he misses the family he once had.

He will probably be going to Crystal's for Thanksgiving. His nieces will be there, but his nephew is not allowed to come. He said something on a previous visit, and Crystal now refuses to allow him to come from his group home this holiday.

"I'm like, Let the little guy come," Bryan says. "But Crystal has talked to him. He understands what he did and says, 'I'm sorry,' and, 'Please, Aunt Crystal, can't I come?' "

Bryan remembers all too painfully the days when his vacations were held hostage by family members he hardly knew. "I didn't have nowhere to go; I didn't have anyone to call to deal with emotions. At least he has Crystal or me to call."

Crystal is adamant. She is sad her nephew won't share the holiday with them, but she's determined to teach him the lesson. She wants to break the cycle of foster care in her family, and if that means teaching lessons the hard way, she'll do it. Bryan understands, but he's still sad.

"Once upon a time I thought that [shop]lifting things was OK," he explains. "Those character flaws needed to be broken, and so do my nephew's now."

While Bryan feels down, he is physically healthy. He works out regularly. He calls it his fail-safe plan to keep depression at bay during times like this.

He eats OK too, he says, as best a vegetarian can on a college student's budget. He's again looking to transfer from Lewis. He has a year's worth of classes to go before graduation. But the bills are mounting. He wants to go directly to graduate school in social work. Spiritually, he volunteers, he's doing great. He'd like to have more time to go to Narcotics Anonymous meetings, but he says he prays a lot and his yearning for drugs has decreased.

He's thankful for the way things have turned out for him. He doesn't believe he could have done it alone. There's too much, too many barriers he faced.

"I'm blessed," he says with a smile in his voice. "I'm a miracle, I must say that."

The modesty rings clear in his voice. Being a miracle means to Bryan that God saved him from his childhood. It wasn't the system. The system banged him around, refused to listen to him, and pulled the remains of his family apart. It didn't save him from the ruts in his environment. While he takes responsibility for his falls, he knows that the system fed him to those falls by keeping him in his stepgrandmother's home and throwing him in and out of the Audy Home. But he's pulled himself up from there, despite slips that at times breathlessly looked fatal.

"I know what drugs have done to me," he says. He's reminded of that every time he goes to work at the Boys and Girls Club, and that's why he's so attracted to that work. It keeps him strong. "I want to live, you know. I want to live. I have a lot of hopes and dreams, and I plan to meet them."

16

Just Watch

▧

On the last day of the year, my husband and I met Bryan near Washington, D.C. He had spent Christmas with his Orphans Foundation mentor and her family. His mentor's husband was angry at her for inviting Bryan into their home. Bryan might steal one of the antiques from the family business, he feared.

Bryan said he understood, but admitted it was a blow. He has worked hard to pull himself out of the system, but still he is faced with the stigma of being a desperate kid raised in foster care, even by those who claim to understand and seek to help.

Bryan expects to be graduated from college this year, then begin study toward a master's degree in social work, and eventually a law degree. He wants to help reform the foster care system.

I asked him how he would react if he were a caseworker faced with a kid like himself.

"I'd be grateful," Bryan said after a thoughtful pause. "I really would. My caseworker, Michael Liberto, calls me up every once in a while and says, 'Bryan you're doing great; you don't know how great you're doing.' I get tired of hearing it sometimes. But then he tells me about the other kids in his caseload and what's happening to them and I'm like, *Man.*" He shook his head low and slow at the children being destroyed and self-destructing.

"Yeah, as a matter of fact, if I had a kid like me, I'd be grateful," he said again.

I laughed at his immodest but honest answer. He smiled back. Then his smile faded.

"I'd give him the world," he said softly in his sincerity, "like Michael gave me."

Two weeks later Bryan is in Chicago court for stealing a school television set a year earlier. He intended to hock it to pay for his books because his Department of Children and Family Services check had not arrived. Initially, the university decided not to press charges. Now, a new administrator reverses the decision.

"I understand why they're doing it," Bryan says. Another youth, who was with Bryan, denies the theft, but Bryan pleads guilty. "It was my mistake, not theirs. I was trying to make it anyway I could. I was dumb and desperate."

Bryan retains an expensive lawyer who had represented his father on recent charges of driving while impaired and threatening a police officer. Bryan believes, as his father does, that a public defender will do him more harm than good. "The judge sees an African-American youth with a public defender and it's all over," Bryan says. "He expects he's guilty."

The lawyer fails to show up in court for Bryan's hearing. He later tells Bryan that he was preparing for a murder trial. A clerk points Bryan to a public defender, who approaches the judge on Bryan's behalf and asks for an extension. The judge agrees. Bryan's hearing is postponed twice more; his spirit flags almost to depression.

"It's just, when I finally get it together, I have to pay," he says. "It's like a roller coaster. Things from the past always catch up."

By the time of his hearing, with a $5,000 lawyer's bill mounting, Bryan just wants it over, no matter what the court decides.

Because of Bryan's prior record of theft and attempted theft, the judge finds it impossible to be lenient. But he offers Bryan a term in boot camp as an alternative to a slightly longer term in prison. Boot camp is an incarceration program modeled after the military program for new recruits, with the same rigorous physical regimen and strict discipline. Prison boot camp aims to reform, even reprogram, young men between the ages of eighteen and thirty-five.

Bryan chooses boot camp, although its reputation on the street feeds his anxiety and fears. He wants to serve his time before college starts in the fall. He remains determined to succeed, despite this setback.

"Don't you worry, Jenny, I'm going to make it," he says just before leaving to serve his time. He sounds exhausted and nervous. "I'm too close not to. I'll do anything to finish school. Then I'll be free and I'll make everyone who's helped me proud. You just watch."

CONCLUSION

❖

"I HAVE a very special charismatic personality," Bryan writes in his most recent letter, which arrived today from boot camp. I smile as broadly as I remember Bryan's smile. His tone reminds me of a year earlier when he phoned from a Chicago hospital bed to declare plainly and without guile: "Jenny, I had a tragedy." He had been stabbed in a robbery attempt, he said. But the real tragedy he saw was that his fragmented family would visit him only individually, and only because they believed he was dying. Despite prompting from his sister Crystal, his family will not come to his boot camp graduation, even though he sees it as one of his greatest accomplishments and the beginning of a new life. Together they won't reassure him at a time when, he writes, "I truly believe inside my heart that this is my final opportunity to challenge myself and achieve my goals." They won't join in applauding his success and reaffirming their bonds in a time of celebration. They come together only for new tragedies. Only tragedy provides cohesion.

I don't smile at Bryan's tragedy, of course, but at his brave words, which again demonstrate his matter-of-fact honesty and refusal to give up. A distant smile, too, of encouragement and admiration and thanks. For it has been the sincerity of Bryan and the other young people in this book, and their sparks of resilience, that has lighted my way through their sad stories.

Still, Bryan's "tragedy" is haunting. It is a common denominator in the lives of foster children—of Angel and Jamie and the dozens of kids I encountered during the course of researching this book. They reach out for a family that was never there for them and probably will never be. They reach out again and again, despite the hurt they experience after each rejection. And because no one has been there for them, they themselves may not be there for others. Studies show that only a small percentage of foster children form a healthy family of their own. Divorce rates are far higher than average, and even when they remain married, their spouses complain of a distance that exists between them and their own children.

None of the young people in this book has formed a trusting, loving bond. Angel, despite her marriage to Mr. Brown, has had several boyfriends and girlfriends, and was unwilling to complete court-directed steps to recover her own children from foster care. Jamie does not believe she will ever be able to love someone completely. Bryan, it seems, never tries. He focuses on his sister Crystal and his nephew and nieces, but seldom on the prospects of having his own children or marriage. I have lost touch with Damien and Sebastian. Their new homes refuse me access to them, although I was told they have asked to speak with me.

JAMIE dropped out of school, temporarily, she says. She hoped to move to Colorado and live with her mother, Pam, while attending university there. Her mother seemed open to the idea during Jamie's visit last summer, until Jamie met a young man at a pool. He took her for a tour of the university. When she returned at 10 P.M., without having phoned to say she would miss dinner, Pam became furious. Living together simply wouldn't work, she told Jamie. Jamie can't understand her mother's reaction. Now, back in Raleigh, she holds down two waitressing jobs and has registered for fall classes back at North Carolina State University.

FOR several months, Angel became difficult to reach. She occasionally crashed with her sister Maria. "She's given up on everything," Maria says, "herself and everything." Maria is trying to win custody of Sammy and complains that Angel is fickle in lending her support. She will not relinquish her parental rights.

"I don't want to let go of my love for my kids, and I want them to know that I love them and that I'll always want them," Angel told me in a conversation a few months after her suicide attempt. "But I'm afraid there'll come a time soon when I'm so worn out and angry it will look like I don't care."

Two months later, Angel does not see her life as dismally as she did then, or as her sister does now.

"I have a new man in my life!" she says on the phone, with the energetic, happy voice that makes me smile in spite of what she tells me. Angel's actions and her attitude can be infuriating sometimes; but in times of less stress, Angel is a wholly likeable and magnetic person. Of all the kids, I find her life story most heart wrenching and tragic, yet more often than not I find myself smiling after talking with her.

Tonight, it seems, she's finally met her Richard Gere.

Angel met thirty-seven-year-old Joe White at the Florentine Night Club and moved into his South Pasadena apartment soon after. She's been with him for several months now. "He calls me Angel Face and he treats me like a queen. We go out to fancy dinners with candlelight every night. He takes care of me and pampers me," she says for him to hear. "He's my man."

"Oh, by the way, he's *rich,*" she whispers eagerly into the phone as he goes outside to check the grill. Angel quit her job at the strip club because she says it's not appropriate while she's with Joe. "Besides," she says, "I was sick of it. I was tired of all those men."

Joe pays her an allowance of $250 a week and has promised to pay for her to attend cosmetology school. She wants to specialize in hair. She is already thinking of names for their children, but says they won't have babies until they're married. She worries about meeting Joe's parents and thinks she'll first have to remove her nose and tongue rings and cover her new tattoo. On her back she now carries a tattoo of a bear holding a bouquet of balloons with the initials of each of her children floating in the balloons.

She often visits her youngest daughter, Sammy. "Honestly," she says sadly, "I have to say Raul's doing a good job; he's raising her well."

Her other four children have been split up into two new foster homes because their social worker found the two girls sleeping on mattresses on the floor. Angel is upset that the children are separated and sides with their former foster mother, Ms. Montario. She argues that Ms. Montario was simply having new carpet installed when the social worker visited. Angel and Mr. Brown, who is still her husband, visit the children for an hour each Monday, when the social worker brings the children together.

"Someday I will try to get them back," Angel says, unconvincingly. "Right now I have to focus on getting my life back together."

DESPITE his self-inflicted setbacks, Bryan is looking forward. He takes full responsibility for his actions and crimes, he says. He's ready, this time, to avoid putting himself in risky situations.

"I'm learning not only self-discipline, but self-determination, and self-respect also," Bryan writes from the Duquoin Impact Incarceration Program in Ina, Illinois. "Some of my associates have been through difficult times, and I sometimes fall off into their lunacy rather than persuade them toward righteousness. That's a weakness for me. I am truly learning about myself here at this boot camp, and that is good, but I can't wait to get out and begin a fruitful life, spend time with Crystal and Amber and my friends."

At Bryan's request, I pass on a course registration list to his advisor at Chicago State University where he recently transferred to from Lewis University. The first is a sociology class called Family.

"I can't take for granted what lots of people do," Bryan told me long ago. "There's a lot I have to learn that most people seem to be born with. The problem is that I don't even really know what I'm missing, and that scares me some. The problem is, for me and a lot of kids like me, there are pieces we need to build on and we don't even know what those pieces are. We just feel them missing. We just feel different."

His words reminded me of what a graduate of the foster care system warned when I began this project. Nancy is a buyer for a major department store. She was graduated Phi Beta Kappa from her state university. She spoke on condition of anonymity. She prefers that people not know she grew up in foster care because she feels there's a stigma attached to it.

"We leave children's homes and foster care homes knowing how to fill out forms and how to buy the cheapest clothes without looking cheap, but there's this thing we don't know. We don't know how not to always protect ourselves. So there's this hollowness. Some kids fill it up with drugs, or with food, or with religion, but some of us never fill it up. It's just sort of cold and restless. I didn't really notice it until my boyfriends kept telling me that I was sort of distant and cold. You see, I think I learned a lot of things and I've worked hard, but I've never learned how to give a love I never received and, to be honest, I don't really understand. And I'm what they call a success."

ACKNOWLEDGMENTS

✦

CENTRAL Children's Home director Mike Alston, Free Will Baptist Children's Home director James Johnson, social workers Emeron Cash, Willie Marrow, Mike Liberto, state licensers Elsie Roane, Toni Levelle, Brother Dan King of Mercy Home for Boys, and Eileen McCaffrey of the Orphans Foundation of America are among those who, by their conscientious caring for the children and willingness to talk openly about the crisis at hand, give hope that the future will be better for young people in substitute child care. Without individuals like them, the future would be bleak.

This book also could not have been written without the help of my family. My mother, Paula Toth, a Maryland court-appointed special advocate (guardian *ad litem* in some states), helped me understand the system in ways I could not have otherwise. She offered different perspectives and stories that went beyond what I saw, as well as listened to mine. And she buried herself in proofreading this manuscript during the final long stretch. My father, Robert Toth, devoted days (which add up to months) to editing *Orphans of the Living*. His insights and edits saved me in ways I cannot begin to thank him for. His care and passion for *Orphans* matches mine. My sister, Jessica Toth, and brother-in-law, Erol Erturk, kept me well stocked with printer supplies and hope. And my brother, John Toth, kept me happy, levelheaded, and, mostly, amused. They have all been tremendously supportive and patient.

Most important and most difficult to put into words is my deep love and gratitude to my husband, Craig Whitlock, whose unwavering support and belief in *Orphans* kept me going through the most difficult episodes. He patiently put off wedding plans, camping trips, and lots else until we turned in *Orphans*. His editing and insights (as the most thorough and finest storytelling journalist around), as well as his reading and rereading the manuscript, mean more to me than I can say.

I also want to thank my agent, Keith Korman of Raines & Raines, for helping me all the way through, including reading the manuscript and keeping me laughing. Keith far surpassed being a good agent, to being the best.

Journalists Nina Easton, staff writer for the *Los Angeles Times Magazine*, and Alison Jones of the Raleigh *News & Observer,* were very generous in sharing their work and insights into the foster care system. Carol Bowman helped a great deal in accessing computer information. Anne Rosenquist, a true friend, has listened with endless patience and fed me encouragement at many of the most critical times. My roommate through much of this book, Brooke Cain, introduced me to great Southern literature from Faulkner to Reynolds Price, which is a debt I can't repay. I probably wouldn't have started this book without the encouragement of my former editor, Amy Teschner, who pushed me to reach out to the largest possible audience.

And final thanks to my editor at Simon & Schuster, Dominick Anfuso, for taking a chance and betting on these kids and me.

Finally, my greatest admiration and thanks to all the young people and many members of their families who opened themselves up to take part in this book. More than anyone, they put themselves on the line to help save the generation of children following in their paths.

ABOUT THE AUTHOR

Jennifer Toth was born in London and grew up in Moscow and Chevy Chase, Maryland. She graduated from Washington University in St. Louis and received a master's degree in journalism from Columbia University. A reporter for the *Los Angeles Times* and the Raleigh *News & Observer,* she has also written articles for the *International Herald Tribune, The Washington Post, Business Week,* the *Asian Wall Street Journal,* and *Max* magazine. Toth is the author of *The Mole People,* a study of homeless life in the tunnels under New York City, which spurred federal funding to house the underground homeless. Jennifer Toth lives with her husband, journalist Craig Whitlock, in Raleigh, North Carolina.